The Importance of Being Trivial

The Importance
of Being Trivial

Mark Mason

rh
BOOKS

Published by Random House Books 2008

4 6 8 10 9 7 5 3

Copyright © Mark Mason 2008

Mark Mason has asserted his right under the Copyright, Designs
and Patents Act, 1988 to be identified as the author of this work

First published in Great Britain in 2008 by
Random House Books

Random House, 20 Vauxhall Bridge Road,
London SW1V 2SA

www.rbooks.co.uk

Addresses for companies within The Random House Group Limited can be found at:
www.randomhouse.co.uk/offices.htm

The Random House Group Limited Reg. No. 954009

A CIP catalogue record for this book
is available from the British Library

ISBN 9781847945174

The Random House Group Limited supports The Forest Stewardship
Council (FSC), the leading international forest certification organisation. All our
titles that are printed on Greenpeace approved FSC certified paper carry the FSC logo.
Our paper procurement policy can be found at www.rbooks.co.uk/environment

Typeset in Fournier MT by Palimpsest Book Production Limited,
Grangemouth, Stirlingshire

Printed and bound in Great Britain by
CPI Mackays, Chatham ME5 8TD

Contents

Acknowledgements

Thank you to everyone who helped during my search for the perfect fact. Particular gratitude goes to Simon Baron-Cohen, Emrah Duzel and Arthur I. Miller, three professors who undoubtedly had better things to do, but nonetheless found time to show me just how significant trivia can be. I'm also grateful to Vodafone for permission to quote the poster produced during their association with the National Autistic Society.

Thanks to Richard for introducing me to Marcus, and Marcus for introducing me to the Prince of Wales. (Chapter one reveals why this is slightly less impressive than it sounds.) Thanks to David for telling me about Carlsberg Special Brew. Thanks to my parents for, amongst much else, buying me the *Guinness Book of Records* when I was ten, and to my brother for his travel advice, even though I ignored it and went to Blackpool anyway.

Thanks to my publishers – I love the fact that Random House are publishing a book which argues the one thing trivia isn't is random. And thanks as ever to Charlie Viney; I'm only sorry the 'Apple logo' piece of trivia wasn't true.

But the greatest thanks must go, as they always do, to Jo. I hope that one day my parallel parking might be worthy of her.

Introduction

The look or the noise. There's always either the look or the noise.

The party's going well. You're on your second or third drink, you've established how you both know James, you're familiar enough with the other person's job not to sound a complete fool. Then they mention a works outing to the dogs. You swap stories of bets made, money lost, how there really isn't form in greyhounds like there is in horses. It's all sounding fine . . . but you know what's bubbling up. You try to contain it, keep it to yourself, smile and nod as the other person relates how much they won by sticking to trap three. It's no good, though. That fatal two-second gap arises. You find yourself looking them in the eye, opening your mouth . . . *Stop, even now it's not too late to STOP!* . . . and saying, all casual-like, 'Did you know the greyhound is the second-fastest-accelerating animal on the planet?'

That's when you get the look or the noise. It's the noise you want: the intake of breath, hold for a count of two, the whoosh as the air's expelled, possibly in the form of 'Wow' or 'Really?' The look is what you don't want: the marginal hardening of the stare, eyes glazing in discomfort, or even fear. Confusion registering in every feature, a face that says, 'But I thought this person was normal?'

Whichever it is, you plough on. 'Have a guess,' you say, either to increase their surprise or combat their disapproval, 'how many seconds a greyhound takes to go from nought to forty-five miles an hour?' If they made the noise, they'll think about it seriously, relish the challenge, try to get it right. They will give (in my experience) an answer somewhere between three and eight seconds. You hit them with the real answer – one second – and they do the noise again, only this time louder. If they gave you the look, though . . . This is where it finally goes wrong. They give you another look, this time one of real panic, awkwardness verging on disgust, as though you've just done something unpleasant to the carpet. They mumble an excuse, then rush to warn James that a nutter has gatecrashed his party.

Trivia, they call it. And depending on whether or not 'they' like it, other words are never very far away. 'Useless', for instance, applied nominally to the information itself, though with a not-very-well-hidden implication that the person spouting the information is himself without use, or indeed worth. 'Fascinating' is another. This gets used by a different group of people – those spouting the trivia in the first place. It seems the world is divided into two camps: the camp which loves the fact that a jiffy is the name given in computing to a hundreth of a second, and the camp which doesn't.

The other word that's never very far away – for obvious

linguistic reasons – is 'trivial'. But it's more than the addition of a single letter. It's the question at the heart of all this: is trivia trivial? A certain successful board game has clouded the issue, or rather skewed the answer towards yes. But it's more important than plastic cheeses and competitive uncles. Trivia, I'm convinced, has to say something about us, tell us at least a little bit about who we are.

'Of what a strange nature is knowledge!' Mary Shelley has the monster say in *Frankenstein*. 'It clings to the mind, when it has once seized on it, like a lichen on the rock.' Among the lichen clinging to my mind are:

- The stretch of road between the Strand and the Savoy hotel is the only public highway in Britain where you're legally obliged to drive on the right.
- Pete Conrad was the first man to fall over on the moon.
- An HB pencil will draw a line 35 miles long.
- Countries at the United Nations are seated alphabetically, Afghanistan coming first, Zimbabwe last.
- John Lennon's first girlfriend was called Thelma Pickles.
- Hull City is the only one of the top 92 football clubs in England whose name contains no letters you can colour in.

For years I thought it was just me. Or at least just me and my friends. Happily we gurgled away, telling each other that the S in Harry S Truman didn't stand for anything,[1] that Sting wrote *Every Breath You Take* at the same desk where Ian Fleming sat

---

1. His parents disagreed over a middle name, but both their preferences began with S, so they settled on a middle initial.

to write the Bond novels, that dolphins have more teeth than any other mammal. For the currency of our discourse to be this weird coinage called trivia didn't seem particularly significant. We just got on with it, relishing the facts we swapped, the facts that had slipped down the back of life's sofa.

Then, a few years ago, things changed. A strange little book called *Schott's Original Miscellany* was published, and proceeded to fly off the shelves. BBC2 started broadcasting a programme called *QI*, which has spawned a website, a club and the best-selling *The Book of General Ignorance*. Now, from *The Pedant's Revolt* through *The Penguin Book of Facts* to *Does Anything Eat Wasps?*, the nation's bookshops are full of trivia. Whole radio shows are devoted to it. The Internet Movie Database has a trivia category for each film. Never before have tiny facts held such a huge fascination.

And so those of us who were there all along ask: why? Those who would dismiss trivia mutter the usual charges ('useless . . . waste of time . . . pointless information'), presumably as they read Proust while waiting for Kissinger to pick up. But millions of trivia hounds can't be wrong. Or at least, if they are, it says something about them that they go *on* being wrong. 'Don't sweat the small stuff,' they always say. I never got that. The small stuff is where life's *at*. Trivia keeps me, and lots like me, firmly in its grip. Like moths we flutter at its flame, like junkies we suck on its pipe. It provides the background music to our lives, peppering our conversation, attracting our gaze whenever it appears on a page, a TV, a computer screen. Trivia is *there*, it is a part, however small or large, of who and what we are. To write all this off with a snarled 'trivial' just doesn't do it justice. It may not be the most important thing in our lives, but it is *something* in our lives.

I resolved to find out what. As many people in the first week of January will tell you, though, making a resolution and knowing how to carry it out are two different things. Initially my mind was pulled in several directions, question upon question clamouring for its attention, thoughts piling up like sheep in a too-small pen. Most of them had never occurred to me before. The notion, for instance, that as surprising as the trivia we do know can be the trivia we don't. George W. Bush spends two full terms as US President, a position which guarantees you a certain degree of attention at the best of times but which he has occupied in such a way as to catapult his name into virtually every news bulletin for nigh on a decade – and yet how many people know what the W stands for?[2] Starbucks embarks on a programme of global domination that makes *War of the Worlds* look restrained – and yet how many people, as they queue for their tenth grande latte of the week, know where the name Starbucks comes from? Curious what we don't find curious.

Then the key appeared. It concerned the *quality* of facts. All day every day my brain is presented with facts. Newspapers, the net, the books I read, the people I talk to . . . all are giving me facts. This has been happening since shortly after I was born, and will carry on until the day I die. These facts (What do they number? Tens of thousands? Hundreds? Millions?) are all taken in, then some are remembered while others are not. If we discount what might be called the important stuff – what my name is, where I live, what the right-hand pedal in a car

2. No, it's not that.

does – we're left with what's usually called the trivia: the name of John Lennon's first girlfriend, how long the line drawn by an HB pencil would be . . . What makes me remember a piece of trivia – or, put another way, what attracts me to it – is its quality as a fact, how good I find it. That the greyhound is the second-fastest-accelerating animal on the planet (beaten only by the cheetah) I find a very good fact. That the sheep is the fifty-ninth I do not.[3] Some facts are, to be brutal about it, simply better than other facts.

From which it follows that there must be one fact which is better than all the others. Or at least a group of facts tying for first place, for the hallowed title Best Fact. But could you take this one step further? Could there be a fact that was not only the best, but was actually perfect? Could there be a fact so fascinating, so beautiful, so compelling that it flawlessly embodied the very notion of trivia? This was the question that would form the theme of my journey.

I was in search of the perfect fact.

3. Not least because I've just made it up for the purposes of this example. But you take the point.

A note on *TOPOTs*

Throughout this book you will find TOPOTs: Tangentially Occurring Pieces of Trivia. None of these have been specially researched, or even checked; they are all facts already known to me. This is not intended to impress – indeed I'm aware that for many it will have precisely the opposite effect. The inclusion of these facts is simply to illustrate the amount and range of the trivia that can be held in a single human brain.

I

Better not look down

I t starts, as so many things do, in a pub.

My chosen terrain is vast and yet curiously intangible. I need an entry point, a platform nine and three quarters, a wardrobe not into Narnia but into Trivia. What better place than the event in which trivia most clearly crystallises itself: the pub quiz?

My partner for this journey is the *Spectator*'s pop critic Marcus Berkmann. I first heard of him several years ago, when we shared an editor. One day the editor handed me a copy of a village cricket memoir called *Rain Men*, saying it was the book he was most proud of publishing, ever. (This the week after my first novel came out. Thanks, Richard.) He was right, though. The book is a gem, and ever since we've been saying how Marcus and I really should get together for a drink. What prompts me into action now is that another of Marcus's books is called *A Matter of Facts*, and concerns quizzes. Marcus loves quizzes. Every Tuesday night he attends, and often runs, the Prince of Wales quiz, generally recognised as north London's toughest. He has appeared on Radio Four's *Masterteam* (several times), and on Channel Four's *Fifteen To One* (several times).

He runs quizzes for literary festivals, for corporate clients . . . I can think of no better man with whom to sit in a pub in Muswell Hill trying to guess how many Shakespeare plays are in print.[1]

We arrange to do a quiz, but not at the Prince of Wales; Marcus says he'd be too distracted there. I'm a bit worried as the evening approaches. For a start there's the fear that Marcus will be nothing like the man you'd imagine from *Rain Men* – funny, self-deprecating, at ease with a pint of lager and a discussion about whether Matt Prior will be dropped by England. This fear disappears within seconds of our greeting each other, a greeting I initiate. Marcus, as he will happily admit later, is quite shy, and avoids asking me if I'm Mark. I know he's Marcus because, as his email predicted, he's the only person there reading a book. It was a confident prediction – he knows the pub. Soon we're two blokes, a few years either side of forty (Marcus has seniority), chatting away about that day's play in the Test match. But my other worry still lurks: Marcus will know more than me. My woeful showing when it comes to the actual quiz will probably disgust him, lose me his respect. This guy writes for the *Spectator*, after all.

For now, though, we talk trivia. Starting, for the sake of somewhere to start, with what the word actually means. I know its derivation was given in *A Matter of Facts*, and ask Marcus to reprise it. He takes a sip of his pint, obviously preparing for the explanation.

'Erm . . .' he says. Another sip. 'Er . . .' He puts down the glass. 'I can't remember.'

1. 38. We guessed 37. Damn.

This is encouraging. Perhaps the quiz won't be so daunting after all.

'Wasn't it something to do with the seven university subjects?' I prompt.

'Oh, that's it, yeah.' We gradually piece it together from memory: medieval universities taught seven 'artes liberales', three of which – grammar, rhetoric and logic, known as the 'arte trivialle' or 'trivium' – were seen as less challenging, a sort of media studies for the fifteenth century.[2] Going further back, the actual Latin derivation is *tri*, meaning three, and *via*, meaning road: 'where three roads meet', or the street corner. The adjective *trivialis* meant 'commonplace or vulgar'. The English 'trivial' came to mean 'of little importance or significance'. Lop off the l and you find yourself in a pub in Muswell Hill trying to guess how many Shakespeare plays are in print. But could you say that Shakespeare was of little importance?

Having sorted the dictionary definition, I ask Marcus how *he* would characterise trivia.

'I'd say it's those things that stick in your head when other more important things have gone. For instance, I spent three years in the late seventies and early eighties doing a maths degree. Now I can remember virtually nothing about it. But the other day, when I walked past the cricket pitch in Highgate Woods with my five-year-old son and he asked me if I'd ever played there, I knew that I had. Even though it was twenty years ago, I remembered that my friend Stephen forgot to bring his box, so went out to bat with a scrunched-up Skol can stuffed

2. The four more difficult subjects, the 'quadrivium', were arithmetic, geometry, music and astronomy.

down his pants. Note how I remembered it was a *Skol* can. I also remembered that he got his highest-ever score – fourteen.'

By now it's time for my round. We're drinking Carlsberg, as the pub, for some strange reason, doesn't serve strong lagers. (Actually, given the number of rounds in the quiz and the fact that Marcus and I will continue discussing trivia – and cricket – long after the quiz has ended, this is probably a good thing.) Seeing the logo on the pump reminds me of a great fact. Carrying the drinks back, I debate whether to tell Marcus. Will trivia about a brand of lager seem *too* trivial? Then I remember this is the man who's just recalled a Skol can from two decades ago.

'Pint of Carlsberg,' I say, handing it over. 'By the way, do you know the thing about Carlsberg Special Brew?'

'No,' says Marcus. 'What thing?'

'It was invented for Winston Churchill.'

The glass stops an inch from his mouth, which now hangs open in amazement. '*No*.'

'Carlsberg brewed it as a thank you from Denmark for Britain's help in the war. Churchill had said no lager was strong enough for him. Norway gives us a Christmas tree for Trafalgar Square every year, Denmark gives us a brand of lager that's usually drunk in shop doorways.'

'That's amazing.'

It's the reaction that truly great trivia always produces. The astonishment, the wonder, the pause to savour.

'That's going straight in my next quiz,' he says. '"For which British Prime Minister——"'

We're interrupted by a tap on the microphone. 'All right, ladies and gentlemen. Round one.'

Oh God. This is it. No sooner have I earned credibility by knowing one fact than I'm going to lose it by not knowing any others. But it transpires that this worry is just as unfounded as my first. Marcus knows pretty well the same amount of stuff as I do. We both know who had an eighties number one with 'I Owe You Nothing' (Bros); we're both uncertain of our guess as to the location of Rockefeller University (New York, which turns out to be right) and both certain of our guess as to whether it was six, 26 or 60 cars that started the US Grand Prix in 2005. (Twenty-six, which turns out to be wrong. It was six. Argument over tyres, apparently.) Marcus knows that the country represented at tennis by Elena Baltacha is Great Britain, while I provide our guess that the pop singer who played Adrian's mother in *The Growing Pains of Adrian Mole* was Lulu. It was.

Between rounds, I delicately broach the subject of how much Marcus knows. 'I suppose you must get questions you've heard before?' I ask. 'What with having done so many quizzes in the past?'

'Not really,' he says. 'I don't view quizzes like that. I have a real prejudice, for instance, against numerical questions. Like that Shakespeare one just now. No one's going to know it, so you're just guessing, and even if you guess right it's no real triumph. A really good question should contain the clue to its own answer. You should be able to work it out. Like that Churchill fact. If I ask, "For which British Prime Minister was Carlsberg Special Brew invented?" people will be able to go through the Prime Ministers, working out which ones liked strong drink, how long Special Brew has been around . . . Eventually you'll get to Churchill.'

I'm feeling quite pleased with myself at this point.

'The perfect question,' continues Marcus, 'is one where no one knows it, but they argue about it for ten minutes, and work their way towards an answer, and then when you read out the right answer everyone goes "*Yes.*"'

'So you never sit down to learn facts, just because they might come up in a quiz?'

Marcus nearly chokes on his beer. 'That is somewhere I *never* want to go. I've got this code with my friends Chris and Sally-Ann: "Barry From Leeds". One of the times we did *Masterteam* we played a side from Leeds. Barry had these ledgers full of facts. He'd sit there reading them before every recording. It was sad. Very sad.'

I'm reminded of the Amazon reviews for *Schott's Original Miscellany*. One of the first books to spark off trivia's noughties renaissance, *Schott's* was a beautiful (in every sense of the word) collection of trivia, ranging from the odds on poker hands to the specifications of Noah's ark. Utterly pointless, utterly brilliant. Most of the reviews are raves, five-out-of-five jobs, citing facts from the book as evidence of its genius. The fact, for instance, that three of the first five US Presidents died on the same date.[3] Only one review is a stinker. It's from 'A Quiz Fanatic' – his/her chosen name – complaining that *Schott's* is no use in preparing for quizzes. You might as well complain that an orchid is no use in changing a car tyre.

Marcus clearly relishes setting quizzes as much as – perhaps even more than – taking part in them. This is something I can

3. Bizarre enough in itself. The fact that that date was 4 July is uber-bizarre.

relate to. A couple of years ago, owing to what can only have been an administrative error, I was given a weekly one-hour programme on BBC Radio Suffolk.[4] Asked what they wanted me to do, they said 'whatever you like'. The slot was three o'clock on a Sunday afternoon. Pubs were likely to be full. A quiz it was: two pubs, against each other, on the phone (local radio doesn't run to satellite links). Setting the questions became a weekly treat, a chance to put all my trivia to use for once. 'Which crucial role in the history of English football,' for instance, 'was played by Tofic Bakramhov?' You could hear the regulars at the Bear and Bells trying to work it out: '*English* football? With a name like that? He can't have been English. What sort of name is it? East European? Russian? Hang on, Russian . . . Russian . . . Was he the Russian linesman who gave the goal in the 1966 World Cup Final?' He was indeed. Two points.[TOPOT]

Sometimes, however, working the trivia in required excessive use of the crowbar. Questions were usually in matching pairs: if one team got 'What is Sting's real name?' the other would get 'What is Adam Ant's real name?'[5] A piece of trivia I was dying to include, all the more preeningly because I'd

> TOPOT
>
> *Had the 1966 World Cup Final still been level at the end of extra time, it would have been decided by the toss of a coin.*

---

4. I'd recently moved to the county from London, and was citing 'local author' credentials in a shabby attempt to plug a book.
5. Gordon Sumner and Stuart Goddard respectively.

worked it out for myself, was that the text alert sounded by many mobile phones – three short beeps, two long, three short – is Morse code for SMS.[6] So one pub was asked 'What's the Morse code for S?', the other 'What's the Morse code for M?' Cue smart-arse explanation from yours truly. Except, it dawned on me as I was asking the first question, everybody knows S, because of the SOS signal. No one knows M. Not even the armed services; they haven't used it in years.[7] This was a really unfair question. What's worse, incompetence compounded my guilt: asking the second team about M, I forgot to fade down the first, so you heard their captain saying 'That's a much harder question than ours.'

Later in the evening Marcus will mention that he compiles *Private Eye*'s 'Dumb Britain' column, the stupid answers given by quiz contestants. I tell him about the team who answered my question 'Which Liverpool club became famous as the venue for many of the Beatles' early gigs?' with 'Everton.' He relates 'Name the funny men who once entertained kings and queens at court. Contestant: Lepers.'

Round two gets underway. We know which road inspired Chris Rea to write 'The Road To Hell' (the M25), we think we know which TV character had a Morris Minor called Miriam (Nurse Gladys Emmanuel in *Open All Hours* – it was actually Lovejoy), we have no idea which ball game was invented by Dr James Naismith (we guess baseball – it was basketball). Question seven – 'Which coloured day of the week was a hit

6. SMS standing for Short Message Service.
7. When the French navy abandoned Morse code in 1997, the last message sent was 'Calling all. This is our last cry before our eternal silence.'

for New Order?' – highlights one of the most famous pieces of pop trivia, namely that 'Blue Monday' is the best-selling 12-inch single of all time. What I don't know, but Marcus does, is that because the record sleeve was so expensive to produce the company lost money on every copy sold. Question nine is 'Barbara Harmer became the first female pilot of Concorde in which year of the 1990s?' Marcus calls this 'the epitome of a boring question. We're just guessing again. Why not make it "In nineteen-ninety-whatever-it-is, Barbara Harmer became the first woman to do which transport-related job?"' A good point. It seems that trivia's appeal, like that of food, depends on how it's presented.[8]

There's another break between rounds. Marcus and I fall to talking about the fascination of trivia.

'For me,' he says, 'I think it's because I've got an intellect that's broad and shallow. I'm interested in lots of things, but there's no depth to my learning. I'm an intellectual dilettante.'

Has he always been like this? At school, for instance?

'I was a very good pupil, certainly when I was younger. Later on I got bored. I remember walking out of my last university maths final saying "That is the last exam I ever sit."'

This strikes a chord. My own experience was the same, except the degree was in politics. And I like the fact that Marcus has come up with a word, dilettante, to replace the one I've always feared could be applied to me: lazy. A love of trivia, goes the worry, shows you haven't got the depth/application/courage to tackle the big questions, to engage in formal study, or at least serious reading. But Marcus's answer has also reminded me of something else. A quote, funnily enough from another *Spectator*

8. 1993. If you're bothered.

TOPOT

> TOPOT
>
> *Jeffrey Bernard, like Mother Teresa, died in the same week as Princess Diana.*

writer, Jeffrey Bernard.TOPOT Of the many brilliant things in his 'Low Life' column, one has stuck in the memory above all others: 'Thinking is the greatest cause of unhappiness. I've never seen an unhappy village idiot.'

I mention this to Marcus, suggesting that perhaps our intellectual lazin— dilettantism is the safest way to be?

He agrees. 'I'm a basically cheerful person. Basically quite sunny. And I don't think too much. Yes, I suppose you could call it a bit "village idioty". But that's how I am. I'm an uncynical person, I find the whole world interesting. My love of trivia is part of that world view.'

But isn't it easy to slip from finding the world interesting into questioning what that world is all about, what the universe is all about, what the meaning of life is? That's when depression can strike. Marcus clearly *isn't* a village idiot, he's a highly intelligent man. Isn't he scared of where that intelligence might lead him?

'No. I know depression can be the curse of cleverness, but I'm essentially an emotional person. My thinking is always secondary to my feeling.' He pauses. 'I have a friend who used to be a Catholic priest. He said his intelligence was "in service to his emotions". I'm the same. I'm like that.'

Intelligence in service to your emotions. I envy Marcus this. If your default emotion, like his, is happiness, your intelligence will always follow. You'll be able to delight in trivia without being sucked down into the meaning of life. I've not always managed this. With no religious belief to cling to, I view life as essentially meaningless. On a good day my mind translates this as 'Enjoy life for what it is,' allowing me to wade happily about in trivia, relishing the fact that three of the first five US presidents died on the same date, that New Order's record company lost money on every copy of 'Blue Monday'. But on a bad day life's lack of meaning can translate as 'Why bother, then?' The same brain that stores all that trivia makes me question the point of gathering it in the first place. On balance, though, trivia – life – always wins. B.B. King knows. 'Better not look down,' he tells us, 'if you want to keep on flying . . . you can keep it moving if you don't look down.' Maybe trivia is the best way of not looking down.

After the first two rounds Marcus and I are fifth out of a dozen teams. Rounds three and four establish that we won't even be finishing in the top half, so we resort to standard male behaviour in such situations: bitching about the quiz-master, chatting about the few questions that interest us. We're intrigued to discover that the spirit on which Pimms No. 1 is based is not our guess of whisky but gin, and that Billy the Kid was twenty-one when he died (clue's in the name, really). Neither of us knows which British bank issued the first cheque guarantee card, but guess Barclays because, as we both know, they had the UK's first cashpoint machine, opened by Reg Varney from *On The Buses*, who withdrew ten one-pound notes. I further know that this happened on 27 June 1967, 40 years to the day before Gordon Brown became Prime Minister; I read a 'fortieth anniversary of the cashpoint' newspaper article on Gordon's big day.[9] Marcus says he thinks that just as Varney was the first to use a cashpoint, Ernie Wise was the first to use a mobile phone. A later check proves him right: Wise made the call on New Year's Day 1985, from a mobile phone in St Katharine's Dock, near the Tower of London, to Vodafone's headquarters in Newbury.

Eventually, the quiz over, we settle into more talk of trivia. Unlike me, Marcus has children. I ask if he can spot his own sense of curiosity in them.

'Oh, sure. My daughter especially. [Martha is eight.] She's like me – she's got an eye for the silly fact. The other day I was telling her about centipedes and millipedes, how there are centipedes with a hundred legs, but no millipedes with a thousand legs. The top millipede is seven hundred and fifty. She loved that.'

That must take him back to his own childhood?

'Yeah. When you're a child you've got this sense of wonder at the world. Everything's amazing. And as you grow up you either lose that or you don't. That sense of wonder either gets eroded or it doesn't. Mine hasn't. I find the whole world interesting.'

Hence the love of trivia?

'I think that's what quizzing is all about. It's about the need to play. As an adult you have a very serious life, most of which is very boring. So you need to have the chance to play. We'd love to be international sportsmen, but we can't. Quizzes take the place of that.'

9. Our Barclays knowledge leads us astray. The cheque guarantee card was the Midland.

This answer both convinces and troubles me. Sure, the international sportsmen point rings absolutely true. If there's a queue of grown men wanting to be Ian Botham at Headingley in 1981 – and believe me there is – the only reason I'm not behind Marcus in that queue is because I'm hitting him over the head with a cricket bat and pushing him out of the way. But equally there's something in what he's just said which bothers me, which *doesn't* ring true. I can't quite put my finger on it.

The pub's TV is showing yet another replay of that day's fumbled catch by Matt Prior. Marcus thinks it will be the end of Prior's Test career. I'm not sure. As our discussion continues, the sports bulletin moves on to rugby, and footage of Lawrence Dallaglio is shown.

'You must know the bit of trivia about him?' I ask.

Marcus shakes his head.

'He's one of the backing singers on "We Don't Need Another Hero" by Tina Turner.'

Again the wide eyes. Again the open mouth. 'Really?'

I nod. 'He was in a choir at school. They were used on the recording session.'^{TOPOT}

'That's fantastic.'

'I know. Don't you just want to share that fact with everyone?'

Marcus looks horrified. 'No way. I'm saving that for a quiz. "Which future England rugby captain . . ."'

> **TOPOT**
>
> *A ten-year-old Keith Richards was one of the choirboys at Queen Elizabeth II's coronation. Yes, that Keith Richards.*

Now I get what was troublesome: Marcus equates trivia with quizzes, and only with quizzes. For him a piece of trivia is a question in the making, so he'll keep it to himself. In conversation it's a caterpillar; only in a quiz can it become the butterfly.

'But the delight you got on hearing that fact just then, don't you want to share that?'

'Yes. In a quiz.'

'What about if you were in the position I was just then? You're in the pub, Dallaglio's on the TV. Don't you just *have* to tell the people you're with?'

'I'd be tempted. But I'd bite my lip.'

'Do you think you could?'

'I know I could.' He smiles. 'Coming here tonight I bumped into some friends, and we got chatting. Basil Brush came up in the conversation – as he does – and I almost physically had to stop myself saying that he'd won *The Weakest Link*. I've got it planned as a question, you see. "Which is the only puppet to win *The Weakest Link*?"'

'So you won't be telling anyone about Churchill and Special Brew?'

'Too right I won't.'

'What if you were talking to a friend who you knew was never going to do your quiz?'

'In the end they all will. There's no escape.'

He's teasing now, but the essential truth remains: Marcus keeps trivia to himself.

'When someone tells me a great piece of trivia,' I say, 'I want to shout it from the rooftops.'

'I write columns for a living,' replies Marcus. 'I get to shout all the time.'

Fair point. And it's not that I can't see the attraction of quizzes. But also I've realised that quizzes are only one small part of this land called Trivia. To explore the rest of it I need some help. I need someone who does shout this stuff from the rooftops, someone who does share snippets about Lawrence Dallaglio and Carlsberg Special Brew.

Someone like my friend Tim.

2

Bombs of delight

The stone column in front of me, I happen to know, is 202 feet tall. What's more, if you were to lay it flat, away from the Tube station behind me, pointing due east, its top would reach the exact point where the Great Fire of London started. It was designed that way, after all, being Christopher Wren's monument to said event. Now known simply as the Monument.

This particular corner of the City is where I'm meeting Tim. He's late, on account of some studio software messing up the levels. After a couple of decades acting and playing in bands, Tim now plies a successful trade as a voiceover artist. One minute he'll be extolling the virtues of a leading brand of shampoo, the next he's adding his silken tones to a Japanese bank's corporate film. Or possibly breathing life into a cartoon rabbit. His proudest moment, however, was being Elvis. It was the King who got him into showbiz originally: 16 when Presley died, Tim was chosen to play the young Elvis in a stage show based on his life. When Radio Two wanted someone to voice Presley for a television trailer, Tim got the gig, the only time the Elvis estate has ever sanctioned anyone to do an impersonation. Not, Tim would want me to point out, that he's an Elvis impersonator. Yes, he can do the voice, yes, he can play the songs – but he has never worn fake sideburns in a Greek restaurant in Enfield on a Tuesday night. Not for the purposes of being Elvis, anyway.

He bounds up the steps from the Tube, as compact and dapper as ever, alternately apologising and slating the software. We make our way up Bishopsgate, passing an *Evening Standard* billboard reading 'Fleet Street Legend Dies'. We say the *Standard* is always doing that, it's bound to be someone we've never heard of,[1] and I give the example of 'Rock Star Dies', which made me buy the paper because I thought it might be Charlie Watts (he'd recently been diagnosed with cancer) but turned out to be someone from Herman's Hermits. This leads to rock star deaths, and Tim's revelation that the policeman who attended the car crash in which Eddie Cochran died was Dave Dee, of Dave Dee, Dozy, Beaky, Mick and Tich. Which reminds me that one of the young British soldiers guarding Rudolf Hess in Spandau Prison after the Second World War was Bernard Manning . . .

It's always like this with Tim. The very reason he's here, of course. Eventually, once we're settled in a bar off Leadenhall Market, I drag the conversation back to its intended purpose. I start by telling him about the quiz.

'I nearly won a pub quiz once,' he says. 'My team put me up for the tiebreaker. I had to stand in a spotlight. I've stood in a few spotlights in my time, but this was worse than any of them. It was ritual humiliation. The question was "What's the world's highest observatory?" The irony was I thought I knew it, but it had changed in the last couple of days and I hadn't seen it.'

1. We're wrong. It's Nigel Dempster.

I tell Tim about my evening with Marcus, how he views trivia merely as quiz fodder.

Like me, Tim disagrees. 'Trivia isn't about pub quizzes. It's about . . .' He searches for an example. 'It's about walking along a Cornish coastal path and seeing a beautiful flock of birds and saying to the person you're with, "Daphne du Maurier wrote *The Birds* after seeing a flock like that and thinking, what if they attacked?"'

I fight the urge to respond with another *Birds* fact,[2] knowing we'll only get sucked into film trivia. One of my first memories of Tim is us both knowing that *Sleuth* is the only film to have its entire cast nominated for Oscars.[3] Instead I ask Tim why snippets like that fascinate him so much.

'They're bombs of joy,' he says. 'They're real treats, they make the world a better place. Trivia makes the journey a little bit more entertaining. Knowing this stuff gives me a feeling of security, in a funny sort of way. It's an affirmation of my own existence. Not that I need that, but it makes me feel alive.'

2. The scene in which Tippi Hedren is attacked by the birds took several days to film, Alfred Hitchcock insisting on retake after retake with live birds (he'd promised Hedren mechanical ones) to elicit the distress he wanted.

3. Its entire cast being Laurence Olivier and Michael Caine. A fact of which my friend Patrick is painfully aware: as a junior reporter on the *Sun* when Olivier died, he and a colleague were told to get quotes from as many of the great man's co-stars as possible. A doddle, they thought. But as deadline approached, they'd only managed one: Dave the barman from *Minder* (Glynn Edwards). Imagine how relieved Patrick was when Michael Caine returned his call. So relieved, in fact, and so awed to be talking to Michael Caine that he forgot to write down a single word Caine said. In true *Sun* style, he made it up.

The bomb image is one Tim will return to. Over the course of our conversation he'll refer to trivia as 'bombs of delight', 'bombs of happiness', 'little electrical charges', 'bolts of lightning'. I like this. It gets across the power that trivia holds – the power to make you say 'No way', to stop a pint glass reaching your lips. But it's a safe power. Trivia is a bomb that can never harm you. It's an explosion of pleasure.

And crucially, Tim points out, that pleasure is all the greater because it's shared. 'The delight in someone's face when you tell them a piece of trivia is brilliant. Something like that Bernard Manning fact – already I'm thinking, I have to tell that to so-and-so. A fact like that is another egg in the basket. It's part of your armoury.'

Armoury? This sounds a momentary note of alarm, reminiscent as it is of the *Secret Policeman's Ball* sketch in which Peter Cook sits on a park bench and annoys John Cleese with so-called 'interesting facts'. ('The whale isn't a fish, it's actually an insect.') Does coming out with trivia, albeit factually correct trivia, make me – make Tim – a bore? A bore who's even worse because he is trying to be a show-off?

Tim laughs. 'Of course not.' His tone is confident without protesting too much. 'It's not about impressing people, it's about pleasing them.'

This seems fair enough. Tim is an affable, charming, socially adept forty-something who has never had trouble forming friendships or attracting women. He knows in which situations he should and should not tell someone that the policeman who found Eddie Cochran was Dave Dee of Dave Dee, Dozy, Beaky, Mick and Tich. And on a good day I'd like to think some of those things apply to me too. Trivia, at least for us, isn't about scoring points, whether in quizzes or conversation. It's about sharing delight.

Has Tim always been like this?

'Oh yeah. Ever since I was a kid.'

What was his family like? What was their attitude to learning?

'Voracious. Whenever we went on holiday my brothers and sister and I would do diaries, keeping ticket stubs and all that. And my dad, who was a headmaster, always told me "Look up." That's really good advice in a city like London. [Tim actually grew up in Suffolk, coincidentally about half an hour from where I live now.] The nose in Meard Street, for instance.'

'Eh?'

'There's a nose halfway up a wall. I don't know what it's about, but I don't know anyone who hasn't gone and found it after I've told them.'

Inevitably, several days later, I maintain the record. Stuck to a building on the south side of this pedestrianised Soho street, about ten feet up, is a nose. Roughly six inches long, it's made of what looks like plaster of Paris. Who knows what it's doing there? Someone's snide comment on the number of media clubs in the vicinity? All I know is I've walked down that street hundreds of times and never noticed it.

For now, though, the mention of Meard Street has me laughing. Tim asks why.

'It's that Peter Cook thing again.' My brain has, as a trivia hound's brain will, done its tangential thing. 'I had a friend who lived on Meard Street. We used to drink in the pubs round there, and one day we were in the Coach and Horses.' Jeffrey Bernard's old haunt. I always wonder how much it helped his thought avoidance. 'Somehow we got talking about *The Day of the Jackal*. Paul knew I liked it and asked when it was written. For a moment I weighed up whether to say it or not. In the end it was irresistible: "The first thirty-five days of 1970." Paul gave a little smile, paused, then said, "*Slightly* more precise answer than I was expecting."'

'Impressive knowledge, though,' says Tim.

'It was just a fluke. I'd known for years that Forsyth wrote it in thirty-five days. But then recently I'd seen a collected edition of his first three novels, which he'd written an introduction for. It explained how he'd got the story mapped out, but couldn't get the name right, couldn't get the right animal. Then, on New Year's Eve 1969, it comes to him: the jackal. He sits down the next morning and starts writing. First of January, start of a new decade – it's going to stick in your memory, isn't it?'

Tim's the same. He recalls being on tour with a play. 'We were in digs in Oldham. One night we bought a takeaway curry, and we're all sitting round eating it, chatting away. Every subject that comes up, at least one of us knows a bit of trivia about it, some little snippet, some fact. The guy whose place it was just ate his curry, watched us, listening to all this stuff. Eventually he said, "Is there nowt you've got nothing to say about?" But he was amused, he wasn't being offensive. Then he said, "Go on, Tim, I'm eating chicken tikka masala, tell me something about that." I tried to stop myself, but I just couldn't. I said, "It was invented in this country, to suit British tastes, it's not actually an Indian dish at all."'

We gaze out at the commuters heading towards Liverpool Street.

'It's to do with recall,' says Tim. 'Stand-up comics always tell you about that. Their job is all about recall, and you find most of them are massively into trivia as well. Recall is uncontrollable. You can't stop yourself remembering this stuff.'

No, but as we've said, sometimes you have to stop yourself saying it.

'True. Depends on the company you're in. I learned that at school. I'd come out with a bit of trivia, and some dour farmer's boy would say, "I'm going to hit you, Whitnall."'

'Do you look for trivia,' I ask, 'or does it look for you?'

'I never search it out,' says Tim. 'But when you find it it's beautiful. Like the fact that the mosquito has twenty-seven teeth. I got that from a beggar at Southgate Tube. Bought it from him.'

'*Bought* it?'

'That was his pitch. He came up to people and said, "I'll sell you a fact for fifty p." So I gave him fifty p, and he told me.'

'Did you check it?'

'Yeah. It's true.'

Thank God I never came across that beggar. The encounter could only have ended with me inheriting his spot as he left Southgate Tube with the deeds to my flat.

Tim confesses to being a 'nightmare in conversation. I get distracted too easily. Anna [his girlfriend] is always trying to bring me back to the point. Equally, she's always asking me, "What do men talk about?" and I always tell her, "It's not sex, it's trivia."'

The first ten minutes of our meeting today were a perfect example. It's not that conversations between Tim and me consist solely of trivia. We're more than capable of discussing serious topics, and frequently do. But sometimes talk gets temporarily kidnapped by trivia. And when that happens it's a nightmare keeping up. Your mouth works more slowly than your brain, and more slowly than the other person's brain, so at any one point you've got half a dozen bits of trivia stacking like planes. It's not a competitive thing, either. In fact it's the opposite: you're disappointed if the other person *doesn't* have a fact to top yours.

Tim's also right about never searching. Trivia is an incidental beast; it should never become a hobby in itself. You don't think, 'let's see what piece of trivia I can learn today'. Then you *would* be Peter Cook on a park bench. Instead it comes when you're least expecting it. Reading a newspaper, a book, watching TV. The information you're presented with is passing you by, failing to register, maybe even boring you . . . and then it comes. One dazzling little fact, a diamond among pebbles, a bomb of delight. The greyhound thing, for instance. It came from *Top Gear*, in a feature where they raced a sports car against a greyhound. Not really being into cars (I like the programme more for its humour) I certainly wasn't expecting to learn anything. Yet when they pointed out that the greyhound was the second-fastest-accelerating animal on the planet, going from nought to 45 miles an hour in one second, I was staggered.

So staggered, in fact, that the statistic was still buzzing around my brain the next day. I mentioned it to my girlfriend.

'How do you remember that sort of thing?' said Jo. Then, a few seconds later, '*Why* do you remember that sort of thing?'

'What I should have responded,' I tell Tim, 'was, "How can you *not* remember something like that? Nought to forty-five in *one* second?"'

Tim's expression is that of the converted being preached to. 'Anna's the same,' he says. 'What did Jo say when you told her about writing this book?' Tim, it should be pointed out, knows and likes Jo, just as I know and like Anna.

'She said, "I know what trivia's about. It's about you and your mates hiding from real life."'

Tim doesn't seem surprised. 'Whenever I mention the JFK assassination, Anna says, "Why won't you talk about something real?" And I say, "It's getting shot in the head with a Mannlicher-Carcano rifle – how real do you *want* it?" Then she says, "But it didn't affect *you*, Tim." But it did. It affected the whole Western world.'[TOPOT]

He's got something here. Our fascination with this stuff is precisely *because* it's real. We're not science fiction fans with an encyclopedic memory of every episode of *Star Trek*. The facts we remember are about the *real* world. 'If you showed me a fictional creature that could go from nought to forty-five in one second,' I tell Tim, 'I wouldn't be interested.'

'Of course not,' he says. 'It's the reality of a piece of trivia that makes it great.'

It's that sense of wonder Marcus talked about. A fascination with the world, the incredible things its creatures can do, the bizarre coincidences it throws up. Reality, as we're so often told,

TOPOT

JFK was assassinated on 22 November 1963, the same day Aldous Huxley died. And C.S. Lewis. Two great writers chose about the only day to pop their clogs that would guarantee them zero attention.

is stranger than fiction. Very frustrating for novelists, that. You learn early on that the uncanny incidents in real life have to stay there; put them in a novel and you'll ruin its credibility. Michael Nyman, for instance. I saw the composer on a Tube train once. Just another minor celeb sighting, common in London. A few months later, walking down a New York street, I heard some British voices, turned round – one of them was Michael Nyman. A few months after that, in Amsterdam, scanning the blackboard outside a bar to see if they were showing the English football, I sensed someone beside me doing the same. It was Michael Nyman.[4]

Tim's gone silent. Eyes half-closed, he's scouring his memory, searching for . . . what? After a few moments, it comes to him. 'J.B. Priestley. He wrote a book called *Delight*. We had it when we were kids; my parents have still got it. It's just a collection of things – a couple of hundred words on each – that delight him. A soak in the bath, the smell of a pipe, that sort of thing. And one of them is . . .' Tim's searching again, trying to remember the exact words . . . 'It's something about truth always being stranger than fiction. He gives the example of a couple who've got married, and . . . Oh, I can't remember it exactly. Anyway, *that's* what we're on about. That's what great about trivia. It's only beautiful because it's true.'

As I walk back to Liverpool Street station,[TOPOT] the evening sun glinting off the Gherkin, I have a real sense, for the first time in my search, that trivia might really be important. That underneath its pub-bore veneer there might be real quality, a message

4. The court order now specifies 400 yards.

to be heard, a revelation –
maybe several – about who
we are, how our minds work,
what makes us tick. Jo's 'real
life' barb (echoed, it seems,
by Anna) is making me . . .
not cross – it was a tease, not
a barb – but animated. Even
the word 'trivia' is getting to
me. Or should that be the
word 'trivial', the assumption that telling friends useless bits of
info about anything and everything is meaningless, insignificant,
a sign of nothing more than that you having nothing better to
do. And, while we're on the subject, the assumption that those
bits of info are indeed useless in the first place. I feel a ridiculous but undeniable urge to rail in defence of Knowledge. Who's
to say that a piece of information is useless? Why should anyone
be allowed to judge a fact?

> ### TOPOT
>
> *The City of London has
> no roads. It has Streets,
> Lanes, Alleys and a host
> of one-off oddities . . . but
> no Roads.*

At first this urge is hard to rationalise. But slowly it starts to
make sense. Trivia, far from being trivial, is a symptom of one
of mankind's most important traits, the urge to discover. Fired by
a sense of wonder at the world, we want to find out about it. The
same curiosity that drives explorers and scientists and inventors
drives me and Tim and Marcus. OK, our facts are a little different
– they're swapped in pubs rather than scientific journals, and
concern Bernard Manning rather than nuclear fusion – but the
central point still holds. Indeed sometimes the facts *aren't* different.
If a biology teacher tells his students there are no millipedes with
a thousand legs, it's called learning. If Marcus tells me the same

thing in a pub it's called trivia. And serious explorers can get trivial too. If George Mallory, asked why he wanted to climb Everest, could reply, 'Because it's there,' can't we trivia hounds cite the same reason for knowing that the man who first said 'Because it's there' was George Mallory? You might say an unquenchable appetite to climb the world's tallest mountain is just as pointless as an unquenchable appetite to collect trivia.

A big difference, of course, is that at least Mallory got off his backside and did something. Climbed most of the way up Everest, to be precise.[5] Tim and Marcus and I just read books about people like him, watch documentaries, discuss those books and documentaries with each other. But mightn't our reading and watching and discussing have their roots in the same urge that inspired Mallory? It's called the Discovery Channel for a reason. And even when we know trivia that isn't about serious topics like mountaineering and millipedes – trivia like Hull City being the only one of England's top 92 football clubs whose name contains no letters you can colour in – isn't that still evidence of our enquiring minds? Laugh if you will at what those minds enquire *after*. But the minds themselves are only doing what human minds have always done, and always will do.

And that seems pretty important to me.

Something else. It strikes me at Liverpool Street, as I wait for the train back to Suffolk.

Tim and I mentioned four people, two of whom 'get' trivia

5. If you believe some people he got all the way up, only dying on his way back down. We'll never know of course. That's a trivia egg which can never be hatched. Does that make it more or less fascinating?

and two of whom don't. The two that get it are me and him. The two that don't are our girlfriends.

Small sample size, granted. But I think of the other trivia hounds I know. All of them are men. Then I think of the people I know who have raised eyebrows, made tutting sounds and shaken their heads when those men discuss trivia. They are all those men's wives and girlfriends.

At some point this is going to need looking at.

The train pulls out of Liverpool Street. Over to the right, three or four miles away, stands the Canary Wharf tower (One Canada Square, to give it its proper name). For years the only tall building on the Isle of Dogs,[6] it is now surrounded by an ever-growing cluster of junior skyscrapers. It's still the daddy, though, still Britain's tallest building, and still beautiful, particularly on an evening like this when the setting sun bathes the whole thing in red.

And I remember a day, years ago, round at Paul's, the same Paul who now knows (or, probably more accurately, has forgotten) that Frederick Forsyth wrote *The Day of the Jackal* in the first 35 days of 1970. He was having some decorating done by a guy who'd worked as a brickie on several London skyscrapers, including the NatWest Tower.[TOPOT] What about Canary Wharf? I asked. No, he hadn't worked

> TOPOT
>
> *The Empire State Building contains ten million bricks.*

6. So-called because it was where Henry VIII kept his hunting dogs.

on that, but a mate of his had. In fact he'd worked right at the top, one of the team laying the final few layers of bricks in what was to be, briefly, Europe's tallest building. And he'd deliberately set one of his bricks ten millimetres higher than all the others, so he could say he'd laid the highest brick in Europe.

I always think of that when I see Canary Wharf. It's that rare thing – a piece of trivia not in the public domain, known only to the brickie and his mate and the people they tell. Private trivia, you might call it, an equivalent of the private income enjoyed by old-fashioned gentlemen.[7] For me it's always made an already-great building even greater. Tonight it seems a perfect example of what Tim's been saying. A real bomb of delight.

A few days later an envelope hits my doormat. Tim's photocopied the J.B. Priestley thing.

Number 73 in *Delight*: 'Truth's determination to keep right on being stranger than fiction'. Priestley gives the example of a newspaper reporting a marriage between a woman of 70 and a man of 43. Their romance began with bread pudding ('a speciality of the bride's cuisine'), so instead of a wedding cake they had a bread pudding weighing eight pounds. A honeymoon was impossible as 'the bridegroom must return to his work at the Dogs' Home'. Priestley complains that novelists and playwrights aren't allowed such 'glorious extravagances.

7. Trivia about the tower that *is* in the public domain includes the fact that its aircraft warning light flashes 57,600 times a day, and that its thirteenth floor contains no rentable offices, only the building's air-conditioning equipment. This is thought to be for reasons of superstition, much as many hotels omit a thirteenth floor.

But Reality pleases itself and does not give a damn, throwing eight-pound bread-puddings about and whisking bridegrooms back into Dogs' Homes . . .'

And that's the point. Reality pleases not only itself but also us, in a way fiction never can. Trivia, if it's true, is indeed a glorious extravagance.

Ah – *if* it's true. This has been playing on my mind. It's far from unknown for trivia – quite widely believed trivia – to be untrue. This is that horrible grey area where trivia meets urban myth, inhabited by such 'facts' as the one about TV presenter Bob Holness playing the saxophone solo on Gerry Rafferty's *Baker Street*. For several years in the 1990s that was a commonly touted piece of information. Touted almost as commonly now is the explanation of how the myth got into the public domain. A music journalist called Stuart Maconie used to write a spoof 'Ripley's Believe It Or Not' column for the *New Musical Express*, containing obviously untrue pop 'facts' like 'Michael Jackson owns the rights to the board game Connect Four'. Someone picked up his Bob Holness snippet and believed it. The rest was history. Very unreliable history.[8]

You could say that the popularity of even an untrue piece of

8. I had to check all this while working as a researcher on a Radio Four documentary about urban myths. Holness himself was far too canny to deny it (though he never actually confirmed it either), knowing that the fifty quid interview fees from programmes like ours would dry up. Maconie was happy to relate his part in the tale. As further insurance we tracked down the man who really *did* play the saxophone solo, a session musician named Raf Ravenscroft. I recorded him putting his phone into a saxophone and playing the solo down the line. One of the more surreal, though not unpleasant, experiences I've ever had.

trivia shows our desire to be amazed by the world. Plenty of spoof facts appear day after day. Yet not many have the legs shown by Holness/Rafferty. No one spread the thing about Michael Jackson owning the rights to Connect Four. There was obviously something inherently compelling, and believable, about the notion of that particular sax solo being played by that particular celebrity. It surprised us, seized our imaginations, tickled our 'no way' glands. And how more unbelievable is it than the notion of one of the backing singers on a Tina Turner hit being a future England rugby captain? Which definitely *is* true: Dallaglio has confirmed it, saying he was 'very proud' of his time as a chorister, during which he also sang at Andrew Lloyd Webber's wedding.[9]

So as soon as you find out it's untrue, disappointment sets in. It's like discovering that Father Christmas isn't real. Or that the word posh doesn't come from a shipping company charging more for the cabins that faced 'port out, starboard home' on Far East routes. That seems to be the consensus, anyway. Some still cite the claim as true, but P&O deny ever issuing any such tickets. And when it comes to trivia, any doubt is too much doubt.

I realise that my search has reached its first conclusion: *The perfect fact must be true.*

---

9. Holness, it should be pointed out, is far from lacking in accurate trivia. Not only was he the second man ever to play James Bond – in a 1956 South African radio adapation of *Moonraker*, which came two years after the US TV version of *Casino Royale* – but his daughter Ros was in the band Toto Coelo whose only hit was 'I Eat Cannibals'.

3

Truth is an illusory notion

T hat walk back to Liverpool Street, the thoughts about the 'sense of wonder' of explorers and scientists, stay with me. The relationship between trivia and so-called 'serious' thinking – science, academia – intrigues me. I want to delve deeper.

But first, I decide to test my first criterion for the perfect fact. How much of the trivia we come across is, in fact, true? (This isn't, incidentally, to try and find the perfect fact itself. Already I have a sense that it's going to find me, rather than the other way round.) An initial problem, and something that's been there, underneath the surface of my conversations with Tim and Marcus, is that you don't know you know something until you realise you know it. Until, that is, something sparks your memory into action. There's no mental filing tray marked 'Trivia', to be opened at will, so revealing a comprehensive collection of facts. The trivia only makes itself known once an external stimulus is applied. To take an example found by glancing out of the window as I write this: a Peugeot 309 drives past, and I'm reminded that Porsche wanted to call their 911 the 901, but were prevented by Peugeot, who have the copyright on all three-digit car names with zero in the middle. Yet ask me to 'tell you some trivia' and I'm stumped.

This obviously proves rather troublesome when trying to compile a list of trivia. So I reach a compromise: give it a few days to see what pops into my mind, then if necessary look up some trivia from scratch. There's a good start within hours, when *Channel Four News* interviews William Hague from its Westminster studio, whose backdrop is Big Ben. And I remember: if you stand at the bottom of Big Ben with a radio, you hear the chimes on Radio Four (which still takes them live for its news) before you hear them 'for real'. This is because radio signals travel at the speed of light rather than the speed of sound.[TOPOT] A second piece of trivia appears later the same evening, courtesy of Gareth who drinks in the village pub. Of course trivia gleaned in pubs – and I say this the venues for my first two interviews notwithstanding – is traditionally viewed with suspicion. The phrase 'pub fact' has, let's be honest, undertones of 'myth'. But Gareth's credibility has on its side the fact that (a) he's a teacher, and (b) he's a teacher of music, which is what this piece of trivia relates to: Chas and Dave played on Eminem's hit 'Stan'. They were session musicians on Dido's track 'Thank You', sampled by Eminem for 'Stan'. My gut instinct is 'Unlikely.' Chas and Dave, session musicians for Dido? Especially on such a quiet, tender song as 'Thank You'? But I add it to my list: if true, Eminem–Chas and Dave will be almost as unlikely a collobaration as Turner–Dallaglio.

After that, though, things go quiet. An email exchange with Tim throws up a

TOPOT

The speed of light is 186,000 miles per second (give or take).

mention of *Brief Encounter*, which in turn reminds me of a great piece of trivia. Unfortunately, however, I know for sure that it's true – having spotted it while watching the film – so it seems unfair to add it to the experiment. Instead I settle for emailing it to Tim as a question: 'Which actress appeared in both *Brief Encounter* and *The Italian Job*?' Tim guesses Irene Handl, then says no, it can't be her . . . but he can't think of anyone else. Either way he's had the 'good grace' not to Google it. 'Surely the mark,' he writes, 'of a gentleman trivialist.' This chimes with my thought on the train about gentlemen and 'private' trivia, but more importantly it also solves the noun problem: 'trivialist' is much better than 'trivia hound', and will replace it forthwith.[1]

So internet trivia lists, as opposed to trivialists, it has to be. This takes some of the fun out of things, because as we've established the best trivia is the stuff you don't look for. Nevertheless, some gems do leap out. Eventually, a hit list of 'facts' is finalised:

- The Big Ben/Radio Four one
- The Chas and Dave/Eminem one
- An ostrich's eye is bigger than its brain.
- Heinz ketchup, at the moment it leaves the bottle, is doing 25 miles per year.
- All polar bears are left-handed.

1. Tim should have had the courage of his convictions. It was Irene Handl. In one of the most entertainingly overacted performances in film history, she plays the organist at the cinema visited by Celia and Trevor. Research undertaken for this footnote (to check her age at the time – 44) throws up the additional fact that Handl was born on the same day – 27 December 1901 – as Marlene Dietrich.

- More money is printed each day by Monopoly than by the US Treasury.
- The housefly hums in the key of F.
- The only country Germany declared war on in World War II was America; all the others declared war on Germany.

I'm really hoping the housefly one is true, because then the fly will be in the same key as Big Ben.[2] This is one of the things about Big Ben I *do* know to be true. Along with the facts that there are words to its chimes,[3] that the minute hand (so memorably held back – or rather, of course, its filmset replica was – by Robert Powell in *The Thirty Nine Steps*)[TOPOT] is 14 feet long, and that the hour hand is 9 feet long. As for the chimes on the radio/in real time thing, though . . . well, it's repeated widely on the internet. But then what isn't? The safest way of settling this one, it seems, will be to do it for real. I make a note to take a radio on my next trip to London.

As three of the queries relate to nature, I decide to group them together and contact a suitably august body who can, with any luck, do the lot. The Zoological Society of London tell me that yes, they have a library, but it can only by consulted by those visiting in person. This seems overly time-consuming; could they recommend anyone else? Yes, 'the Natural History Museum tend to be good on this sort of thing.' Soon I'm

2. Or rather, to be a fundamentalist pedant, the four smaller bells that ring out Big Ben's tune. The big bell itself only does the 'how many hours' chimes, and of course as a single note can't really be said to be in any particular key at all.
3. 'All through this hour, Lord be my guide, And by thy power, No foot shall slide.'

TOPOT

The number of steps up to the Royal Box at the old Wembley stadium was thirty-nine. There are far more at the new one, though Wembley's PO box number remains the same – 1966.

chatting happily away to Claudine in the museum's press office. She sounds intrigued by my book, and will be glad to help. Ostrich, polar bear and housefly details are emailed over. She will forward to the appropriate experts. Three in the bag already – nearly halfway there. By this rate I'll be done by lunch.

For the Heinz ketchup one I go straight to the horse's mouth (the bottle's neck?) and email Heinz themselves. An equally direct route is available for Monopoly's manufacturers Hasbro, and for the US Treasury. The former receives an email asking how much money it prints every day, while the latter saves me even that bother by posting on its website the fact that 'during fiscal year 2006, the Bureau of Engraving and Printing . . . printed . . . currency notes each day with a face value of about $529 million'.[4]

The 'official website' trend continues with a visit to www.chasndave.com. Surely if they've collaborated with Eminem, even indirectly, they'll want the world to know about it? The 'About Us' FAQ section seems most likely. 'Which is

---

4. They also add that 'about 95 per cent of the currency notes printed each year are used to replace notes that are already in circulation'. A very comprehensive website, though sadly it doesn't include the function offered by Hasbro whereby you can download and print their money for free.

which?' tells you that 'Chas is the slightly bigger one sitting at the piano, Dave is the slightly thinner one on the bass.' There is information about the drummer, including a denial that he's either Chas or Dave's father. There's a big paragraph about which Chas and Dave CDs are official and which aren't . . . and then, just as hopes start to fade, I catch sight of the magic word Eminem. *Please* let it not be another denial. 'In the seventies . . .' it starts. Eh? Dido wasn't making records in the seventies. '. . . Chas and Dave were prolific session musicians, playing on many albums for a wide range of artists. One such album was Labi Siffre's "Remember My Song" from 1975.' Already, then, it's clear that Dido is out of the window. But that doesn't matter. The charm of this piece of trivia is the Eminem–Chas and Dave link. 'One of the tracks on this album – "I Got The" – was sampled by Eminem on his breakthrough hit "My Name Is" and is the main musical refrain of the track. Chas is playing guitar and Dave is playing bass.'

There's the sound of a small explosion, as delight makes itself known. The track with which bad-mouthed, trailer-trash rapper Eminem burst shockingly onto the world stage, representing the rebellious instincts and alienated emotions of teenagers by the million, is actually performed by Chas and Dave, previously best known for their lyric 'snooker loopy nuts are we, we're all snooker – loopy'.

Savouring this thought properly demands an early lunch.

On my return, an email awaits from Nigel Dickie. Nigel is no less a person than 'Director, Corporate and Government Affairs, Heinz UK and Ireland'. 'I can confirm,' he writes, 'that Heinz Tomato Ketchup has a speed limit. If during manufacturing, Heinz Tomato Ketchup pours unaided at more than 0.028 mph, it is rejected.' Quick reach for the calculator: 0.028 miles per hour equates to 0.672 miles per day, which equates to 245.28 miles per year (assuming the year in question isn't a leap year). I don't know whether to mark this down as a success or not. The original claim was that ketchup does 25 miles per year, which is out by a factor of ten. But surely the charm of a piece of trivia like this lies not in the figure itself, merely the notion that, as Nigel himself puts it, ketchup has a speed limit. It gives rise to images of crash-helmeted dollops of the stuff driving past miniature speed cameras in a laboratory. Yes, this piece of information is stupid. It might even be useless.[5] But so are jokes, so are sitcoms, so, even – if you want to be strict about it – are the paintings of Rembrandt. But some people get a lot of pleasure from looking at Rembrandts. Just as some people get a lot of pleasure from trivia. The relative merits of the two things can be debated, and you'd be hard pushed to contend that 'Heinz ketchup does 0.028 miles per hour' is as great a contribution to civilisation as *Belshazzar's Feast*. But should we ever cite uselessness as a criticism in itself?

Back at the coalface, only one query remains: that of whether Germany's sole declaration of war during World War II was on America. I'm in the early stages of Googling it when another email arrives. It's Claudine from the Natural History Museum, saying she has farmed out the ostrich and the housefly (as it were), but can tell me already that polar bears are indeed left-handed. It is 'something that we have printed on the pencils that we sell in the Natural History Museum shop'. This is, in anyone's book, a dream

5. Though is it? It's only a particular phrasing of the fact that Heinz doesn't allow its ketchup to be too runny, which is very useful. Not just to the Heinz boffins, either; to anyone who consumes that ketchup.

start. At worst I've proved two out of three, and if you're generous about the ketchup it's a hundred per cent record.

Returning to the search results, Wikipedia's entry for 'Declaration of war' gives a list of all such declarations from World War II. Early September 1939 looks promising, as the United Kingdom, France, Australia, New Zealand, South Africa and Canada all declare war on Germany. Then, as if that wasn't bad enough for Hitler, 9 April 1940 sees Norway join the fray. But tragedy strikes in the very next line: 'May 10th 1940 – Germany declared war on the Netherlands, Belgium, Luxembourg and France.' Damn. Continuing, I find Germany (with or without Italy and/or Romania) declaring war on Yugoslavia, the Soviet Union and, yes, the United States. This piece of trivia has been comprehensively blown out of the water. Scrolling disconsolately down, I reach the 'See also' section, which includes a separate entry for the German declaration of war against the Netherlands. In for a penny, I think, clicking on the link: might as well complete the disillusionment. The entry tells how 'at 6:00 in the morning (Amsterdam time). . . the German envoy Count Zech von Burkensroda gave Dutch minister of foreign affairs Van Kleffens the following German declaration of war. At least, it was later interpreted as such by the Dutch; from the German side it was at the time seen as a mere warning, hopefully intimidating the Dutch enough to accept German military protection . . .'

Hang on. Was it a declaration of war or not, then? Back on the original Wikipedia entry, the 'External links' section refers readers to worldatwar.net, and in particular their 'Chronology of World War II diplomacy'. This list of who did what to whom and when differentiates between 'declares war on', 'invades', and 'breaks diplomatic relations with'. Citing in its own links section the Avalon Project at Yale Law School (a collection of diplomatic documents including declarations of war, armistices, etc.), this was compiled by Richard Doody, who the web soon reveals to be a respected chap in these matters. And he says that on 10 May 1940 Germany *invaded* Belgium, Luxembourg and the Netherlands. France isn't mentioned on that date; their next dealings with Germany are on 22 June (signing of an armistice). On 6 April 1941 Germany *invades* Yugoslavia (and, seeing as they're in the area, Greece). I'm just starting to build up hope again when I reach 22 June 1942: 'Germany, Italy, Romania and Bulgaria declare war on the Union of Soviet Socialist Republics.' Double damn. Buggered by Barbarossa.

And yet still I don't want to give up. The fact that this is only a web page – albeit a seemingly authoritative one – bothers me. A call to the Imperial War Museum's library is answered by a very helpful woman who says she too has heard this 'fact'. Indeed she encountered it while reading war studies at King's College, London, but having mentioned it to friends since, she's never been able to track down the exact source. 'You could try,' she suggests, 'Joe Maiolo at King's. He taught my course.'

The King's website announces Dr Maiolo as, among much else, the current UK editor of the *Journal of Strategic Studies* and a member of the editorial board for another journal, *Intelligence & National Security*. More importantly for my purposes, his research 'focuses on the history of diplomacy, strategy and intelligence in the era of the two world wars'. Despite what must be a busy schedule, he's happy to take my call.

I explain the question under discussion.

'You know what,' he says, with a reassuringly firm American burr, 'I think that's right.'

Think? 'You're a doctor,' I want to say. 'Don't you *know?*' Instead I wait as he voices his thoughts.

'Poland – definitely not. Germany was just responding to a Polish attack, albeit a set-up one. The Soviet Union – no, there was no declaration of war before Barbarossa.'

I'm confused now. This is how I'd always seen Germany's attack on the Soviet Union: the whole point was that it was a surprise. Hitler was hardly going to give Stalin a clue by declaring war, was he?^{TOPOT} After seeing the worldatwar.net mention, I assumed that Hitler declared war *after* invading. About to raise this with Dr Maiolo, I stop myself. He's just said he's sure there was no declaration. Saying 'But I've seen this thing on the internet . . .' is unlikely to impress.

Besides, I'm reaching a conclusion. Not on the question of whether America was the only country Germany declared war on in World War II. On the question of how easy it is to reach

---

TOPOT

The British embassy in Moscow was directly opposite Stalin's private apartment in the Kremlin. Hating the fact that the first thing he saw every morning was his sworn capitalist enemy, Uncle Joe ordered that the British be offered the choice of any other building in the city. Knowing why this had been done, the British opted to stay put.

---

conclusions. Life is full of apparently simple statements, whose truth or otherwise would, you assume, be equally simple to prove. Not just trivia; information in general. And yet here I am, talking to an academic who specialises in the area, and even he can't give me an absolutely definite answer. I respectfully say that it would be unfair to take up too much of his time, and ask if he knows of anyone else who has studied the question in depth. There's no one, apparently; it would be a case of looking up the detailed events, country by country.

I thank Dr Maiolo for his time and hang up. This search is leading into unnerving territory. How much of the information you hear can you actually trust? How much of what you're told in life is true? For a while it troubles me. I stare at my list of facts to be checked with growing despondency. But not for long. Only halfway through, I tell myself. Who knows what tomorrow's research will bring? To take my mind off things I download the Labi Siffre song from iTunes.

Chas and Dave sound great. There's not a 'gertcha' to be heard.

The next morning, mid-seventies pop-funk still running round my brain, I resume work. Claudine has emailed to say she's not had much luck with the housefly but there has been progress on the ostrich. Only partial, though. They can't 'easily get a response on this without undertaking much more extensive research. However, one of our scientists in our bird group has said that in a 1958 book entitled *1001 Questions Answered About Birds* (that he's found to be generally accurate) the following is written: "The eyes of birds are the largest structures in their heads and often weigh more than their brains. Of all land animals in the world, the ostrich has the biggest eye.'" Claudine knows this doesn't absolutely answer the question, but hopes that it helps.

It certainly does. For a start it's amazing that the ostrich is the land animal with the biggest eye. And it gives you a warm feeling inside to know that there's a book in this world called *1001 Questions Answered About Birds*. But a definitive answer will have to be found elsewhere. Again, the internet repeats without proving. The BBC's *Newsround* site mentions the 'fact'. Wikipedia's ostrich entry includes 'it is often said that their eyes are larger than their brains'. Yes, and it's often said that Elvis is still alive. Wikipedia cites other web pages (including *Newsround*) as evidence, but none of these offer actual measurements. Somone at Eden Ostrich World in Cumbria tells me the brain is the size of a pea and the eye that of a large marble, but asked how she knows this mentions our old friend 'common knowledge'. The American Ostrich Association (www.ostriches.org) provide a comprehensive general information page. While it doesn't actually answer the eye/brain question, it does say that if you require any further information, the AOA will be 'glad to hear from you'. An email is dispatched.

Still no reply from Monopoly, and with several days to go before my next trip to London, when Big Ben can be tested, I'm at heel-kicking stage. Reading between the lines of Claudine's last email, however, it doesn't sound as though I should be putting all my housefly eggs in the museum's basket. I set to work on finding an alternative expert. A few minutes on Oxford University's website introduces George McGavin, Assistant Curator of Entomology at the University's Museum of Natural History. As if this title doesn't confer expert credentials enough, he even *looks* like an expert (largely on the grounds that he has a beard).

He answers my email within the hour. Warning that the 'wing beat frequency of insects will vary with species, size . . . sex, age, ambient temperature, relative humidity, etc.' he goes on to mention a study of the *Musca domestica* (housefly) which gave a frequency of between 141 and 164 cycles per second.

Another web page soon reveals that this range covers the D, E flat and E below middle C on a piano. You can't make much of a tune with those notes, certainly not one in F. I email George to thank him for his time anyway. He replies that, for the sake of completeness, I might like to contact Dr Graham Taylor of the university's zoology department. Taylor makes the clinching point that insects vary wing-beat frequency continuously, resulting in a glissando rather than a scale of any sort.

So at least, unlike the German declarations of war, I know for sure. The housefly does not buzz in the key of F. The more you consider it, this piece of trivia smacks of someone having a laugh, much as a music journalist once made a joke about Bob Holness. But then so does the idea that all polar bears are left-handed, and that one *is* true. Talking of which: *why* are they all left-handed? Not wanting to bother Claudine too much, I get back on the internet. Soon the website of Polars Bears International appears. An esteemed non-profit conservation body, these people clearly know their polar bears. Which is why I'm horrified to find, on their 'Myths and Misconceptions' page, that the left-pawed (as they correctly call it) belief is *un*true. 'Scientists observing the animals,' they write, 'haven't noticed a preference. In fact, polar bears seem to use their right and left paws equally.'

Eh? But it's on the Natural History Museum's pencils. I communicate the bad news to Claudine, who admits she didn't consult an expert on this one. (Who can blame her? If you can't trust the Natural History Museum's pencils then whose pencils *can* you trust?) She'll get straight on the case. Hopefully we'll soon be pitting the museum against Polar Bears International. Experts at dawn.

By now my faith in this supposedly concrete structure called Knowledge is beginning to shake again. It gets even worse when my friend Rob calls. Telling him about Chas and Dave, I realise that the original Labi Siffre track is in reality two tracks put together. The second, which starts about two minutes in – and from which the 'My Name Is' sample was taken – has a different chord struc-ture, different melody, different everything. Often when this happens the second part will be recorded days later – or earlier – than the first. . . and sometimes with different musicians. Checking the exact wording on Chas and Dave's website, I notice they don't claim to have played on both halves of the track, though they don't say they didn't. And the last twenty-four hours have proved that to be absolutely certain of something, if indeed you ever can, 'i's need dotting and 't's crossing. All of them.

'Only one thing for it,' says Rob. 'You've got to call Chas and Dave.'

He's right. Sod it, he's right.^{TOPOT}

Ten minutes after we hang up, Rob sends a text. It's occurred to him that Eminem's character in *8 Mile*, the film in which the rapper plays a thinly disguised version of himself, is called Rabbit. Perhaps there's more to this Chas and Dave link, says Rob, than meets the eye.

Thanking him for his input, I break for lunch.

* * *

TOPOT

Chas and Dave are the original Chas and Dave. The same cannot be said of 1960s soul duo Sam and Dave. Following an argument, Sam sacked Dave and recruited a replacement. Following another argument, Replacement Dave sacked Original Sam, recruiting a Replacement Sam in his place. A musical equivalent of the philosophical conundrum about whether a broom with a new head and a new handle is still the original broom.

Key to these questions of accuracy and trust – key, indeed, to the whole issue of trivia in the twenty-first century – is the internet. Not only has the net made it so much easier to spread trivia, both via websites themselves and via email, it has also made people less trusting of that trivia. I think back to my chat with Tim. As our discussion widened out from J.B. Priestley's *Delight* to books in general, Tim said he was wary of the net, being more inclined to believe the trivia he came across in books. I understand this. It is, of course, the very ease with which the net disseminates trivia that makes one so hesitant to believe it. 'Web of deceit' has taken on a whole new meaning.

But the more you consider this, the more it seems unfair. Or at least a matter of degree rather than principle. Books can repeat mistakes too, and frequently have.[6] The problem is not

6. Even dictionaries get things wrong. Some early ones mistakenly picked up the non-existent word 'slughorn', supposedly a kind of trumpet. Believing them, Robert Browning used the word in a poem.

the medium by which information is transmitted, it is the checking of that information in the first place. And as that's a process carried out by humans, it will always be prone to error. Yes, it might be argued, but aren't the checks carried out by authors and publishers before the printing of a book more stringent than those carried out (or not) by a 14-year-old cyber-geek in his Kansas bedroom? On balance, you'd have to say yes. But it is only on balance. Some authors, some publishers are less stringent than others. Some website builders are more stringent than others. And even where every effort *is* made to check facts, as my last few hours with World War II and polar bears have shown, absolute certainty is rarely on offer.

Besides, just as the internet has made it easier to commit errors, it has also made it easier to correct them. If, in the 'good' old days, you read something in a book, and found yourself inclined to doubt it – less likely in itself, of course, these *being* the good old days – you had to track down another book to check it. Say that book disagreed: which would you believe? No use saying 'the book whose author seemed more authoritative', because that applies to websites too. You had to track down more books, and yet more, to establish where the weight of evidence seemed to lie. Exactly the same is true on the internet, yet it takes a fraction of the time. You don't have to wait for libraries or bookshops to open, or for those libraries and bookshops to locate the book you require. That's assuming you *knew* the book you wanted, of course. No search engines to point the way in those days. No 'Ctrl F' either, quickly finding the word or phrase you needed among thousands of others.

And of course sometimes the truth doesn't stay the truth. It will always be the case that Spencer Perceval was the first British Prime Minister to be assassinated. At the moment, he's the only one. If that changes, it's a fair assumption most of us will hear about it. But other changes won't be so widely publicised. Heinz might change the speed limit of their ketchup, for instance. And some changes happen without *anyone* knowing about them, certainly for a while: natural selection must have been making fish smaller (so they could get through fishing nets) for at least a short time before fishermen and scientists noticed.[7] But when a truth does stop being true, surely the internet is quicker to reflect that than books? Web pages can be altered in seconds; books take months.

Despite my head being convinced of all this, though, my heart can't help agreeing with Tim. I'm aware of the inconsistency between saying that internet lists take the fun out of trivia because they make it too easy to find, and saying that *Schott's Miscellany* is a thing of beauty. But that's how I feel. There is something about a book that says 'authority', 'worth', 'weight'. It demands your attention – your respect, even – in a way no website ever can. Why should this be? Is it because a book, unlike a website, physically exists? Does its actual weight translate into moral weight? If so, aren't we book snobs guilty of the crime we're often known to accuse others of: choosing style over substance?

Perhaps. But I think there's a different reason. Those of us over, say, 35 are the last generation who had an entirely non-internet-assisted education. Our whole experience of school – and, if we went there, university too – was conducted through

7. It's like the old one about whether a tree falling over in a deserted forest makes a sound. Is a fact that no one knows really a fact?

books.[8] To learn was to read from a printed page, not from a screen. Maybe our preference for books is no more than the nostalgia any generation attaches to its childhood, a bound-volume fetish that will soon seem as ridiculous as the Monty Python 'tougher in my day' Yorkshiremen. Maybe to today's schoolchildren it already does.

But being ridiculous doesn't stop a feeling holding you in its spell. The power of a book-gleaned fact is more than the combined weight of paper, ink, cover and glue. It's the work you put into finding it. When, as a child, you went to the library and searched for the three books that would be your companions for the next week, you were actually choosing three authors whose world views would shape yours for those seven days. To read a book was to see things, see *everything*, through the prism of the person who wrote it. Whatever the subject – insects, astronomy, horse-riding – you learned what that person thought you should learn. A limited number of facts were chosen by them, ordered by them, explained in the way they thought best. Now Google lets you search a trillion facts through whichever prism you want. Or no prism at all. A Wikipedia article, peppered with its clickable words and terms, can have you three subjects away quicker than you can say 'attention span'. If you'd given me that option as a boy sitting in the library of a small Midlands town in the 1970s, I'd have bitten your hand off. Yet now, in a perverse way (and what could be more perverse than nostalgia?), I prefer things how they

8. Except, possibly, for the 'schools television' programmes broadcast during class hours. These were preceded by a clock that counted down the seconds to transmission with disappearing dots, which pupils would shoot away with imaginary guns.

were. The exhilaration at unearthing an amazing fact was all the greater because you'd worked so hard for it. Waited so long. Waded through so many boring pages.[9]

Even now, when I drive past that modest Georgian building (which has long since ceased to be the library), I can recall the thrill of going through its stone porch, pushing open the heavy wooden door, causing the leaflets to flutter on the noticeboard in the hall . . . Then turning right into the – as it seemed back then – huge room housing the books. You'd spend ages examining the shelves, reading back covers, flicking through pages, deciding which books excited you the most. Finally you would carry your chosen three to the desk, where a wooden tray held all the slips denoting volumes on loan. The librarian would take the books you were returning, find their slips in the tray, remove them from the three triangular green cardboard jackets bearing your name. Then your new books would be stamped with a date, the date until which they were yours. Carrying the books home, you'd wonder what secrets they were going to reveal. Because that's what this was all about: secrets. That library, to my eight-year-old eyes, contained every secret in the world. All human knowledge collected together in one building.

It could be argued that the day you find yourself saying 'I appreciate something more the harder I work for it' is the day you grow old. You could dress it up intellectually, declaring that 'Facts have a higher value when they're harder to find' is no

9. And, if it was a fact you needed for an essay, copied out in longhand. Has any research been done into the effect on spelling ability of cut-and-paste? This innovation means we no longer have to spell difficult (or indeed easy) words or names for ourselves; the computer does all the work.

more than a statement of the most basic law of economics. Either way, the relationship between a love of reading and a love of facts, of trivia, is best summed up for me by one book: the *Guinness Book of Records*.

I only ever owned one copy. It was the 1982 edition, which I got for Christmas 1981. When you're ten years old the very fact that something has next year's date on it causes excitement enough, but this book – hardback, 350 pages, measuring 30 centimetres by 21[10] – soon won a place in my affections that wouldn't be lost until well after 1982 was history. I would read it for hours on end. Or rather delve into it. That was one of the joys: you could open it up at any page and be guaranteed something interesting. Inclusion in this book depended, by definition, on being world-beatingly special. There was seemingly endless scope for poring over its facts and figures and pictures and captions and special boxes, learning about the world through its extremes, marvelling at the universe and related stuff.

The fact that the *Guinness Book of Records* exists at all is due to trivia. In November 1951 the managing director of the Guinness brewery, Sir Hugh Beaver, was on a shooting party in the exquisitely named North Slob, an area near the River Slaney in Ireland's County Wexford. He got involved in an argument (as people often will, though thankfully they're not usually holding guns at the time) over which was the fastest game bird in Europe, the golden plover or the grouse. Back at his host's stately home, he found it impossible to confirm the answer from reference books.[11] There must be countless arguments of that type, he

10. Information which I have, of course, just obtained from the internet.
11. It's the grouse.

realised, in pubs the length and breadth of Britain every night. Why not compile a book to settle them?

The job was given to twins Ross and Norris McWhirter, students who were running a fact-finding agency. A thousand copies were printed and distributed free in pubs. 'It was a marketing giveaway,' Beaver said later. 'It wasn't supposed to be a moneymaker.' Conversation-starter it may have been. But so many conversations got started that the McWhirters' collection of trivia, issued the next year as the first *Guinness Book of Records*, went straight to the top of the British best-seller lists. Half a century and over a hundred million copies later, no one could deny that there's gold in them thar facts.

Even as a schoolboy, though, I knew it wasn't *just* the facts: it was the stories behind them. Time after time I would return to the entry for 'highest individual score in any first-class cricket match': 499, by a player called Hanif Mohammed from somewhere called Pakistan. And the sentence that got me every time, which I would stare at for literally minutes on end, was the one stating that he was *run out going for his five hundredth run*. Every time it made me cringe, imagining his agony at having so nearly made it. It was almost as though if I came back to it often enough, one day I'd open the book and find he *had* got to 500.

Another compelling record was that for tallest human being ever. This was (and remains) an American from the early part of the twentieth century, his name scored into my memory by countless readings: Robert Pershing Wadlow. He was eight feet eleven point one inches tall. Again, part of the reason for coming back was a vague expectation that he might make that final point nine of an inch. Yet also I knew this was one record you wouldn't want to hold. Quite apart from the horror of living your life as a freak, there was the fact that Wadlow's height resulted from a medical condition. He died in his twenties. That made me sad every time I read it.

It was an early lesson that trivia is never just about trivia.

All that can be achieved after lunch is a phone call to Chas and Dave's manager, who is called (what else?) Barry. In no way wishing to cast aspersions on the reliability of Chas and Dave's website, I explain, it would nevertheless be a real help if either of them could spare a few moments to go over the finer details of the Eminem thing. Barry says Chas does all the interviews. He'll see what he can do.

Apart from that, it's a case of sending reminder emails and/or sitting back to wait. Ostriches, Monopoly, polar bears, Big Ben – all hang in the balance.

Over the next few days, doubts set in as to whether any piece of trivia, indeed any fact at all, can ever be seen as totally, categorically, undeniably true. For a start there are the deep philosophical questions which epistemologists spend their days tackling. How can you be certain there isn't a tiger under your dining room table, that sort of thing. I find myself trawling internet discussions in which people say things like 'If we claim that we can never be 100 per cent certain of anything, aren't we 100 per cent certain that we can't be 100 per cent certain of anything (which proves by contradiction that we can be 100 per cent certain of something)?' I feel a sense of relief at not being an epistemologist.

But it's not just angels-on-a-pinhead stuff. Even the apparently simple questions I'm trying to answer give rise, on further inspection, to all sorts of doubts and uncertainties. The Monopoly/US Treasury one, for instance. What does the wording actually mean? That Monopoly prints more *US* money every day than the US Treasury? Or more money of all denominations, in all the game's versions around the world? Surely the latter is pretty meaningless? It would only be fair to compare that figure with all the money printed by every treasury around the world. I send a qualifying email to Hasbro, who still haven't responded to the first.

Then there's the issue of whose testimony to believe. Take one of the most famous pieces of trivia ever: that Henry Stanley, encountering the man he'd been scouring Africa for, said, 'Dr Livingstone, I presume?' For well over a century this was accepted as fact. Yet the most recent biography of Stanley concludes that it is untrue.[12] Insecure about his lowly, uneducated background, goes the argument, Stanley invented the phrase subsequent to the meeting, in order to make himself sound witty. (Perversely, people then castigated him for flippancy at a serious moment.) The claim appears in his autobiography, yet the relevant pages in his diary have been torn out, and in the days following the encounter Livingstone mentioned the phrase to no one. The biography makes a convincing case. Yet as you follow the logic through you realise that we will *never* know. The only people who could know for sure were Livingstone, Stanley and their groups – all of them long dead.

Not that certainty is guaranteed even when witnesses are still living. Self-interest, desire to protect your reputation – or destroy someone else's – simple errors of memory . . . all can conspire to frustrate the seeker after truth. Peter Morgan, author

12. *Stanley: The Impossible Life of Africa's Greatest Explorer*, Tim Jeal, 2007

> TOPOT
>
> *David Frost is five feet eleven and a half inches tall. When filling in forms he makes a point of answering this precisely, feeling that to round it up to six feet would be deceitful.*

of the play *Frost/Nixon*, researched it as thoroughly as he could. Yet in the end he had to admit that 'truth is an illusory notion . . . everyone I spoke to told the story their way. Even people in the room tell different versions. There's no one truth about what happened in those interviews.'TOPOT

It makes you realise how many of the everyday statements we toss around so casually, and accept as gospel, rely on individual perspective, generalisation, average values, approximations and a million other niceties. The exercise changes my view of just about every piece of information I hear. A survey in the news, for instance, states that 'teaching is now the most stressful profession in the UK'. But what does this actually mean? How big was the sample size, how was the survey conducted? Did it include *every* profession? How did they measure the stress? Were all respondents medically examined, or merely asked how stressed they felt? And of course even when results were obtained, they were only averages. There will be plenty of people in 'less stressful' occupations far more stressed than some teachers. There will even be some people in the *least* stressful occupation more stressed than the *most* stressed teacher.

Forget what they say about lies, damned lies and statistics. Do we really know *anything* for sure?

* * *

Gradually, replies start to appear. Yes, Chas will talk to me. I phone at the appointed hour, and he's happy to confirm that he and Dave played on the whole track. He remembers the session well, and that Labi Siffre himself played the keyboards. The first he heard of the Eminem connection was from his son. 'He came into the room and said, "I can't believe it – my dad's on a worldwide hit!"' What about royalties? 'We ain't had any yet, but someone's chasing it up. We've signed something, anyway.'

Douglas Osborne of the American Ostrich Association responds: 'Wet or dry, sir?' Confused, I seek clarification. He means the 'eye of a freshly killed ostrich still full of fluid or the dried version'. Figuring that the former increases my chances, I opt for that. He confirms that the wet eye is bigger than the brain. Pressed for measurements, he confesses to only 'eyeballing' it (very apt), but puts the brain at one and a quarter inches in diameter, the eye at one and a half. Not much in it – and how many one-and-a-quarter-inch peas do you see, Miss Eden Ostrich World? – but I mark it down as a victory.

Hasbro finally get back to me. Their latest figures show an average printing of $144,007,671,232 per day, over two hundred times the US Treasury's output. Though this is only because of their Here and Now edition of Monopoly, which includes $165,500,000 worth of currency per set. The property market really has gone mad.

Bad news, however, from Claudine. 'We try our best,' she writes, 'to check all facts about the natural world on the items we sell in the Natural History Museum shop. The polar bear pencils were created by an external company. As you know, research into animals and their behaviour is continually shaping our knowledge of the natural world, often challenging commonly held beliefs. Indeed we now believe it is a myth that polar bears are left-handed and we will no longer be selling them [the pencils, not the bears] in the shop.' It's stupid, but a genuine pang of guilt appears at the thought of all the children who have bought those pencils. Then I realise it's not just the children. I'm disappointed too. I *want* all polar bears to be left-handed.

The disenchantment lingers. It's still there, two days later, on the train up to London. Big Ben has taken on a far greater burden of responsibility than is strictly fair for a single bell, even one as weighty and famous as this. If it can't be heard first on the radio then another ray of wonder will be extinguished. I desperately want this fact to be true.

But *can* it be true? Yes, we know the theory: the only part of the note's journey travelled at the speed of sound is the few feet from bell to microphone. After that – down the line to the BBC, up to the transmitter, out over the radio waves – it travels at the speed of light. It doesn't *feel* believable, though. It just seems counter-intuitive that that whole journey can happen quicker than a sound wave reaches someone standing at the bottom of the tower.

I make my way to Westminster. It's a sunny day. Tourists are milling around, smiling as they pose for relatives crouching to get the famous clock in shot. A stallholder selling Beefeater teddy bears exchanges cheery banter with his customers. Yet my demeanour is closer to that of Churchill on his statue in

Parliament Square: grim determination in the face of all odds. Tempted to stay on the other side of the square to maximise my chances, I nevertheless force myself up Westminster Bridge Road until I'm right next to St Stephen's Tower.

Portable out, earpiece in, Radio Four selected. To make differentiation as easy as possible, I stand with my right ear facing Big Ben, my left, containing the earpiece, facing away. The *PM* programme is coming to a close; just the weather to go. When that finishes, the presenter bids farewell. Then there is silence. The next thing I hear will be Big Ben. Or rather, it dawns on me now, one of the four smaller bells that play the tune. Still, the principle's the same.

Despite the traffic noise, nerves and concentration mean that all I can hear is the radio's gentle hiss of static.

The seconds – they feel like hours – tick by.

And then there's the sound of a bell.

It's in my left ear.

A third of a second later it's in my right ear. As the next few notes sound, the same thing happens. And I know it for sure: you hear Big Ben on the radio first.

Five minutes later, walking up Whitehall, I phone my girlfriend to share the good news. Jo's happy for me. As we carry on chatting, I cross the road by the statue of Field Marshal Earl Haig, and notice that his horse has its front left hoof[13] raised. An ancient piece of trivia appears from behind the clouds of memory: one hoof raised means the rider was injured in battle; two hoofs raised means they died in battle; no hoofs raised

13. Or, as I absentmindedly call it, 'paw'. Jo finds this very amusing.

means they died of natural causes. Instinctively I begin to look for Haig's dates. But no . . . Quit while you're ahead.[14]

Thinking back over the pieces of trivia I've tested, a distinction emerges. There was a yearning for Big Ben to be true, as there was for polar bears to be true, though with a different result. But ostriches? Despite it proving correct, I could take or leave ostriches. Had the brain been bigger than the eye it wouldn't have been upsetting. Why should this be?

The word, it seems to me, is 'charm'. There's something undeniably charming about the world being so mixed up, the laws of nature so perverse, that you can hear something before you hear it. Likewise the notion – even though it's a completely unfounded notion – of all polar bears being left-handed. Here the charm is slightly different; it's a childlike charm (the Natural History Museum must have thought so, to put it on their pencils), a charm rooted in humour – I keep getting the image of a polar bear struggling with a right-handed guitar. But the difference in size between an ostrich's eye and its brain doesn't have that charm. It doesn't engage the imagination.

The search has reached its second conclusion:

The perfect fact must be charming.

14. A wise move. Later research shows that Haig died of old age in 1928, and that the hoofs thing is a myth.

4

Apophenia rules

Time to pick up where I left off with Tim. Namely the idea that there are links between trivia and proper learning, that the information spectrum doesn't span from important at one end to trivial at the other. There was also the sense of wonder, a notion that trivia might represent the explorer instinct in cerebral form. Somewhere, I'm sure, there will be an expert who can develop this. But who? To help me find the right expert, I need the right non-expert.

Toby, in his way, is one of the most intelligent people I have ever met. If the 'in his way' sounds patronising, it isn't meant to be. All I mean is his intelligence marries the trivial with the serious, and at the moment that's exactly what's required. We know each other from my BBC radio days in London, when he was one of the performers in a weekly satirical show. In the bar afterwards, and no matter who the other guests were (fifty-something political editors, stand-ups barely out of their teens), Toby always had something to contribute. Tales of debauchery at the Royal Shakespeare Company, insights into *The Simpsons* . . . and great trivia.

We meet, for the first time in a while, in Soho. Toby looks

well; at 42 he's still not put any weight on, and impending marriage – a day some of us thought would never come, though not for the reason you get with a lot of actors – has given him a distinctly healthy sheen. We're at the Courthouse Hotel, which, in its former life as Great Marlborough Street Magistrates' Court, provided the venue for my one and only brush with the law (busking, fined £20).[TOPOT] The courtroom itself is where guests now take breakfast, while the cells have been incorporated into the bar. Still replete with toilets, whose bowls now contain nothing worse than flowers, they accommodate two comfortably, four at a squeeze. Feeling like Fletcher and Godber in *Porridge*, Toby and I take up residence.

> ### TOPOT
>
> *Great Marlborough Street Magistrates' Court was where a pre-fame Michael Caine appeared on a palimony charge.*

'You don't need to convince me that trivia isn't always trivial,' he says, toying frustratedly with a packet of cigarettes. The ban on smoking in public places has just come into force. 'Do you know which the first government was to have a smoking ban? The Nazis.'[1]

Trivia that makes a point, I say.

---

1. This sounds suspiciously convenient, but Toby's right. If you discount Pope Urban VII in 1590 (which you should, because his ban only applied to churches, and also he only lasted thirteen days), Hitler got there first. In 1941 he created the Institute for Tobacco Hazards Research, and forbade smoking in any German university, post office, military hospital or Nazi party office.

'Yeah. Like the fact that there have only ever been two communist MPs in Britain, and they were thrown out of Parliament for fighting – *with each other.*'

Has Toby always known this sort of stuff?

'Pretty well. At school I'd remember factoids from biology or whatever, though I never bothered with exams. I'd already decided I was going to be an actor, so I didn't really see the point. Except for the year my Latin teacher said, "Oh, well, you must be stupid then." I worked really hard and came top just to prove him wrong.'

What about his family?

'We were all very knowledge-based. Even as children we weren't allowed to have childish views; we were always encouraged to debate things sensibly. I suppose my trivia comes out of that, the idea that knowledge about the world is good, valuable. *Any* kind of knowledge is a good thing: it's a starting point for discussion.'

That evening at Liverpool Street comes back to me. The unfairness of judging facts . . .

Toby mentioned school. What sort of 'factoids' did he remember?

He thinks for a moment. 'There was a textbook that had two pictures next to each other, and a caption saying "Look how the shape of this river delta is similar to the veining structure of this leaf." It fascinated me. The book was saying it was just coincidence, there was no meaning to it. But years later, after I'd left school, it transpired there *was* some fundamental link, to do with fractals. [Toby explains that these are shapes made up of smaller copies of the same shape.] Even at the time though,

I loved the fact that there was a pattern, a link between these two completely different things.'

At the time, this strikes no real chord. Conversation continues, dotted liberally with trivia to illustrate the points being made. Not that there are many points; a central theme remains elusive, the trivia itself threatening to take over, to become trivia for its own sake. Not that this isn't fun. Toby reveals, amongst other things, that the first ever episode of *Dr Who* was broadcast the day after JFK's assassination (pity – Huxley would probably have liked it), and that first choice for the role of Indiana Jones was Tom Selleck. I mention that there's only one of the top 92 football teams which shares no letters with the word 'mackerel' (Swindon Town), to which Toby replies there's only one Tube station which does likewise (St John's Wood).[2]

Then, returning to films, Toby mentions one he's noticed himself. 'There are three Charlton Heston films in which he spots that the world has ended, or is ending. *Soylent Green, The Omega Man* and *Planet of the Apes.*'

Which reminds me of a list that's formed in my brain over the years: songs about heroin that no one knows are about heroin. Toby gets *Golden Brown* by the Stranglers and the Stones' *Brown Sugar* straight away, is soon led towards *Perfect Day* by Lou Reed, but struggles with the seventies soft-rock classic (*Horse With No Name* by America) and the jangly nineties British pop hit (*There She Goes* by the Las – 'there she goes . . . pulsing through my veins . . .').

Toby likes this one. 'It's patterns, you see. I think a lot of

2. This depends, of course, on not spelling it 'Saint'. Which London Underground don't, so we're fine.

> ## TOPOT
>
> Midnight Cowboy *was the first X-rated movie to win the Oscar for Best Picture. The scene in which Hoffman yells 'I'm walking here' at a cab that nearly runs him over happened for real; they were shooting in New York traffic, and the taxi driver wasn't an actor.*

trivia is about patterns. I love finding connections, bringing together disparate items. The Six Degrees of Kevin Bacon is all about that.'[3]

A recent rewatching of *Midnight Cowboy* comes back to me.[TOPOT] 'The last scene, when they're on the bus and Dustin Hoffman dies,' I say. 'It made me think of *The Graduate*, because that was another movie whose last scene featured Dustin Hoffman sitting on the back seat of a bus.'[4]

'Happens all the time,' says Toby. 'Of course the ultimate example is that list of similarities between Lincoln and Kennedy.' Pausing only to wonder why there's so much trivia about JFK, we assemble some of the list from memory: Lincoln had a secretary called Kennedy, Kennedy had a secretary called

3. The game in which you link Kevin Bacon to any other actor in six steps or fewer. For example Robbie Coltrane: Kevin Bacon was in *Sleepers* with Minnie Driver, who was in *Good Will Hunting* with Ben Affleck, who was in *Shakespeare in Love* with Judi Dench, who was in *Goldeneye* with Robbie Coltrane.
4. Despite their supposed age difference in the film, Hoffman was 30 and Anne Bancroft 36. The leg in the famous poster isn't hers; it belongs to Linda Gray, who played Sue Ellen in *Dallas*.

Lincoln; both were shot on a Friday; JFK's assassin ran from a warehouse and hid in a theatre, Lincoln's ran from a theatre and hid in a warehouse; both presidents were succeeded by a Johnson; both assassins were shot before their trial . . .

Over the coming days, example after example will occur to me of patterns playing a part in my trivia, or rather in how my mind has *stored* that trivia. Within a few weeks in the spring of 1992, Manchester United narrowly failed to win the First Division title, Jimmy White narrowly failed to win the World Snooker Championship, and Labour narrowly failed to win the general election. Each was the latest in a long line of such failures. Ever since, mention of one has reminded me of the other two. Also on snooker, the rules say you have to keep at least one foot on the floor – as did the rules of old Hollywood love scenes. Learning that the one thing the SAS never say before a mission is 'Good luck,' I filed them away with actors. Sometimes the pattern can be of opposites: Ringo Starr has never eaten a pizza, while Shane Warne *only* eats pizza, often forcing upmarket restaurants to cook him one. While each of those facts might be memorable in themselves (not least because they're exactly what you'd expect of the people in question – if you had to pick one of the Beatles who'd never eaten a pizza it would be Ringo, wouldn't it?), they now nestle in my mind side by side, cross-referenced as bastard twins of trivia.

Toby is scrabbling in his jacket pocket. He brings out a copy of the *Fortean Times*.

'Oh God, Toby, not this again.' The *Fortean Times* is where he and I part company. A monthly magazine devoted to what Toby would call 'the paranormal and associated phenomena' and I would call 'mad stuff', it covers UFOs, conspiracy theories, cults . . . everything, in other words, that trivia *isn't* about. At least not my kind of trivia – it's not true. Certainly not provably true. It's closer to fiction than fact.

Toby, though, begs my indulgence. He's searching for a particular page. 'There you are,' he says, showing me a picture. 'Simulacra.'

'Eh?'

'Simulacra. Patterns where there aren't any.'

I examine the picture. It's a rock in which the sender of the photo claims to have perceived a face.

'It's a regular feature,' says Toby. 'Simulacra are significant pictures or patterns appearing in the natural world.'

'Yes, but it's not significant, is it? It's different shades of moss. Which, if you squint, look a bit like a face. It's the same as those people who see Jesus in their toast.'[TOPOT] And indeed Esther Rantzen. She made a career out of this sort of thing on *That's Life*, though in her case it was carrots resembling genitals.

'Of *course* it's not significant. That's what I'm saying. There

---

TOPOT

Jesus probably wasn't born on Christmas Day. His exact date of birth being uncertain, early worshippers appropriated an existing festival on 25 December. Someone who definitely was born on that date, in 1964, is ex-Scottish footballer Gary McAllister.

isn't a face in that rock, but the guy who sent this photo in has *perceived* a face. He's seen a pattern even though there isn't one.'

'You mean we're geared up to see patterns, whether or not those patterns are actually there? That this is just how our brains work?'

Toby nods. 'There's a word for it . . .' He clicks his fingers. 'Apophenia. The definition's something like "the propensity to see meaning in random data or events". A lot of it's to do with madness.'

Later, at home, I look it up. The word apophenia was coined in 1958 by Klaus Conrad, a neuropsychologist who described it as an 'unmotivated seeing of connections' which gave the 'specific experience of an abnormal meaningfulness'. Commenting that we 'often see what we expect to see, we interpret the world through our own personal lens', Conrad talked of apophenia exclusively in connection with psychosis. It's easy to see why. What is paranoia, for instance, but the perception of a pattern where there isn't one? And the mathematical genius John Forbes Nash (played in the film *A Beautiful Mind* by Russell Crowe) saw what he thought were Soviet conspiracies behind random magazine adverts. But since Conrad's time the term has become more widely used, referring to healthy people as well.

People who spot that there are three films in which Charlton Heston notices the world has ended or is ending, for example. 'It's something we do all the time,' says Toby. 'Looking for links, connections, patterns – seeing form in things . . . It's a facility your brain has got. You can't turn that facility off.'

Up until now I haven't seen this. Whatever significance I've suspected trivia of having, the idea of that significance being tied to, or rooted in, *order* simply hasn't occurred. Seeing trivia as tangential, I've assumed it to be random. The phrase 'going off at a tangent' is a loaded one, carrying undertones of dottiness, mess, disorder. But a tangent is still connected to the thing it goes off from, just in an unexpected way. A tangent might lead somewhere you hadn't thought of, but it *does* lead somewhere. There *is* order here. There is a pattern.

'Very often it's how science progresses,' continues Toby. 'Scientists will see patterns in things, realise there's a connection – like the connection between a river delta and the veins in a leaf. Most of the time there's no meaning to those patterns, but occasionally there is, and scientists make a discovery.'

That's why they're always calling for more funding? For pure science, that is, research where there's no immediately foreseeable benefit?

'Yeah. You never know, they might hit on something. We don't know what we don't know.'[5]

This idea is appealing: a connection between the mind of the trivialist and that of the scientist. This isn't to claim that Toby and I are essentially Newton and Einstein. Or that spotting a similarity between three Charlton Heston films will lead to a cure for cancer. It is merely to note that the human mind works

5. A more concise version of Donald Rumsfeld's famous musing: 'There are "known knowns" – there are things we know we know. We also know there are "known unknowns" – that is to say we know there are some things we do not know. But there are also "unknown unknowns" – the ones we don't know we don't know.'

– or can work – in a particular way, one that is common to both trivia and 'serious' thinking. To develop it further I'll need someone who knows far more about science than either Toby or I do. But for now there's the realisation that this stuff in my head called 'Trivia' isn't a drawer crammed haphazardly with scruffy Post-it notes – it's a filing system. A heavily cross-referenced one at that.

In the village where I grew up there is a sign giving the distance to the next town as four miles, and the one past that as nine. A few days after my chat with Toby I visit my parents. Driving past the sign, I remember how as a child I would always note that the two figures were, respectively, the squares of two and three. Now I realise that that thought has never really gone away. However subconsciously, it gets noted each and every time.

I remember an old address of mine: flat 4, number 25. That the two figures multiplied together made a hundred always seemed satisfying. I think of astrologers looking at the stars – now that *is* a case of seeing patterns where there are none. (Even if you can make out a bear or a plough, however oddly shaped, it's only because you're standing on Earth. Look at them from Jupiter, see what significance you can find then.) I think of wallpaper and curtains and tiles – not much randomness there. And I remember an interview with Victoria Beckham in which she said that whenever there was an odd number of Coke cans in their fridge, David would throw one away to achieve symmetry.

Whether or not you take it to superstar extremes, there's something undeniably comforting in a pattern.

* * *

Also going round my mind are the words of Klaus Conrad: 'we interpret the world through our own personal lens'. The idea seems particularly suited to trivia. To have a conversation with Tim or Toby or Marcus is to open yourself up to all the facts they've accumulated over a lifetime. (All right, maybe not Marcus: he's holding on to them for a quiz.) Each and every trivialist views the world through a personal lens, collecting the items that seem interesting to them, storing those items, retrieving them as and when the occasion demands. Some trivia will be common to all. Most of us, I daresay, know that Margaret Thatcher once said, on a children's TV show, that there wouldn't be a female Prime Minister in her lifetime.^TOPOT But not everyone knows there was once another Margaret Thatcher: Denis's first wife shared that Christian name. Chatting to another trivialist, I might mention that, then receive another fact about Thatcher in return. Or, taking the Tangential Line, a fact about someone else's first marriage.

It's as though each trivialist has a personal library, stocked with the volumes they find pleasing. When you talk to them you're visiting that library, just as they're visiting yours. No membership is required. You simply photocopy whatever you want. Then you take it away with you.

So no one library, no one person, holds every piece

> ## TOPOT
>
> *The letter box of No. 10 Downing Street bears the words 'First Lord of the Treasury' – the PM's other title.*

of trivia. It reminds me of the library (the real one) I used as a child: each visit was exciting because I saw it as the place where every piece of knowledge in the world was collected together. Of course it wasn't. No library can do that, not even the British Library. No one space, be it physical or cyber, can hold all human knowledge. Things are happening all the time; new facts are being born quicker than new people.

But even though such a place is impossible, is that what the trivialist dreams of? Is that what lies behind my search? More than the perfect fact, am I yearning for access to *every* fact?

When the British do 'professor in his sixties', they go for a stoop, a shambling gait, a tweed jacket (quite possibly flecked with dandruff), someone whose unworldly air puts him halfway between a vicar and a member of the House of Lords. The Americans, on the other hand, go for someone who could recently have retired from the Marines.

At least if Professor Arthur I. Miller is anything to go by they do. The man who meets me in a very swish gastropub in a very plush part of north London – must be more money in academia than I thought – carries his six feet of height with the taut, muscular control of Someone In Charge. His dark hair is cut short, and while his jeans, black shirt and black jacket look good, they could easily be replaced by the uniform of a lieutenant colonel.

Not that Arthur isn't friendly. Far from it; a warm smile creases his tanned face as we shake hands, and his deep voice reminds me why so many things, from movie trailers to platform announcements, sound better in an American accent. This particular New Yorker, though, has come a very long way from the Bronx. After a PhD at the Massachusetts Institute of Technology, he has been (among many other things) visiting professor at L'Ecole Pratique des Hautes Etudes in Paris, an associate editor of the American Journal of Physics, and chairman of the American Physical Society's History of Physics Division. Currently Emeritus Professor of the History and Philosophy of Science at University College, London, he is a corresponding fellow of L'Academie International d'Histoire des Sciences, as well as a member of the International Academy of the History of Science. He is the author of several books, and has received fellowships and grants from bodies such as the John Simon Guggenheim Memorial Foundation, the American Philosophical Society and the National Endowment for the Humanities.

And I'm interviewing him for my book about trivia.

There is method in my impudence, though. Arthur's special area of interest is the nature of creative thinking: what is it that makes a mind creative? What particularly caught my eye about his work was that, despite a background as a scientist and then a historian of science, he is equally interested in the creative minds of artists. In fact he argues that the thought processes of great artists and great scientists can in many ways be seen as similar. His Pulitzer Prize-nominated *Einstein and Picasso: Space, Time and the Beauty That Causes Havoc* is just one example of his work highlighting the need to see science not as a specialist pursuit confined to its own corner, but as something whose methods and thought processes have links with the rest of us.

We settle down with our glasses of wine, and I tell Arthur a little about my book. In particular, I say, I'm keen to explore the notion of patterns in science. Would it be fair to say that they're sometimes how science progresses?

'There's a theory of scientific discovery,' he replies, 'which says that scientists look for patterns. They might see the results one point one nine, two point three, three point eight . . . They'll see the pattern that these are powers of two. Two to the zero, which is one, two to the one – two; two squared – four . . . That's the way you do theoretical science. You're working with mathematics that gives exact results, but in laboratory experiments you only get approximate results.'

For what won't be the last time tonight my brain struggles with some of the details. I thought two to the zero would be zero rather than one – isn't anything multiplied by itself no times zero? But the general point is clear.

Arthur recommends a book entitled *Patterns of Discovery* by Norwood Hanson. Written in 1958, this is an attempt to understand how senses and perception play a part in scientific discoveries. Hanson differentiated between seeing *as* and seeing *that*. 'What's important,' says Arthur, 'is being able to interpret data in new and different ways, getting something else out of it that nobody saw before. Like seeing a pendulum going back and forth. The real trick of it is to note that it's essentially about falling down. Seeing the so-called "deep structure". That's how Galileo made his great discovery of the law of falling bodies. They didn't have clocks in his day, in the sixteenth century. Things fell too fast to time them with water clocks, but he worked out a theory of the pendulum from which he could extract information about how bodies fell straight down. So seeing things differently is another way of seeing patterns.'

In other words, Galileo saw a connection between the way a pendulum swings – it takes the same amount of time no matter how long its arc – and the way bodies fall vertically to earth: they take the same amount of time no matter their mass. Disappointingly, the famous piece of trivia about him dropping objects of different masses from the Leaning Tower of Pisa to prove his theory is now thought to be untrue. But he was working with patterns.

Hanson's book amplifies the notion with such thoughts as 'in a growing research discipline, inquiry is directed not to rearranging old facts and explanations into more elegant formal patterns, but rather to the discovery of new patterns of explanation'. But its most striking entry comes in the acknowledgements: among the people thanked is one A.J.T.D. Wisdom. He was a philosopher. With four initials and a surname like that, what else could he have been?

Another lover of patterns, it transpires, was Isaac Newton. Whether or not an apple really did fall on his head ('It could have happened,' says Arthur), the point is that he saw what no one else had seen: that the apple behaved in the same way as the moon. 'Apples fall on lots of people's heads. Lots of people see the moon go up, but they don't see the moon falling towards the earth. That's the connection –

> **TOPOT**
>
> *A blue moon is a second*
> *full moon in the same*
> *month.*

the apple falling, the moon falling . . .'TOPOT And so Newton deduced the theory of universal gravitation.

Not that he saw this as his main work. Newton, Arthur tells me, was far from the model of sober scientific endeavour we all think. 'His main interest wasn't physics, but to find out how big the city of Jerusalem should be to receive the souls on Judgement Day, and to do a biblical chronology . . . The idea of his physics was to be able to differentiate between relative distances – between you and me, me and the table – and also between us and God. He probably died a virgin. He did optical experiments by sticking knives in his eyes. He was very good at word association. He always had to have a pencil in his hand. He advocated hanging for spies.'[6]

Tempting as it is to discuss whether Britain's most famous ever scientist was, in fact, barking mad, I stick to the subject of patterns. In particular, spotting patterns where at first glance they don't exist. 'Science,' says Arthur, 'is when you have apparently disparate items and someone puts them together. That's what produces the big breakthroughs, like relativity theory, quantum theory. That's the hallmark of creative thinking. What Einstein did was to see a connection between the laws of motion for objects and the laws of motion for light. They both obey what's called the "principle of relativity".'

6. Another piece of Newtonian trivia with which Arthur regales me is that Isaac was born the year after Galileo died (1642/3).

Ah, the good old Theory of Relativity. Long experience has taught me never to ask scientists to explain this, even friendly scientists like Arthur who are good at putting things into layman's language. They start by saying 'It's very simple, really' and 90 minutes later your brain is bleeding. Everything about the Theory of Relativity is hard. For instance you'd think it would make sense to start with the General Theory, then move on to the Special. Wrong. The Special Theory is the basic one (a relative term, no pun intended). It took Einstein another decade to develop the General Theory. And he was Einstein. What chance have I got in half an hour in the pub?[7]

Spotting patterns, Arthur continues, isn't always a case of thinking abstractly. Sometimes it concerns data. 'Look at DNA. Rosalind Franklin had the requisite data but didn't know what to do with it. Then Watson and Crick spotted patterns in the data.' The double helix. 'They had to interpret two-dimensional data in a three-dimensional way. How you visually represent data is important.'

Visual imagery is central to much of Arthur's work. His book on Einstein and Picasso, for instance, looks at the similarities in their work – which took place around the same time – in terms of perspective. 'Cubism is looking at an object from different perspectives,' he says. 'That's the idea of a cubist painting. That's similar to the situation in physics, where there's no preferred viewpoint.'

7. Mention of the speed of light inspires me to tell Arthur about my Big Ben experiment. It doesn't surprise him, of course, and also he tells me that the speed of sound, unlike the speed of light, is affected by temperature.

TOPOT

One of the German plans uncovered by Bletchley Park was the bombing of Coventry. But countering it would have revealed that the code had been broken, thereby eliminating the chance of more valuable intelligence in future. Churchill watched the bombers fly over London, knowing their destination but powerless to act.

Arthur also mentions Gestalt theory, the notion that our brains have self-organising tendencies. The Gestalt effect is the capacity of our senses to perceive forms, to visualise whole shapes or figures where only limited information is given. This happens in different ways. Some are merely the basis for optical illusions, such as 'multistability' (a famous example being the drawing that can be seen as either a candlestick or two faces in profile) and 'reification', for instance three circles each with a missing segment – arrange them so that those segments face inwards and you'll see a triangle even though none is there. But other Gestalt principles can have practical results. Invariance, our ability to recognise shapes even when they're distorted, is what allows us to pass a CAPTCHA test: Completely Automated Public Turing Test to tell Computers and Humans Apart. Alan Turing (he of Enigma fame)[8] was the first to propose a test that would stop computers imitating humans.[TOPOT] Now

8. Though not of Apple computers fame. Sadly the piece of trivia about their partly eaten apple logo being inspired by his suicide method (said fruit injected with poison) is untrue.

CAPTCHAs are used on websites to do precisely that, so preventing terrible things like spam. They're the boxes you have to fill in with numbers and letters which look slightly melted. Computers, clever as they are, can't make out those numbers and letters. Only the human mind, with its uncanny ability to perceive form, can manage that.

Is there something about the brain, I ask, that *needs* to make sense of the world?

'You have to classify,' replies Arthur, 'or you can't succeed at our level – you can't live. When you're walking down the street and you see a dog, there's this massive parallel processing that tells you "It's a dangerous dog," so you walk the other way. You can't think about it, say, "Right, it's a German shepherd, blah blah blah" – you just know.'

I like this idea that our brains work independently of us. They're machines doing what they're designed to, computers working as programmed – indeed, as Gestalt theory shows, computers way more sophisticated than anything Bill Gates can manage. It's not my fault I put Ringo Starr and Shane Warne in a file marked 'pizza preferences'. It's my brain's.

We talk a little more about my book, in particular the search for the perfect fact. 'In science there's no such thing as a raw fact,' says Arthur. 'Even something like "This is on the table," [he points at my tape recorder] that doesn't mean anything until you talk about how the table is supporting it, its weight is being balanced off by the upward push of the table, and so on.'

I tell him he's bringing back the doubts that assailed me in my trivia-checking enterprise.

And this is obviously what he intended. 'The notion of a fact is very tricky. An experimental fact, something you get out of an experiment, depends on data. But data are taken on instruments. Data also are usually folded into a theory, they're interpreted in terms of a theory – it's called the "theory dependence of data". How much theory-ladenness is in your fact? Also, scientists choose between facts. They present the best facts they have, throw the others away. Actually, sometimes the facts they throw away, some years down the line turn out to be the meaningful ones.'

He gives the example of electroweak theory. The details are complex – they would be, it's particle physics – but essentially a group of scientists working in the 1970s discarded data that didn't fit their theory. Only when they reincluded it and discarded other data did the electroweak theory finally work. 'A trivial fact isn't wrong,' says Arthur. 'It's just not important. But there are cases where people assume that a fact isn't important, until someone says, "Wait, let's take a look at this again." What's trivia at one point in time isn't trivia at another.'

Later, after we've finished the interview proper, it crops up in conversation that Arthur is friends with Dave Scott, the seventh man to walk on the moon. They met several years ago through a mutual friend, though at first Arthur didn't know who he was ('He's a very low-key guy'). Then Arthur mentions that he himself worked on the Apollo programme, as a young scientist at MIT in the mid-sixties. 'I worked on the navigational system. Some of my equations were up there with them.'

It's a good thing this has happened at the end of the evening rather than the beginning. Abandoning my interview for an hour-long conversation about the moon landings wouldn't have been a very good idea, but that's not to say it wouldn't have happened. As it is, I settle for swapping Apollo trivia with Arthur. We mention Buzz Aldrin's mother's maiden name: Moon. We mention the advice given to the crew of Apollo 12 when their entire computer system was affected by a lightning strike shortly after launch ('Turn it off then turn it on again,' proving that computer help desks have been the same down the ages). And we mention, also from Apollo 12, the three weightless astronauts holding on to the rails in their command module as they headed to the moon, dancing to the song 'Sugar Sugar' played on a tape recorder.

And I reflect that this last fact sums up what trivia, at its very best, is capable of: lending an already impressive story an extra layer of charm. Of course it doesn't matter that the three astronauts did that dance. It wasn't 'Sugar Sugar' that got them to the moon. That was achieved by the billions of dollars and millions of man-hours that produced the ground-breaking Apollo technology. That really *was* rocket science. But 'Sugar Sugar' always brings a smile to my face. The human angle. Trivia about a very untrivial subject.

I ask Arthur if Dave Scott ever talks about his moon landing. 'We were walking down the street one night, and there was this beautiful moon, and I said, "How do you feel when you see it now?" He said, "Ah, I've put it all behind me."' It seems that any experience, even one that only eleven other people in the history of the species have shared, can get filed under 'trivia'.

Later, at home, I look up Dave Scott's mentions in Andrew Chaikin's *A Man on the Moon*, easily the best book about Apollo.

It takes the evening full circle: one of the things Scott did on the moon was drop a feather and a hammer, in tribute to the man who (never) did the same thing in Pisa, Galileo. They hit the lunar dust simultaneously.

'Nothing like a little science on the moon,' said Scott.

Before tonight, I've seen trivia as essentially a passive thing. It's something that comes to you, rather than you looking for it. Sponge-like, your only role is to absorb it. Even the settings in which you encounter trivia are passive – a comfy armchair in front of the telly, sitting in the pub with your mates. About the most active thing you ever do is open your mouth to pass the trivia on to someone else.

Yet now I see that trivia *is* active. By which I mean more than just the 'sense of wonder' explorer instinct. I mean active and *organised*. Responsive, organic . . . *re*-active, if you like. A trivialist isn't a sponge, haphazardly soaking up whichever random facts he encounters. He is a machine working on those facts, organising them, constantly sifting, filing, evaluating. Just as a scientist works on data, a trivialist works on trivia.

This isn't, of course, to claim that the two enterprises are of equal worth. Einstein spotting patterns in the laws of motion revolutionised science. Me spotting patterns in the films of Dustin Hoffman will revolutionise nothing. But the point isn't the result, it's the process. The human brain does more than receive information, it engages with it. This applies to the trivialist watching a DVD just as it applies to the scientist in a laboratory. Trivia isn't a passive accumulation of rubbish, it's an active engagement with the world. The information might be received randomly, but our brains do more than just store it; they get to work on it. Connections are made. Patterns appear.

Without in any way thinking I'm a Newton or a Galileo – or even an Arthur I. Miller – I nonetheless feel I've learned something about my relationship with trivia.

Something else has come from talking to Arthur, too: the idea that facts aren't separate from the rest of life. Science and art, he argues, have much in common, not least the creative natures of those who practise them. The creative natures, that is, of their minds. This intrigues me. Could it be that trivia – a very hard world of facts, lists, information – has links to other, less precise, more nebulous worlds? Might trivia be artistic as well as scientific?

Less than a week after meeting Arthur, I happen to pick up *Carter Beats The Devil*, Glen David Gold's novel about a 1920s magician. It begins with a quote: 'The most beautiful experience we can have is the mysterious. It is the fundamental emotion which stands at the cradle of true art and true science. Whoever does not know it and can no longer wonder, no longer marvel, is as good as dead, and his eyes are dimmed.'

The quote is by Albert Einstein.

All those years ago, as Toby and I swapped trivia in the BBC bar, one man more than any other swapped along with us. He also swapped trivia in the studio during rehearsals, and, because he was the script editor for the sketches Toby used to perform, in the production office as the programme was prepared. In fact whenever I saw Steve, we would fall to swapping trivia. Films, music, why the Elephant and Castle is called the Elephant and Castle[9] . . . you name it, Steve Punt knows trivia about it.

We arrange to meet near Broadcasting House, where Steve has spent the morning working, in a square. In a reassuring confirmation that some things will never change, he arrives twenty minutes late. Despite the fact he's nearly three decades past the school-leaving age, Steve still has the air of a sixth-former: genially distracted, heavily overdue a haircut, shirt *almost* tucked into his trousers. We get coffees from a nearby Starbucks – inevitably Steve knows that the name comes from a character in *Moby Dick*[10] – then, as it's a nice day, park ourselves back in the square.

I tell him about Arthur's work, the idea of factual thinking being linked to artistic creativity. As a comedy writer, does he think trivia can be an inspiration?

'Sure. I'd say that almost every comedy writer and performer I've ever known has been into trivia. Comics tend to be inter-ested in all sorts of stuff in a random way. It's a prerequisite of what they do. You have to connect disparate items together, that's what comedy is. Like Monty Python having philosophers play football. Or *Shaun of the Dead* – zombies in suburban London. Or Bill Bailey doing the BBC News music as a rave track.'

9. It was the area of London where a Spanish princess, to whom Charles I was betrothed, came to live. She was known as Infanta de Castille. The locals weren't renowned for their Spanish pronunciation . . . At least that's the explanation Steve's heard.
10. Equally inevitably, he knows that the same novel inspired Moby's stage-name: the musician, real surname Melville, is descended from Herman. Neither of us can remember Moby's real Christian name.

Disparate items? Has Steve been eavesdropping on my interviews?

'Trivia,' he continues, 'is really another word for detail, and in comedy the laughs are in the detail. They're not in big generalisations. It's no good saying, "Aren't train announcements funny?" You

> TOPOT
>
> *The escalator at Angel station is not only the longest on the Tube network, but the longest anywhere in Western Europe.*

have to give specific examples. Like, I will never forget being at East Croydon station and hearing the announcer say, "We are sorry for the cancellation of the 18.46 to London Victoria, this train has failed." Or one at Reigate: "The train is slipping on the line at Deepdene."'

He's right: another station name wouldn't have been funny. You must need a good memory to be a comedy writer, I say.

'A memory for details like that, yeah. Though because I use that line a lot I could do you the whole of East Croydon to Brighton. And probably to Littlehampton too. Dave Tyler [another comedy writer] can do you the whole Piccadilly Line. You'll find London Underground has a fascination for trivia buffs.'TOPOT

Is it always a case of finding things funny at the time?

'No, not at all. The great thing about trivia is it's like that drawer in the kitchen where you store the little presents you get in Christmas crackers, things you think you'll never use but you hang on to them just in case. Then one day you say, "Have we got one of those special screwdrivers for glasses? Hang on, yes, we have – it's in the drawer." You never know what scrap of info you'll need to make a joke work.'

Steve says he owes his whole career to finding comedy in the detail. 'We had a German textbook at school. I found the examples in it so funny I used them in the school revue, which was the first thing I'd ever done in front of an audience. All I did was read them out. It started, "Is the cat green?" "No, the cat is not green." "Is the cat blue?" And so on, until you got to sentences like "Hans is wet because he is standing under a waterfall." Another one was "'Hooray, the countryside,' says Hans. 'It's full of insects.'" One I didn't use was in book two: "'Herr Aylers, a gorilla has entered the office.'" It went so well I hung on to it. When I got to university [Cambridge] I did it as my audition for the Footlights.' Which was where Steve met his future comedy partner Hugh Dennis, as well as David Baddiel, and indeed Piccadilly Line expert Dave Tyler.

We talk more about the appeal of trivia. 'I think it's the propensity to remember detail rather than the big picture,' says Steve. 'Detail is more *appealing* than the big picture. I've got this theory about architecture, why lots of people prefer a classical building. It's because it's got details – columns, arches, friezes . . . A modern building looks good from a distance, but up close it's just a sheet of a glass. When you're close to a classical building, though, there are lots of details to enjoy. Trivia's like that. And comedy. It has to work on different levels. American sitcoms have different people for every level: there'll be series story editors, episode story editors, and then writers working on individual jokes.'

Not that it just applies to comedy. Steve goes on to mention

Stanley Kubrick. 'The reason it took him years to make each film was because he was absolutely determined to get every last detail right. His films were built from the detail up. Like the instructions for the anti-gravity toilet in *2001*. There's a whole long list of them, way more than you've got time to read in the split second they're on screen, yet they're all written down in precise detail.'

For a few moments we get sidetracked into Kubrick trivia, from the reason the computer in *2001* is called HAL – the letters are one back from IBM – to the fact that Stephen King, author of the novel on which *The Shining* is based, tried to talk Kubrick out of casting Jack Nicholson: the story is a normal man descending into madness, whereas Nicholson looks mad at the best of times. Then I mention that, not for the first time in my research, an interview about trivia is getting derailed by trivia.

'It's bound to happen,' says Steve. 'Trivia is such a social thing. It breaks a conversation down from generalisations into specifics, and that's what conversation needs. Especially when people meet for the first time. You need details to talk about; you can only talk in generalisations for so long. Unless you're a politician. It's even called "small talk". You've got to talk small if you want to be socially adept.'^{TOPOT} There are problems here, though.

> **TOPOT**
>
> *Richard Nixon was notoriously bad at small talk. Sitting down to record an interview with David Frost he asked the crew, 'So, any of you guys do any fornicating over the weekend?'*

'As modern life gets more and more disparate – more TV channels, for instance – the less people have in common. Trivia was easy in the playground in the 1970s because there were only three channels. But it's harder for the modern child. If their favourite game is Pro Manager and their friend's is Age of Empires, they have no link.'

People of our age, I say, have seen all the Bond films, so we can swap Bond trivia.

'Yes. But in future, if you haven't got the references, you won't get the trivia. With some people it's music, with some it's sport – but you need the references . . .'

I mention apophenia, and the concept of patterns in trivia.

'Our brains just have a facility for doing that,' says Steve. 'I looked into it a lot for my dissertation [Steve's degree was in English], which was about metaphor. You know it must be natural because children do it all the time. They see things in terms of other things. A friend of mine has a three-year-old daughter. One day she picked up a magnifying glass. She'd never seen one before, didn't know what it was. But she examined it for a while, then said, "It's a saucepan for your eyes." The ability to see resemblance is intrinsic to human nature.'

It can also apply to language. 'T.S. Eliot wrote a lot about the "objective correlative". As a writer you might be trying to conjure a feeling for which there are literally no words, but if you can find the right phrase it gets *exactly* the right feeling. The brain has this amazing ability to construct sense from just a couple of focal points. "A face like a smacked arse", for instance. The face looks nothing like an arse, but somehow we get the point instantly.'

Back to disparate items again. Steve says they can work for documentaries as well as for comedy. 'I wanted to do a radio programme about famous people who wouldn't fly. There was Dennis Bergkamp, Kate Bush, Aretha Franklin, Stalin . . . A list like that, you'd think they had absolutely nothing in common – and yet there was this one characteristic they all shared.'

We agree that Stalin may have had more reasons than most for being scared of flying. Either way, says Steve, it's certainly true that his insistence on going by train kept Roosevelt and Churchill waiting at Yalta for two days.

The talk returns to my interview with Arthur. I mention his reference to the Theory of Relativity, how I've given up trying to understand it.

'I remember an evening,' says Steve, 'a very long evening, in Dave [Tyler]'s room at Cambridge. He was doing science, and tried to explain the Theory of Relativity to me. In vain. I think the early twentieth century was when science got hard to understand. Until then you could pretty much follow it all, but now it's getting harder all the time, more and more counter-intuitive. There are only a few thousand people in the whole world who really understand the Theory of Relativity.'[11]

'Perhaps that's why we stick to trivia,' I say. 'Science is too hard now.'

'I think it's certainly true that it was easier to be a Renaissance man four hundred years ago. We didn't know so much then.'

---

11. The English astrophysicist Sir Arthur Eddington was once told that only three people understood the theory. 'Who's the third?' he asked.

'Da Vinci had it easy.'

'Now if you want to be an expert on anything, you have to accept that you'll know about nothing else. When I was at university I looked around for a PhD to do, and realised how incredibly specialised it all was. My director of studies spent three years on whether the Gawain poet [an anonymous writer responsible for a poem of that name] also wrote 'Pearl' [a fragment of fourteenth-century verse]. Three years just on *that*.'

Flotsam and jetsam. That's how I viewed trivia at the start. Random snippets of info, bobbing about on the sea of knowledge. But Toby, Arthur and Steve have shown me it's not like that. Yes, they may be snippets – but they're not random. Patterns and connections and linkages are the way of trivia. And of the trivialist: our brains work that way, whether we know it or not. Our brains have a desire for order. Nothing we love more than a category. Even if a trivialist doesn't see it, that tendency to organise information into groups is always there. It throws together the most unlikely combinations of people, facts, events. The more unlikely the combination, the better the trivia.

Which has an implication for my search:

The perfect fact must link together two or more disparate items.

5

The female of the species

Time to take stock of my interviewees so far. Marcus, Tim, Toby, Arthur, Steve. They all have one thing in common. Something pretty fundamental to their natures. Something which might – how shall we put this – skew the results of my research.

Even as a man, I can see what it is.

Trivia, like many things – nuclear fission, the internet, garlic – can have consequences both good and bad. More specifically, in the ongoing chess-game-cum-soap-opera that we call 'male–female relationships', trivia can be, if not the most beautiful thing, then at least a mildly humorous bond – or it can be poison. Just watch the collective look of bewilderment creep across a group of women as their partners discuss a Chelsea back four from 1978. For many women, the sight of 22 men kicking a pig's bladder around while thousands of other men watch is the very definition of 'trivial'. The scores resulting from that activity are the very definition of 'trivia'. No wonder the word's got such a bad reputation.

But given a fair wind, a blossoming romance and a little bit of subtlety on the man's part (note the 'little' – we're not expecting miracles here), trivia can be good for a relationship.

Walking in Central Park with a girl who lived in New York (we'd met in London), I noticed the stone obelisk that stands near the Metropolitan Museum. It was thousands of years old, I told Allison, originally from Egypt but transported to New York in the nineteenth century, a team of horses taking months just to bring it from Manhattan's east coast to the park, and there are similar ones in London, on the Embankment, and Paris, in the Place de la Concorde. She laughed, said she'd lived in the city all her life and never noticed the obelisk, let alone known its history. Needless to say I felt ten feet tall. *Hey, aren't you the cool one – you can make trivia sexy.* It would be a lie to say smugness wasn't there. Trivia can be cool, if you throw it in at the right angle, with the right deftness. Humour counts. So does self-parody. *Yeah, I know I'm a nerd, but . . .*

Is it intensity? That's how it feels. Tell a girlfriend a piece of trivia about something that means a lot to you – a song, a film, Botham at Headingley in '81 – and the look she gives reminds you (reminds me, anyway) of the look a mother gives a young son enthusing about his new hobby. The loving smile, the glassy-eyed stare, only half an ear on what he's actually saying, her real affection reserved not for the subject of his intensity, merely the fact that he *is* intense. And that he's hers. Back in the days before iPods, when you made compilation tapes for your girlfriend – and Nick Hornby wrote novels about making compilation tapes for your girlfriend – I accompanied one C90 with several sheets of paper full of trivia about the songs on it. Who they'd been written for, stories about the recording sessions, which keys they were in . . . As my then girlfriend read it tears formed in her eyes. 'You went to so much trouble,' she said.

Intensity isn't always a good thing, however. Intensity can get dark. Men go to their sheds, and have their hobbies – and their trivia – and women smile, with greater or lesser degrees of affection, saying, 'Men will be men,' 'Each to their own,' 'Space is important in a relationship' . . . But in the end, is it the relationship a man wants – *really* wants – or is it the space? For all that trivia gets painted as harmless blokery, charming women at best, puzzling them at worst, perhaps it goes deeper than that. Goes somewhere less pleasant. Trivia's pretty narcissistic, after all. It's always about what interests *me*, what's fascinating to *me*, quirky, amusing, intriguing to *me*. And it can be a weapon rather than a bond. Once, in my mid-twenties, during what was always going to be (we would both have told you this) a dalliance, never a relationship, a woman and I walked through central London. Low-key irritability had marked the day from the start. Within the space of half an hour I came out with two or three pieces of trivia.[1] Maybe it was a subconscious attempt to provoke; I don't know. But when my companion said it irritated her, a decidedly conscious attempt began. As we walked down Spanish Place, I announced that this was the first street in the UK to have parking meters. Big argument, end of trip.

Ever since then Spanish Place has always made me feel a little ashamed.

Lunch with my editor. We discuss how the book's going, and I mention the need for the female point of view.

Nigel agrees, only too aware from his own experience how

---

1. Including, as we passed the store bearing his name, that it was Gordon Selfridge who coined the phrase 'The customer is always right.'

'male' trivia can be. 'My wife just doesn't understand how I can get so excited about this stuff. The Tichborne thing, for instance.'

Ah. The Tichborne thing. Nigel first told me about this in his office. His colleague Sophie was there at the time. She listened as Nigel related the four elements: the Hampshire Tichbornes, a family who have to give flour (the Tichborne Dole) to the poor each year to avoid bad luck; Chidiock Tichborne, who wrote a famous poem on the eve of his execution for plotting against Elizabeth I ('my prime of youth is but a frost of cares . . .'); the Tichborne Claimant, a Victorian con man claiming to be the missing heir Sir Roger Tichborne, who fooled even Sir Roger's mother; and finally Little Tich, a music hall star who took his name from the Claimant, so giving us the adjective titchy. The point was that even though Nigel had heard of the first three separately, they were all in fact the same family.

'Every time you tell this . . .' said Sophie.

Nigel and I awaited something along the lines of '. . . it amazes me how fresh it sounds.'

'. . . I wonder just how many more times you're going to make me sit through it,' said Sophie.

Nigel's wife, it seems, takes a similar view. 'She can't understand why I remember numbers, either. The catalogue numbers from my first job, for instance. It was in a classical music shop. Knowing the codes for each record was very useful. I've never forgotten that the classic du Pré vinyl recording of the Elgar Cello Concerto was ASD 655.'

Nigel gives his wine glass a contemplative swirl. Then he

puts it down, stares into the mid-distance, and says, 'It's a wonder I'm still married at all.'

Deep into the countryside now. The roar of the A12 has subsided, and as the Essex coast beckons the lanes narrow. I'm very glad Andrea's emailed directions are so precise.

Andrea Barham is the author of *The Pedant's Revolt: Why Most Things You Think Are Right Are Wrong*, and *The Pedant's Return: Why Things That You Think Are Wrong Are Right*. Both are compelling collections of trivia which despite their titles exhibit none of the mean-spiritedness associated with pedantry. Instead they delight in uncovering the truth or otherwise of trivia down the ages. It's because of Andrea that I know about the S in Harry S Truman (and indeed the H in Harry H Corbett, an invention to pacify Equity);[TOPOT] about Virginia Woolf writing all her books standing up, in imitation of her artist sister Vanessa; about the unrepealed English law forbidding the beating of doormats in the street after eight a.m.; about Charlie Chaplin failing to make the final in a Chaplin lookalike contest, but a

TOPOT

Peter Cook was told by the actors' union that there was already a member with that name, so he'd have to adopt a pseudonym. Reluctant to do so, Cook replied with an increasingly absurd list of suggestions. The name at which Equity finally gave up was 'Sting Thundercock'.

young Bob Hope winning one . . . It cannot be denied: Andrea is a woman who knows her trivia.

I reach a lightly built-up area, and find the close where Andrea lives. She's a tall, slim woman in her forties, her smile welcoming, her eyes large and bright. Immediately off the hall is a lounge with ornaments, pictures, a computer in the corner – but hardly any books. My assumption of shelf after groaning shelf of encyclopedias and gazetteers dies a death. Amid the initial chat I'm about to thank Andrea for her excellent directions, when her husband Andy appears from the kitchen. Friendly in a blokey way, he explains that he won't disturb us for long, he just needs to check the computer for something to do with his course.

Andrea tells him not to worry, we haven't even started yet. She goes to make coffee.

'What's your course?' I ask.

'Open University,' says Andy. 'I'm studying history.'

'How's it going?'

He shrugs, gives a weary sigh. 'Oh, you know – essays to do . . .'

'Not like Andrea writing her books, eh? She can stick to the bits that interest her.'

Andy nods. 'Guess that's what trivia's all about.'

I feel a twinge of guilt. Despite Marcus suggesting the word 'dilettante', there's still that suspicion of intellectual laziness. Virtually the whole of my working life has been spent swimming in the cerebral shallows. Moving to London after university I stayed with a writer friend successful enough to give me occasional work researching his books and newspaper columns. After that it was the BBC, researching and producing radio programmes.[2] Then writing. Non-fiction (like the *Bluffer's Guide To Bond*) which, as with my previous work, required research into – *only* into – the Interesting Bits; and novels, which required no research at all. Any trivialist must ready himself for the accusation of levity, of never sticking at a subject. Jack of all trades, master's degree in none.

Andy disappears to another room, while Andrea and I move through to the conservatory. I mention the lack of books.

'I try not have too many,' she says. 'They only mount up.'

Most of her research is done on the internet, then?

'Well, yes, but often it's books on the internet. The online version of the *Encyclopædia Britannica*, *Oxford English Dictionary*, books of quotations, the Bible . . . Then of course there's Google book search [the function allowing you to search the entire text of a book].'

What about Wikipedia?

'I'll use it as a starting point, but never as confirmation.'

Has she ever corrected it?

'Yes. And I've corrected the *OED*. Which isn't like Wikipedia, of course – you can't just log on, you have to write to them.

2. The broadcast of the Princess of Wales's funeral among them. Four of us were assigned to the research, splitting her life into topics. Mine included 'alternative medicine', the cuttings for which revealed that her colonic irrigation treatment had averaged ten gallons a week. Putting completeness before delicacy, I included it. The coffin's long journey from Kensington Palace to Westminster Abbey was undertaken in complete silence; fine for TV, but the radio commentator had to keep talking. He began to read out the notes compiled merely for back-up use, in their entirety. During the medicine section there was a short pause. The nation was spared that particular detail.

It was only a minor thing, on the spelling of someone's name. But I had seen the original text, so they checked it and accepted my change. I'm thinking of contacting them again, about koalas. They've got it as "koala bear'" but it isn't actually a bear, it's a marsupial.'

Would it be fair, I ask, to call Andrea someone who doesn't like inaccuracy?

She laughs. 'Yes, that's fair enough. I like things . . . I like things to be *right*.'

But it's as apparent from her conversation as from her books that she's no pedant-for-its-own-sake, no tut-tutting Apostrophe Nazi. Her desire for correctness is born of enthusiasm – an enthusiasm for trivia.

'I particularly like debunking fallacies,' she says. 'Don't know why – I always have. If I hear something, a piece of trivia that sounds intriguing, I have to check if it's true. Something's only enjoyable if you know it's true. Take the *Titanic*, for instance. The Kate Winslet film is terrible.[TOPOT] The other film about it, *A Night To Remember*, is better because it's more realistic. But neither of them are as good as watching a documentary about it.'

> TOPOT
>
> *Leonardo di Caprio is six feet one inch tall. Other surprising six-one-ers include Robbie Williams and Jamie Oliver.*

I ask if it's true that the musicians' widows had money deducted from their settlements to cover lost uniforms and failure to finish the journey. Andrea hasn't heard that one, but does confirm that the band continued to play as the ship went down.

Though whether or not the last tune was 'Nearer My God To Thee' or 'Songe d'Automne' depends on which survivor you believe.

'Some fallacies,' continues Andrea, 'are believed really widely. Like Nelson wearing an eyepatch. He was blinded in his right eye during a battle but wasn't disfigured.'

'His statue in Trafalgar Square has got an eyepatch, though, hasn't it?'

Andrea shakes her head. 'Complete myth.'

I could swear blind (half-blind?) that I've seen pictures of the statue wearing a patch. But later, a Google Image search proves me wrong. Both eyes present, if not correct.[3]

'It is true, though,' says Andrea, 'that Napoleon was late for Waterloo because of his piles.'[4]

I've never thought it wasn't. Largely because I've never heard the fact in the first place. Though now I have it's very unlikely I'll ever forget it. 'How do you check something like that?'

'Wherever I can, I go to an original source, or at least as far back as you can go, as close to the event as it's possible to get.'

3. Other myths about Nelson's Column are that its base contains a one-man police station – it's a separate hut, at the south-east corner of Trafalgar Square – and that the lions are made from melted-down French cannons captured at Waterloo; they're not, though the panels depicting battle scenes are. The most fundamental myth, though, is that the column is 185 feet high; restoration work in 2006 discovered it to be a mere 169 feet 5 inches. A spokesman for Trivial Pursuit said the game would be amended.

4. The late journalist, diarist and insufferable snob Woodrow Wyatt was once asked by a French hotel receptionist to spell his surname. 'Waterloo, Ypres, Agincourt, Trafalgar, Trafalgar,' he replied.

In this case Andrea's sources included *Non-neoplastic Diseases of the Anorectum* by P. Fruhmorgen et al. Probably not the best choice for a loo book.

I ask Andrea if she's always been interested in trivia.

'Oh yes, even as a child.'

What about the rest of her family?

'My mother was the same. She still is. Andy cycled all the bridges in London this summer, for charity. When I mentioned it to Mum she listed them.'

What was her mother's line of work?

'She was in unit trusts. She's always had an enquiring mind, always absorbing facts like a sponge. She's great at crosswords. My sister's the same, too. She likes globes and maps, loves reading about geography.'

And her dad? Does he have that sort of mind?

'Not so much. He's the odd one out in the family.'

It further emerges, as we discuss books and reading, and the *Guinness Book of Records* gets mentioned, that Andrea's thirteen-year-old niece has the current edition, and loves it.[5] Her nephew, on the other hand, prefers playing sport. Andrea's whole family, I say, seem to prove that trivia isn't an all-male club.

'Maybe,' she says. 'But then I would admit to not being a typical woman.'

Meaning?

5. Something else to emerge is that Andrea's US publishers removed her reference to Emily Davison (the suffragette who threw herself in front of the King's horse during the Derby), saying that people wouldn't have heard of her. Why do you *read* a book?

'I prefer the company of men. Men talk more about facts, women talk more about feelings. I can get slightly interested in relationship talk, but I'm much happier talking about facts and concepts.'

It's a point that confuses me, almost to the extent of being irksome. Is Andrea saying that her interest in trivia makes her an honorary bloke, that actually she *isn't* a Woman Who's Into Trivia, at least not a properly feminine one? Certainly this isn't how she comes across.

'Why do you think trivia is traditionally seen as male?' I ask, throwing in my 'explorer tendency' theory: instead of conquering the world, we conquer its trivia.

'It could be that,' says Andrea, nodding. 'And also, of course, it's about being a collector. That's a very male trait.'

I've never collected anything in my life. Or at least I didn't think so, until Andrea said that.

How do men react to women who know lots of trivia?

Andrea laughs. 'I don't think men like women who sound knowledgeable.'

They see them as a threat?

'Yeah.'

This saddens me. Not that I haven't heard it before. But is it one of those 'truths' that's actually an assumption in disguise? To my mind knowledge – be it trivia or in the wider sense of being well-read, having thoughts and opinions – is one of the most attractive qualities a woman can possess. Judging from their partners, all my male friends feel the same. How could a bimbo ever be truly attractive? Knowledge is sexy.

Saddening, too, is the growing sense that Andrea doesn't,

after all, have a truly female take on trivia. Perhaps it really is a male domain after all, women only allowed in on day passes? Her next comment reinforces the fear. 'Trivia might also be a male thing because of the survival instinct. The better informed you are, the safer you are in the world.'

This makes sense, certainly if you buy into caveman theories of human development. Men having a better sense of direction because they went out hunting prey, for instance. It's hard to imagine how knowing that Gordon Selfridge was the first man to say 'The customer is always right' would aid you in a one-on-one with a woolly mammoth, but the theory's general thrust seems plain enough. Do I buy it? Instinct says there's something there. Though if true, surely it would apply to useful knowledge as well as trivia? And no matter how many times I'm told – by my girlfriend, naturally – how to check the oil in our car, I keep forgetting where, in the sprawling mass of components under the bonnet, you find the dipstick.

How is Andrea's memory? Is it just trivia she remembers?

'I don't have a very good memory. But I can remember fallacies for some reason.'

What about dates?

'I don't do dates. Andy and I chose the day after our day-we-met anniversary for our wedding so I'd find it easier to remember. We did actually try and get the same day itself.'

Numbers in general?

Andrea shakes her head. 'I shun numbers. I'm prejudiced against numbers.'

Earlier she mentioned using her library number online. Surely that sticks in the memory?

Another laugh. 'I can barely remember my own phone number.[6] But I'm good with names.'

And directions, I add, mentioning her email.

'Don't be silly. They were from Andy.'

Ah. Until now, it strikes me, I've taken the memory as a given. You like trivia, you remember it. But perhaps things aren't so simple. Perhaps two people watch the same programme, read the same book, hear the same fact – but only one of them remembers it? Interest doesn't differ, merely memory capacity? Could the sheer volume of trivia out there be the problem? It's often the way with jokes, after all. How many times have you heard a comedian tell twenty jokes, loved them all . . . then not been able to remember a single one?

Andy, reappearing for something else from the computer, is soon drawn into our discussion. A theme develops: is it possible to learn too much, so that new information starts pushing out the old?

'I've got the opposite problem with my course,' he says. 'I can't get the information to go in in the first place. Remembering some of it is a real problem.'

Andrea's not sure about the 'full memory' question. 'And even if it did work like that, I wouldn't care. The new fact could only push out the old one if it was more interesting.'

Sherlock Holmes certainly took this view of memory, I say.

6. We have a woman to thank for pin numbers being four digits long. The inventor of the cashpoint (as first used by TV's Reg Varney) initially took inspiration from his old army number and chose six digits. But tests with his wife found she could only remember four.

He calls it an attic with limited room.[7] Then, warming to the theme, I remember Al Bean, the fourth man on the moon (he was there when Pete Conrad fell over). In the run-up to Apollo 12, he deliberately ignored the names of people he was introduced to, scared that to remember them would be to forget something for the mission.

Andy warms even further. 'There's a *Simpsons* with something like that in it.' He consults Google. Google obliges. 'How is education supposed to make me feel smarter?' muses Homer. 'Besides, every time I learn something new, it pushes some old stuff out of my brain. Remember when I took that home wine-making course, and I forgot how to drive?'

We feel pleased with ourselves. Of course we do: we've established a pattern. Two fictional characters and an astronaut all saying the same thing. But I know this question of memory will need looking into. Exactly what happens when we remember a piece of trivia? How does the brain actually manage it? And how does it retrieve that trivia? What are your grey cells up to in the split second before a complete stranger learns about accelerating greyhounds?

Exam revision gets mentioned. Andy says the only method that works for him is the mind map — key facts written on a

---

7. *A Study in Scarlet*. Holmes astonishes Watson by not knowing that the earth goes round the sun. What's more he doesn't *want* to know; it is of no use in his work. 'I consider that a man's brain originally is like a little empty attic . . . It is a mistake to think that the little room has elastic walls and can distend to any extent. Depend upon it, there comes a time when, for every addition of knowledge, you forget something you knew before. It is of the highest importance, therefore, not to have useless facts elbowing out the useful ones.'

single piece of paper, with arrows and lines denoting connections. Andrea agrees.

'In fact I did one for today,' she says.

Today? For this interview?

'Yes.' She reaches down by the side of her chair, and hands me a sheet of A4. In its centre is written 'Popularity of Trivia'. The space to its right is headed 'Traits Common to Males', the one to the left 'Traits Common to Females'. Branching off into the former are lines marked:

- Status (sound knowledgeable, impress)
- Competitiveness (sport for the non-athlete – quizzes)
- Analytical (amassing, processing and extrapolating from data)
- Collecting (obsessive personalities)
- Ordering (control through categorising)
- Survival instinct (knowledge = safety)

From the last entry branch subcategories such as 'quick info (short attention span)' and 'understand world better'. I ask Andrea about this.

'The world is a big jigsaw,' she says. 'The more trivia you can assimilate, the bigger your understanding of it.'

A jigsaw? Jigsaws are about completeness, one big picture, everything connected. My search has already thrown up the notion of connections in trivia, but only a limited one. The patterns that Toby and Arthur Miller talked about were self-contained. Yes, they linked disparate items together – Charlton Heston films, the laws of motion for objects and those for light – but once linked, the items were still distinct from everything else. The pieces of trivia became beads on a necklace; the necklaces, however, remained separate. But Andrea's metaphor can be seen as going one stage further: *everything* is linked. This sounds an appealing notion. Perhaps a love of trivia is more than a love of facts for their own sake, more even than a love of spotting patterns in those facts; perhaps it's a desire to understand the world as one, organic whole? Maybe we're not just collecting jigsaw pieces because they look pretty. Maybe we're trying to complete the puzzle.

The left-hand side of Andrea's page, denoting female aspects of trivia, is almost blank. Only one line surges out from the centre, labelled 'Human interest'. At its end are the words: 'Understand people better, e.g. Napoleon's piles.'

Andy's examining the mind map too. 'That's right,' he says, pointing at the 'female' side. 'Understanding people.' He looks at his wife. 'That's what your trivia is about. You're interested in people. I'm more interested in events.'

Andrea nods. 'That's true.'

A quick recap of her trivia backs this up: Harry S Truman, Virginia Woolf, Charlie Chaplin, Nelson. And, of course, Napoleon. While the emperor's problems with his derrière might not be the most revealing piece of trivia in terms of his polit-ical or military leadership, the wider point seems fair: trivia can help you understand people. To read that Virginia Woolf was close to her sister, but also worried that people would view her writing as less worthy than Vanessa's painting, is to learn – if indeed you do learn it – a fairly dry, mundane fact. To hear that Virginia countered those fears by standing at a special desk to write, so putting her art on literally the same level as her sister's, is to have the fact sealed into your memory.

Further evidence of Andrea's mindset comes with her revelation about Abraham Lincoln and Charles Darwin. She knows they were born on the same day, but can't remember what that day was.[8] This reminds me that Margaret Thatcher was born on the same day as profanity-loving, heroin-using US comedian Lenny Bruce (surely the ultimate argument against astrology?), and that Catherine Zeta-Jones was born on her husband's twenty-fifth birthday. Andy refers to the recent deaths, announced on the same day, of ultra-bleak film director Ingmar Bergman and cheeky cockney comedian Mike Reid. We're disappointed that Reid actually died the previous day, so robbing us of a beautiful coincidence. Two people who really did cash in their chips on the same day, however, were Benny Hill and Frankie Howerd. Except no one knew about Hill at the time; his publicist, asked for a quote about Howerd and unable to reach Hill, made one up. Only two days later was his flat broken into and his body found. Another instance of trivia encapsulating a wider truth: Hill always lived alone. Preferring his own company, he shunned relationships.

I wonder if he was into trivia?

That evening, pleased that there is, after all, a distinctively feminine take on the subject, I discuss Andrea's thoughts with my girlfriend. Jo agrees about the 'people' point. While ordinarily she may have little time for the trivia I 'keep coming out with' (her term, and one I can't help feeling is a touch loaded), she does like a 'person' fact. She laughed, for instance, when I told her about Reg Varney. There was also, we recall, a chuckle on hearing that Sophia Loren was once addicted to peanuts.

8. 12 February 1809.

Imagine my annoyance, therefore, when all efforts at confirming the Loren fact prove unsuccessful. The internet contains not a single mention. Her biographer Warren G. Harris tells me he's never heard it either. He very kindly gives me contact details for various representatives and associates of Miss Loren. Their lack of response to my emails provides its own answer. God knows where I first heard it. Warning: this rumour does not contain nuts.

I do, however, learn that Sophia Loren's sister was once married to Benito Mussolini's son. He was a successful jazz pianist.

Several days later. I'm sitting on the terrace of Somerset House. Two centuries ago I'd have been very wet; before the Thames was artificially narrowed to build the Embankment, it came right up to the building, thereby allowing ships to reach the then home of the Admiralty. Now the same premises house a smart café and bar, serving expensive bottled beers to the likes of me and Liz.

Liz Anstee is head of radio at the production company responsible for *Who Wants To Be A Millionaire?* Smart, vibrant and animated, Liz is the human distillation of zeal. Every sentence begins before the last one has ended, every phrase contains an idea, a thought, a point worth making. Or, as often as not, a great piece of trivia. I have seen Liz with groups of male comedy writers, swapping pop facts from the eighties as though her career depended on it. Though given that she was the producer, it was probably the other way round.

'Of course there's a feminine approach to trivia,' she says. 'Most women could name you five diets, and what's that if it's not trivia? It's the same with fashion – most women could name you five designers, five models . . . That's more trivial than football, and football's bloody trivial. Who buys *Heat* magazine? Women. That's *crammed* with trivia.'

But that, I tell Liz, isn't the sort of trivia I associate with her.

'I think I do both male and female trivia,' she replies. 'I could name you five diets if I had to, but it doesn't really interest me. I do music, films . . .'

But not sport?

'I don't like sport, but I like the stories that go with it. My brother tells me about the characters in his cricket team and I love it. Also things like the Busby Babes. They're interesting, whereas Man United's current signing isn't.'

What about stupid football trivia? The Hull City no-letters-you-can-colour-in thing, for instance?

'I did like that one about players whose surnames were TV programmes. What were they again?' This is from ten years ago, but Liz gets there in the end. 'Lee Sharpe, Gerry Taggart and Dan "Pet-Rescue".'

We move on to films. Liz scares me slightly by proving her claim that she can name Liz Taylor's eight husbands in order.[9] Is this how my girlfriend feels when I name an entire England cricket team from 1984? Liz knows that *It Happened One Night* was the first film to win all five major Oscars (actor, actress, director, screenplay and movie). I ask if she knows the only case of two actors winning Oscars for playing the same character. Liz starts by assuming it must be a real person ('Churchill? Nixon? Malcolm X?'), then is steered towards fictional characters. After

9. Nicky Hilton, Michael Wilding, Mike Todd, Eddie Fisher, Richard Burton, Richard Burton again, John Warner, Larry Fortensky.

a brief foray down a Hannibal Lecter cul-de-sac, she gets it: Don Corleone. Marlon Brando – best actor, *The Godfather* – and Robert de Niro – best supporting actor, *The Godfather II*.^{TOPOT}

I test Liz on Toby's Charlton Heston thing. She doesn't know the answers, explaining that her interest is often in the personal lives of film stars, rather than the films themselves. Though she does get the two Dustin Hoffman films.

'And *Rain Man* as well,' she adds. 'Doesn't that end with him on a bus?'

She could be right. I make a note to check.

Liz sees the point of the 'pattern' theory. 'I think it's that you're trying to make sense of the world. Maybe even *control* the world in a way. Even though you know you can't. Women do it as well as men. Patterns in relationships, for example. You'll look back on past boyfriends, try to learn from the errors you made there when you're choosing a new one.'

Where does Liz think her love of trivia comes from?

'Both my parents were like this. My mum is queen of the weird fact. She doesn't really analyse, she just knows lots, remembers the strangest stuff. She'll watch *Mastermind* and answer along. She's got that sort of sticky brain.'

TOPOT

Researching his role in Taxi Driver, *Robert de Niro exhibited his usual thoroughness by working as a real cabbie. One fare turned out to be a friend. 'What happened, Bobby?' he said. 'You won an Oscar two years ago.'*

I like this phrase. It nutshells one of trivia's key aspects: it finds you, not the other way round.

'My dad was the same,' says Liz. 'He was the sort of guy who'd say "Talking of hedgehogs . . ." when you weren't. And he would *keep* you guessing about things. It would be some obscure fact about . . . oh God, I don't know . . . the first post box or something, and he would make you carry on guessing until you cried. I've inherited that. If I've got a great piece of gossip I'll make people guess before I tell them. Though I don't string it out for quite as long as he did.'

Another inheritance was less happy. 'Dad was never really interested in what you had to say, he was always listening for something he could pin his next fact on. That's why I speak as fast as I do: he was always interrupting me. I had to speak quickly to get it all out. In fact until I was thirty I had a stutter. To this day I've got a hatred of being interrupted. I've got the same approach Dad had to sharing facts, but I'm careful never to interrupt anyone.'

How did Liz get on at school?

'Badly. Both my brother and I were sent to private school [her brother went to Harrow]. My dad had wanted to go to university, but his dad wouldn't pay for it. From then on he saw education you paid for as important in getting on in life. I reacted badly. I got myself thrown out of school at fourteen. I'd worked out early on – when I was about ten – that you could pass exams without working, so why should I work? That was how I stayed until my last year at university [history and French at Cardiff]. Then I decided I wanted a two one, so I worked and got it.'

We veer back on to films. Liz teaches me the game Movie Movie. One player names a film, the other an actor in that film, the first another film in which that actor appeared, and so on until one of you fails. Liz invites me to start.

I pick a film famed for its trivia. '*The Italian Job*.'[10]

'Michael Caine,' says Liz.

'*The Ipcress File*.'

Liz opens her mouth, then closes it again. Such a well-known film . . . she's got to know someone else in it . . . but no. 'They're all "You'd know his face" actors, aren't they?'

I take her point. 'But what about the woman? You must know her?'

Liz is grinding her teeth. 'No. It's gone.'

'Sue Lloyd. From *Crossroads*.'

Liz thumps the table. 'Of *course*.'

Beginner's luck, it transpires: soon Liz is trouncing me. Films and film stars fly past like hundred-mile-an-hour tennis serves: *Cover Girl*, Jean Harlow, *The Poseidon Adventure*, Burt Lancaster . . . When James Dean gets mentioned, I attempt a trivia fight-back.

'Do you know the story about him and Alec Guinness?' I ask.

Liz laughs. 'I've been to the car park where it happened. Barney's Beanery.'[11]

Liz also knows that Dean was 24 when he died. I respond

---

10. It was Noël Coward's last film. The sewer through which the Minis drive isn't in Turin, it runs between Birmingham and Coventry. Corblimey theme song *The Self Preservation Society* was written by king of cool Quincey Jones.
11. Dean proudly showed off his new sports car outside said Los Angeles restaurant. Guinness felt a chill run through him. 'Promise me you will never drive this car,' he said. 'If you do you'll be dead within a week.' Dean died when he crashed the car seven days later.

with Marilyn Monroe being 36, in fact living a mere four days longer than the woman with whom she shares an Elton John song, Princess Diana. I mention that I'm about to outlive them both.

'I do that too,' says Liz. 'I remember realising I'd outlived John Lennon. Then last year it was Elvis.'

This is a trait I've only ever known in male friends: retaining the trivia in the first place (birthdays of the famous, especially your heroes, and how old they were at death), as well as comparing your achievements at a given age to theirs. The American satirist Tom Lehrer once said, 'When Mozart was my age, he'd been dead for two years.'[12] I'm intrigued to find Liz does it too.

'Oh yeah,' she says. 'I was playing bridge with my friend Johnny and his mates the other week. They were all in their mid-thirties. Johnny took out a bottle of port his father had given him. I was so chuffed: it was the one thing in the room older than me.' Liz also knows who shares her birthday of 15 April: Jeffrey Archer, Samantha Fox, Dodi Fayed and Emma Thompson.

Does she compare achievements with those of her heroes?

'Not really. I think the older you get the fewer heroes you have. Also you realise that film stars aren't their characters. As Rita Hayworth used to say, "Men go to bed with Gilda and they wake up with me."'

Later, as we're leaving the café – I'm meeting a friend for a drink, Liz is heading for the Tube – she umms and ahhs over whether Covent Garden or Leicester Square is better.

With a lot of people, I'd think twice about voicing the thought

12. This must have been when Lehrer was 37.

that comes into my head. Not with Liz, though. Not after this conversation.

'You know the distance between those two stations is the shortest between any two stations on the network?'

The friend I'm meeting is Alison. Three years younger than Liz (her fortieth birthday – lots of Human League at a private members' club – was only a couple of months ago), Alison is similarly high-powered in a non-high-powered way; she's a marketing director unafraid to dance to the Human League. She is not, however, much of a trivialist.

Or so I've thought until now.

I tell her about Liz knowing who shares her birthday. 'I've got Ryan O'Neill and Nicholas Lyndhurst,' replies Alison.

And, I add, the most famous April the twentiether of them all: Hitler.

'Yes, I did know that, thank you very much.'

Does she know Hitler's death date?

'No.'

April the thirtieth, I tell her. 'The year's obvious, of course.'

But the look on Alison's face says otherwise.

'You do know he shot himself in the closing days of the war?'

'Yes.'

'And the war ended . . . ?'

Alison thinks. 'I should know this. Especially as I did a history degree.'

'*What?*'

More thinking. Eventually Alison guesses 1945. But it is only a guess.

'That,' I say, 'has to be the definition of a trivialist: someone who doesn't know which year the Second World War ended but does know Nicholas Lyndhurst's birthday.' Alison tries to save face with some First World War trivia: its starting whistle, the assassination of Archduke Franz Ferdinand, occurred on 28 June 1914.

While we're on birthdays, does she know the time of her own birth? 'Yes. Nine forty-five p.m. It goes on Scottish birth certificates, but not English ones.' A piece of trivia in itself.

We fall into a discussion about band names. Alison learns that the Human League were characters in a science fiction wargame, and the Spandau Ballet was the twitching of Nazi war criminals' feet as they were hung at said prison. I, in return, learn that Duran Duran took their name from the Jane Fonda film *Barbarella*, the villain being Dr Durand Durand.

Alison also knows that Donnie Osmond's favourite colour is purple. To which the only possible response is: how?

'*Jackie* magazine. If I liked someone as a child I'd get all the info I could on them. *Jackie* was great for that. I think it was *Jackie* that gave me Lewis Collins's birthday – twenty-seventh of May. I controversially fancied him in *The Professionals* rather than Martin Shaw.'[13]

Does Alison do the age comparison thing?

'Oh yes. It's depressed me for a good ten years now that most of the Scotland rugby squad are younger than me. I always

13. Alison initially remembers the date as 28 May, which was Ian Fleming's birthday. Born in 1908, he gave exactly the same birthday to his villain Blofeld. Whose name he took from the father of cricket commentator Henry Blofeld; they were members of the same club.

used to hold them in such esteem – they were doctors and lawyers and things – but now one of them will be thirty-two and he's the veteran of the team. I still look at them and think, "I wouldn't say no", but they'd think I was on a grab-a-granny night.'

A little later, it strikes me that Alison's trivia, like Liz's and Andrea's, concerns people. The exact moment it strikes me is when Alison says, apropos of Keith Richards singing at the Coronation, that a young Barry Sheene, before he got into motorbikes, once sang at the Royal Opera House.

Despite his blatant fabrication of Michael Caine quotes, my friend Patrick has risen through the journalistic ranks to become political editor of a Sunday broadsheet newspaper. This hasn't stopped him being a trivialist of the first order. Sport, films, music . . . A particular area of expertise is funk. What that man doesn't know about Earth Wind and Fire isn't worth knowing. In fact a lot of what he *does* know about Earth Wind and Fire isn't worth knowing.

Chatting to him about the book, I mention my research into women and trivia.

'You've got to meet Melissa,' he says, referring to his deputy on the paper.

'Is she good on trivia?'

'Is Tony Blair a Catholic?'

We discuss possible dates. It's just before the party conference season, so we'll have to wait. Unless . . . For years I've been meaning to see what a conference is like, egged on by Patrick's stories of hedonistic excess. (Never, apparently, try to hide a hangover from David Blunkett.) Could this be a two-birds-one-stone scenario? Diaries are compared. The Tory conference it is.

Melissa and Patrick and I will meet in Blackpool. Oh the romance of it.

That Sunday, having paid special attention to Melissa's articles in the name of research, I turn to the newspaper's magazine. There, in her regular column, Sandi Toksvig peppers her prose with snippets of trivia. It's her trademark. Recent columns (like every lazy recycler I have my own private newspaper library) reveal Shakespeare using the word pedant to mean 'teacher', Bumper Harris, a man with a wooden leg, being paid to spend his days riding up and down the first escalator at Earl's Court Tube station to show it was safe, and Phedippides – who ran the 26 miles from Marathon to Athens with news of the Persians' defeat – managing to say 'Rejoice, we are victorious' before dropping dead.[TOPOT] She even

TOPOT

The modern marathon's final 385 yards date from the 1908 London Olympics. Aiming to standardise the race at 26 miles, the organisers mapped out a course of exactly that distance from Windsor Castle – where the young princes could watch – to the newly built White City stadium. But the finishing line, unlike that of all other races, was on the opposite side of the track from the Royal box. Queen or Princess Someone-or-Other demanded that the runners complete the extra distance.

writes of 'every nugget of information connect[ing] with a thousand, often unexpected others. The minute I learn something I find myself mentally standing in front of a vast intellectual Tube map with any number of options as to where I might go next.' This is a woman I have to speak to.

Fortunately I did exactly that last year, when she interviewed me on her Radio Four travel programme about my trip to Turin to visit *Italian Job* locations.[14] The skill with which she disguised pity as interest showed what a nice woman she really is. What's more, the programme's producer, Harry, is himself an accomplished trivialist. I know this having worked with him for a short while during my time at the Beeb. An avuncular man in his late forties, his round glasses somehow give him a schoolboyish air, in keeping with the intellectual enthusiasm that makes him a brilliant producer. An email or two is exchanged. Several days later I visit Henry Wood House, next to Broadcasting House. Naming this mid-twentieth-century office building after the father of the Proms is a bit like owning an Elgar Coal Shed. But inside the BBC have done their best with office partitions and pastel colours. Harry and Sandi and I bag some comfy seats in a quiet corner of the fourth-floor communal area, and settle down to talk trivia.

How many of the facts in her columns, I ask Sandi, does she already know, and how many does she look up?

'I know a lot of them, but I look things up as well. Very

14. The trip wasn't solely because of *The Italian Job*. I'm not that sad. I worked in *Day of the Jackal* locations too. My girlfriend was happy to make the journey with me, though only because it visited some of the most stunning parts of northern Italy and the French Riviera.

often you'll say "What about that?" and when you look it up
it leads you to something else entirely. You can take five pieces
of trivia that seem utterly unrelated, and find a way to make
them go from one to the other to the other . . . That's the thing
I take pleasure in. It's like managing some terrible crossword
puzzle you've made for yourself.'

Sandi mentions that her latest column is all about pencils,
inspiration (if that's the word) having come from an opera critic
whose noisy scribbling drove her away at the interval. I ask if
she used the HB pencil/35 miles fact.

'Irritatingly, I didn't know that. But I did find out that pencils
were invented by an Italian couple. They ran a carpentry shop.
I bet you any money – I can't prove it – that she invented the
pencil. I bet he had a piece of graphite and he kept getting it
all over his trousers . . .'[15]

Sandi doesn't care for 'the kind of trivia that wins you a
million pounds on *Mastermind*'. Unless *Mastermind* has changed
considerably since I last saw it I think she means another quiz
show, but I let it pass. Coincidentally, a news story appears
a couple of days later about the programme struggling to
find female contestants. 'I think men are more nerdy,' says
the presenter John Humphrys, 'and more capable of amassing
sometimes useless facts. Women are more interested in the
important things in life.'

Useless or not, facts have an admirer in Sandi. 'My dad
was a journalist. He believed you could capture the audience's imagination through the minutiae, a piece of detail.

15. Harry, unlike either Sandi or myself, knows what HB stands for: hard
black.

Say he was covering the American elections for a European audience. You could see that as a really broad topic. But actually if you look at the frayed collar of a Democratic candidate who isn't quite going to make it, that's the bit that *tells* you he's not quite going to make it.[16] You've got to pay attention to the little stuff, and then somehow you'll get the big picture.'[17] Hence her dislike of 'quiz show' knowledge. 'If you know the highest lake in the world or something you'll win a million pounds. We now reward that as a form of knowledge. I don't really like that. I like it when you take trivia and make it work for you, when it has a place in a bigger context of understanding.'

'It's interesting about quiz shows,' says Harry. 'I'm quite good at remembering those kinds of things – what geological period we're in, all that. I just seem to know. But remembering people's names . . . I'm terrible. It's the unimportant things I remember.'

'I always think my head is like an office full of filing cabinets that haven't been shut properly,' says Sandi. 'There are bits you keep meaning to put away, they're on the floor . . .'

16. A few weeks after our conversation, the Liberal Democrat leader Menzies Campbell is forced to resign. He confesses to being 'irritated, because of the quite extraordinary concentration of trivia which seems to surround leadership. People write articles on what kind of socks I wear.' Actually the article asked whether he wore sock *garters*, an alleged sighting having been made. The trivia only gained currency because it symbolised wider concerns about Campbell's old-fashioned image.

17. Sandi will mention later that her father always made his children read the first three pages of the *New York Times*, on the grounds that 'we'd always have something to say'.

Harry asks about the memory's capacity. 'Do new facts make you forget the old?'

Scribbling a reminder about tracking down a memory expert (perfect subject for a reminder, really), I tell Harry I'm not sure, but Sherlock Holmes, Al Bean and Homer Simpson all thought so.

'I've got room in my head for about five telephone numbers,' he says. 'I absolutely promise you, if I learn a new one, I forget one of the old ones. And three of the five are mine.'

How about birthdays? I ask him.

'I can remember the months, but not the dates.'

'That's what a partner's for,' says Sandi. 'It's their job to remember things like that.'

Harry sees trivia as 'details divorced from their original context . . . You can read a book or an article, but you'll only remember certain details, and years later they will be what's left. For instance I'm reading a book at the moment called *How To Enjoy Paris in 1842*, by an Anglo-French travel writer called Francis Hervé. It's full of interesting bits, so many that you can't remember them all, but certain things stick out. Already I know that the French invented the queue. They'd line up neatly for their theatre tickets, whereas in London they didn't.'

'Who knew that was a French import?' says Sandi.

'Exactly. The English are supposed to be the masters of queuing. The other thing was that Frankish kings were all called Clovis, which is why French kings ended up being called Louis.'

TOPOT

The Duke of Devonshire, whose stately home Chatsworth is actually in Derbyshire, owes his title to a spelling mistake by the medieval clerk who wrote out the original documents.

Sandi laughs. 'History's littered with bad spelling, isn't it?'TOPOT

As an example of the trivia that stays in her own mind, Sandi mentions lobsters. 'I learnt years ago that they're left- or right-clawed in the same way are we are left- or right-handed. Also, by the way, lobsters are benthic, which means bottom-dwellers. I think that word's wonderful; I know so many benthic boys in showbusiness. Anyway, I can't now eat a lobster without checking it was left- or right-clawed. The claw that it favours will be the larger. This is an entirely anecdotal survey – but I do like lobster very much, so I eat it a lot – only about ten per cent of lobsters are left-clawed.'

I mention the sad truth, or rather untruth, of all polar bears being left-handed. Which brings us, by way of the Natural History Museum shop, back to pencils.

I raise the issue of gender, of trivia being seen as a male subject. What's Sandi's opinion?

She thinks for a moment. 'I take an active pleasure in knowing short cuts on journeys, in looking at a map and then memorising it. That's not really a girl thing. I argue with my satellite navigation system. "Oh don't be absurd, that's a ridiculous way to go . . ." I've taught my kids that too – you'll never get lost if you know where the sun is.' Sandi has two daughters and a son. 'They were all brought up exactly the same. But my son, from the age he could make clear his desires, if anyone arrived with a car we had to open the bonnet so he could look at the engine. My girls couldn't care less. It was just extraordinary.'

How does Sandi fare, in terms of practicality?

'I'm quite mechanical. I like fixing things. I've got a beach hut in Whitstable, and I was on the roof one day fixing it. A man came past on his way to the sailing club. He said, "Fixing the roof?" I wanted to say, "No, I'm here for the view." But I said, "Yes," and he said, "You can get rolls of felt from B&Q." I said, "I know, I've got some." Then he told me they do very good adhesive in five-litre tins. "I know, I've got some." He was so irritated that he couldn't advise me on anything. No woman would ever have walked past and advised me on what I should do. I was quite tempted to go and tell him how to sail his boat, which I probably could have. But I didn't.'

Harry, I guess, is a practical man – right?

'Yeah, reasonably. My first car was a Renault 4. The petrol tank had a leak at the top, so although petrol couldn't leak out water could leak in, and it used to clog up the carburettor. I used to be able to get out at a red traffic light, clean the carburettor, then get back in before the light had changed.'

'That's a kind of trivia I like,' says Sandi. 'There are certain pieces of information which actually are useful.'

I wouldn't be able to find a carburettor, much less fix one. I don't even know what a carburettor does. Though I'm with Sandi on maps. My girlfriend isn't. But her driving is better than mine. Recognising this, we happily stick to our specialities.

Even when the roles get switched for whatever reason, we agree to do our best in maintaining the peace. Jo tries not to flinch too much when I parallel park, I try not to say anything when she turns the map upside down just because we're heading south.

'It's the same with first aid,' adds Sandi. 'I know that sort of thing. I'm not a very good swimmer, but I did once save someone from drowning. They were drowning right next to me, which I thought was very inconsiderate. They could have picked someone who was a good swimmer. But I'd seen a programme, years before, about how to save someone from drowning, and although I didn't realise I'd taken it all in, it all came back into my head. I did exactly what I'd seen in the programme, and did indeed save this person's life. My family thought it was hilarious. Someone more unlikely to save a person at sea is hard to imagine.'

Harry sees that this returns us back to the notion of detail. 'The thing about saving someone from drowning, or something like the Heimlich manoeuvre, is that it's all in the detail. Lots of people know what the Heimlich is, but could they do it? Exactly where do you grab them, and so on? The detail is the important thing.'

'Sure,' says Sandi, 'but there was an interesting study done by NASA once about problem solving, and they concluded that they'd prefer to have a woman in charge of a spacecraft. If a meteor is coming at you, a woman will go, "Let's do D". A man will say, "Ah, A is occurring, therefore B means C . . ." by which time you've been knocked on the head. So in a way detail can sometimes get in the way of making an instant decision. One of the things that they've never been able to quantify or scientifically analyse is the thing they call women's intuition. Why does a woman instinctively think she knows what the answer is? She may be wrong, but the fact is she just makes a decision and goes for it.'

Does she think women are wrong very often?

'I do know if a mother tells you there's something wrong with her child there is. I would defy any doctor to be up against a mother who's saying, "My child's not well," and be right when the mother isn't.' Sandi says she has experience of this herself, but has 'no idea' why it should be so.

Later, looking something up on Wikipedia, I check what the site has to say about Sandi. She once mentioned on air, it says, that she 'enjoyed editing historical entries on Wikipedia in order to make unsuspecting children fail their GCSE coursework'. However, the entry continues in all seriousness, 'this was later revealed to be a joke'.

My first ever visit to Blackpool. The town's advance press has not been good. My brother was particularly scathing. A comparison was made with Beirut. To Beirut's advantage.

Yet when I get there, on a blustery but sunny autumn afternoon, the place doesn't seem that bad. It's busy, not just with the assembled journalists and politicos, but day trippers and holidaymakers too. Yes, the amusement arcades are gaudy, the souvenirs cheap and tacky, the candy floss overpowering. But everyone here for a good time is *having* a good time. They've got spirit, humour, a glint in their eyes. There's an energy to the place that's rare in twenty-first-century British seaside towns. The famous tower still stands tall and proud.^{TOPOT}

After settling into my hotel (two doors away, I discover only after paying up front, from the Hotel California – what a missed opportunity), I head for the Hilton, which along with the Imperial forms the epicentre of the conference socialising. Talk is of the general election which Gordon Brown may or may not call, depending on the Tories' performance this week, the opinion poll ratings, the projected state of the economy over the next year or two and a myriad other factors, all of which receive constant in-depth analysis.

Except from Patrick and his journalistic colleagues, whose analysis is of how they tonked the Tories 10–0 at football this morning. Only four of them have made it, via the celebration curry, to the Hilton bar. Patrick, looking as ever like Andy Garcia gone slightly to seed, reports that Melissa is busy tonight, but will be at their newspaper's party tomorrow evening. He offers a report on the match. His colleagues confirm that Patrick's performance in defence was as impressive as the scoreline would suggest, especially for a man of forty-four summers.

Once Patrick has told them about my book, the conversation inevitably turns to football trivia. Thankfully no stats anoraks are present. Instead the taste is for the quirky, the humorous, the downright stupid. The reason for Hull City's uniqueness is soon

> ### TOPOT
>
> *The Eiffel Tower grows by seven inches in summer. How Parisian.*

dispensed with. Though as Dan of the Press Association points out, it does make you wonder who spotted that in the first place, and why.[18] The four clubs whose names begin and end with the same letter take a while, but we get there eventually: Liverpool, Aston Villa, Charlton Athletic and Northampton Town. Until they got relegated a few years ago you could also have had York City. The only club in England or Scotland whose name contains a letter shared by no other club takes even longer, but again the group persist. St Johnstone, says Mike, who works for Sky. Correct: the J is unique.

With each question a hush descends, punctuated only by incorrect guesses and muttered workings. There's no bullish male competitiveness, we're simply relishing the challenge for its own sake. Nevertheless it strikes me that no group of women would ever behave like this. Female bonding requires proper communication. Perhaps we've hit on the explanation for all those surveys about women using twenty thousand words a day to men's seven thousand. The men are too busy mentally reciting the Scottish Third Division.

The Swindon Town/mackerel question soon raises its fishy

18. No one at the club itself knows, though they confirm that the fact's been doing the rounds for at least 15 years. An appeal on BBC Radio Humberside draws a blank. The writer John O'Farrell, who used the fact in his novel *The Best A Man Can Get*, can't remember who or where he got it from. He recognises trivia as a male trait, though doesn't know how long this has been true: 'The Bible does not record whether much of the Last Supper was taken with the disciples testing each other on statistics about the Roman Empire.' In the end the best guess comes from my friend Martin: 'I bet it was a bloke in a bookie's on a Saturday afternoon, passing the time by colouring in teams' names.'

head, leading us to the only US state to share no letters with 'mackerel' (Ohio), from where it is but a short step to the only letter not to appear in the name of any US state (Q). Music gets mentioned, and before we know it Mike is asking us which Beatle was the first to own a video recorder. Playing for time, I mention that Peter Sellers was one of the first people in the UK to own an answerphone. Always doing impressions for his outgoing message, he inadvertently created the catchphrase Michael Caine never said: 'Hello. My name is Michael Caine. Not a lot of people know that.'[19]

None of which gets us any closer to the answer. In the end we plump for John. We're wrong: it was pizzaphobe Ringo.

Thus is another evening passed in learned conversation.

The next day, I visit Blackpool's Winter Gardens, where the conference proper is taking place. The hall is large and ornate, with gilded columns and intricate plasterwork stretching all the way up to the high vaulted roof. But everything is faded and shabby, and though none of the paint is actually peeling, there's the sense of a long-gone age clinging desperately to the present. In fact none of the major parties has any plans to return here. Gazing down from the balcony, I feel sad that half a century of political history is coming to an end.

Several minutes later, I cheer up very quickly. The platform speaker has just mentioned a *great* piece of trivia.

*   *   *

19. Though Caine does confess to a love of trivia, and the way it works along tangents. Hearing on the radio that there was a shortage of salt, he remembered that nowhere in Britain is more than 52 miles from the sea.

That evening, the Hilton again. The Sandringham Room, designed to hold 200 people, is playing host to what feels like 2000. So crammed is the main body of the room that it is in effect a clothed sauna. Patrick and I, in search of cooler plains, retreat to a long corridor-like section through which people are entering and leaving. It feels like stepping from a tropical airport's tarmac onto an air-conditioned plane.

Melissa escapes from a nearby group and joins us. She's mid-thirties, with dark blonde, shoulder-length hair and a disposition that at first I mistake for sullenness. As the conversation develops, though, it becomes clear that Melissa is merely a woman who reserves judgement, waits for the world to impress her. There's a hint of creative stroppiness, a healthy cynicism. Entirely natural in a journalist, it's also a pleasant change from the non-stop glad-handing of a party conference, where too-ready smiles appear fifty times an hour.

I've warned Patrick that a question on political trivia lies in store. He invites me to fire.

'Parliament with the highest percentage of female members.'

They look at each other, instantly intrigued.

'It can't be Sweden or anywhere,' says Patrick. 'That'd be too obvious.'

'You'd think Scandinavia, wouldn't you?' says Melissa. 'Generous maternity leave and all that.'

'Somewhere with a long history of female emancipation . . .' muses Patrick. 'New Zealand?'

'Rwanda,' I say. 'Forty-eight per cent.'

'No way!' exclaims Melissa. 'That is very good trivia.'

She asks about the book, and in mentioning Andrea I relate the Napoleon facts.

'You know he was killed by his wallpaper?' Melissa says.

'His *wallpaper?*'

'He was poisoned by it. There was arsenic in it. They tested his blood after he died, and it showed high levels of arsenic.'

Patrick and I love this fact. As we do Melissa's revelation about King Charles spaniels: they have complete right of way in Britain. 'It was a royal decree. They're the only dog that has the absolute right to go anywhere they want. If you brought one in here and they said "No dogs" you could insist that it stayed.'

None of us knows which King Charles gave his name to the dog.[20] Equally I know that London's King's Road is named after one of them but can't remember which.[21] All I know is that he used it as his private road.

We turn to politics. I ask them what the W in George W. Bush stands for. Melissa knows, but Patrick's struggling. 'Is it . . . is it Whitter or something?'

Shaking our heads, we give him the answer: Walker.

'Have I imagined it,' I ask, 'or was there a rumour about Clinton's staff spending their last day at the White House taking the Ws off all the computer keyboards?'

---

20. It was in fact both of them.
21. It was in fact Charles II.

Patrick confirms there was that rumour. Whether it's true or not is a different matter.^{TOPOT} How many Americans, I wonder, would know the W stands for Walker? The consensus is 'not very'.

> **TOPOT**
>
> *The longest word you can make from the letters on the top row of a QWERTY keyboard is 'typewriter'.*

'Americans don't mind not knowing stuff,' says Patrick. 'It's a new, young, thrusting country. It's all about pioneering and pushing back frontiers. They're on big issues – they've got to do this, that and the other. We're an old, turned-in-on-ourselves island culture. Of course we're going to get obsessed by trivia and facts and history.'

Melissa nods. 'Do they have pub quizzes in America? I bet they don't.'

Patrick points out that there was never one in *Cheers*. Later investigation finds that quizzes aren't entirely unknown in the Land of the Free, but almost always occur where expat Brits and Irish gather, often on the east and west coasts. You never know, give it a few centuries and you might find bars in Yanksville, Alabama offering two points for the answer 'Lewinsky', with a bonus for 'cigar'.

We return to political trivia. I say that for me it brings the media's coverage alive. Patrick and Melissa's piece just after Gordon Brown's accession to the premiership, for instance. For all its incisive analysis, my favourite fact came in the opening paragraph: Brown, who is blind in one eye, had decreed that the font for Number Ten emails would change from Times New Roman 12 to Arial 14.[22] Trivia may be unimportant in itself – but if that detail hooked in someone who might otherwise not have read the piece, surely it's a good thing?

'The details can be fun,' agrees Patrick. 'Like the fact that Gordon's actually his middle name. Our Prime Minister is really called James Brown.'

'That's like Blair,' says Melissa. 'You know his father's surname was originally Parsons? We could have had a Prime Minister called Tony Parsons.'[23]

How do Patrick and Melissa fare on basic political facts? The distance between the red lines on the floor of the House of Commons, for example? Both know that it's two swords' lengths, originally to prevent MPs fighting.

'That's where "toeing the line" comes from,' adds Melissa. 'People often spell it t-o-w, but it's actually about keeping your toe behind the line.'

How about all Prime Ministers since the Second World War?

Melissa shakes her head. 'I'd be useless.'

Patrick looks confident.

'With years,' I warn.

---

22. Brown's blind eye is his left. One of two reasons why Jack Straw securing the place on the PM's immediate left at Cabinet – normally a great honour – was seen as a snub. The other being that Straw is deaf in his right ear.

23. Tony's father, Leo, was born out of wedlock to a man named Parsons, but adopted by a Glasgow couple called Blair.

He completes the roll call, with only occasional prompting required.[24]

'I wish I could reel off dates,' says Melissa.

'Why?' I ask.

'Because it's clever.'

'Isn't it cleverness for its own sake?'

'I *like* cleverness for its own sake. But I don't obsess about things like men do, so I don't get the dates in there in the first place.'

'It's not clever to remember dates,' says Patrick. 'It's just "having a good memory".'

Melissa's not convinced. 'If you're at a dinner party and you reel off those dates you sound clever.'

'To me it sounds boringly anal.'

I ask Melissa if that sort of memory impresses her in a man.

'Yes. It's not the be all and end all, but it's not unimpressive.'

'Even when they do football dates?'

'It would reassure you he was normal.'

I mention Andrea's knowledge-is-safety theory. Does Melissa think knowledgeable men attract women because, at whatever subliminal level, they offer protection?

'I think that's right. Men should know things. OK, if I went out for dinner with a man and he was constantly reciting dates my eyes would glaze over. But if he dropped in one or two –

24. Attlee 1945–51; Churchill 1951–5; Eden 1955–7; Macmillan 1957–63; Douglas-Home 1963–4; Wilson 1964–70; Heath 1970–74; Wilson 1974–6; Callaghan 1976–9; Thatcher 1979–90; Major 1990–97; Blair 1997–2007.

if it happened to crop up, if we wanted to know who the Prime Minister was in a particular year – it would be very impressive. There are women who like being entertained by men reciting trivia. It's entertaining to be fed information.'

Similarly, lack of information is something Melissa doesn't like. 'I find people who parade their ignorance annoying. If you turn on the radio, and it's one of those mainsteam rush-hour programmes, the DJs will be stunningly ignorant. They will relish not knowing who Gordon Brown is. That's so annoying.'

Conversation veers on to attitudes to learning. All three of us, it transpires, fitted in neither socially nor academically at school. 'I didn't do well until A levels,' says Melissa. 'Then it became interesting. It wasn't just reciting verbs any more, it was about things like Peter the Great. I wanted to know about that. My history teacher would just sit and talk to you, with you making notes. Sometimes she wouldn't even tolerate that, she'd want all your attention. She would talk interestingly about the lives of these people.'

While everyone in her class was 'fired up by being anti-Thatcher', Melissa took pleasure in being pro-government. Patrick talks of a similar contrariness, of 'big disciplinary problems'. I'm reminded of Toby – 'I never bothered with exams' – and Liz, who actually got herself expelled. Not every trivialist I've spoken to has been like this, it's true. But the tales correspond with my own school experience. It's not so much that a willingness to be the odd one out – lunchtime spent in a book rather than on the playing field – mirrors trivia's status at the margins of knowledge. Rather it feels like a rejection of conventional learning, or at least the conventional approach to such learning – a querying of which facts are thought important and which not.

Something Melissa said earlier intrigued me: she doesn't 'obsess about things like men do'. What did she mean?

'I think men are more entertained and satisfied by trivia because women are more broad-brush. Women want to talk about grand themes of love and death. Women know that the devil isn't in the detail. That's what men think, isn't it? That it's all about the detail. Whereas women say, "Forget about the detail, let's just get on with it."'

Patrick's nodding. 'Men want to strip things down and see how they work.'

'Men want to analyse things and look at component parts,' continues Melissa. 'Women are more interested in the organic whole, and respond in a more emotional way. Women are feeling their way with their instincts. Men are obsessing about the detail.'

It's not the first time someone's used that word. Steve, Harry and Sandi all talked about trivia in terms of detail. Not just in the literal sense of a piece of trivia being a detail, but detail as opposed to the big picture, a more complete view. Only now, however, does the importance of this really hit home. Men do detail, women do the big picture.

'I have never had a boyfriend who's untidier than me,' says Melissa. 'And I'm not an untidy person. In my experience men are more interested in everything being just so. They read a lot of significance into it.

Patrick refers to a male colleague of theirs whose desk is a monument to tidiness. Woe betide anyone who moves so much as a paper clip.

I'm reminded of recipes. As much as I love cooking and would claim at least a moderate degree of proficiency, I always have to follow a recipe to the letter. It says three sprigs of thyme? Three it must be. Not two, not four. We've run out of caster sugar? Panic grips me, the world's about to end. Then Jo breezes happily in, casts half an eye over the recipe, says why don't I use normal sugar? 'Will it work?' 'Sure.' 'Then why does it say *caster* sugar?' In the end the normal sugar goes in. The recipe works. But still I'm not happy, not totally content. A detail has been disobeyed.

Walking back to my hotel, I call Jo to say goodnight. We talk about Melissa's theory, including the tidiness point.

'There's a difference between being tidy and being clean,' says Jo. 'Men want their CDs in order, but they can live like pigs. I shared a flat with a bloke who was revolting like that.'

There's a pause.

'Not you,' she says. 'You're . . . not bad.'

I settle for that. On the tidiness front, I know Melissa has got me to a tee. While my CD collection isn't large enough to warrant a catalogue (they're not even stored alphabetically), plenty of other things get the 'detail' treatment. I have separate files, or at least A4 envelopes, for all the utility bills. Should we ever need an account number, a customer reference number, a helpline number, I know where to look. Finding an electricity bill in the council tax file was a disturbing experience. Finding a council tax bill in the box where we keep the dog's toys threatened to bring on a seizure.

Although I know now that the best way to deal with it is by counting to ten before I raise it with Jo. That way things can stay polite.

Back at the hotel, I look through my notes. Andrea's mind map is there. I notice a line at the bottom that hadn't stood out before: 'Dangers: a little learning is a dangerous thing.' (Actually, in her haste, Andrea has written 'a little leaning is a dangerous thing'.)^{TOPOT} Details can indeed lead you astray. Just look at conspiracy theories. To extrapolate from a few tiny facts and think you've 'solved' the big picture is to invite ridicule. But the trivialists I know don't extrapolate like that. None of them believe that the moon landings were faked in a Mexican desert. They enjoy trivia simply for what it is.

What *is* it, though? Melissa's comments about men and women have got me thinking: perhaps men *are* looking for the big picture. Not about the moon landings, or who really shot JFK, or any other crackpot theory. About *everything*, the biggest of Big Pictures: an entire understanding of the world. The meaning of life. That's what I got from talking to Andrea, after all. The idea of trivia as pieces of the jigsaw. While women want to understand people, men want to understand the world. Sandi talked about female intuition. Now Melissa has contrasted that with male attention-to-detail.

Is it that women have an

> **TOPOT**
>
> *Double-decker London Routemaster buses can lean further without falling over than a human being can.*

innate feel for the world, while men, lacking such an understanding, search for it in details? You can comprehend something either through its details or through the overall picture. The latter, of course, is made up of the former: every picture is simply a collection of megapixels. Collect all those – join the dots, complete the jigsaw – and the picture will emerge. It might even emerge with just some of the pixels. You don't need every last piece to see what a jigsaw depicts. Maybe that's why trivia, as opposed to comprehensive knowledge, holds such appeal. Perhaps it's a short cut to understanding life.

Or is that just a man talking? Perhaps you can't understand a picture from its component parts. Link every piece of trivia, connect every detail, and you still won't see the picture: maybe female intuition is the key to that. Maybe. But even if it is, my male brain doesn't *know* it is, so carries on collecting trivia anyway.

Not looking down. That's what I thought trivia was about, that evening at the pub quiz with Marcus. Following B.B. King's advice, allowing yourself to delight in the unimportant, the inconsequential – the trivial. Don't bother with the meaning of life stuff. That way madness – or depression – lies. Yet now I'm starting to see that the opposite might be true. Perhaps trivia *is* the meaning of life. Or at least to search for one is to search for the other.

Perhaps I am looking down after all.

The next morning I find Patrick on the press balcony, gazing gloomily down on the conference proceedings, wondering how he can turn them into readable copy. I run him through my thinking from last night.

'If you want to see someone trying to understand every last detail about the world,' he says, 'sit on a train from Teddington to Waterloo with Joe.' Patrick's son, aged six. '"What's the next station, Dad?" "Raynes Park." "Why is it called Raynes Park?" "Because there's a park there." "Why is there a park there?" "I don't know, there just is." "How long is it to Raynes Park?" "About five minutes." "What's the next station after that?" "Wimbledon." "Is there a park at Wimbledon too?" "There's Wimbledon Common, yes." "Why is it Wimbledon Common and not Wimbledon Park?"'

'What about Georgia?' I ask. Joe's sister, a year older.

'She just says, "This is boring. We've been on a train before."'

Why are we curious? Why does every answer produce another question? Why is it always why?

Once upon a time scientists wanted to know why molecules behaved as they did. Then they wanted to know why atoms behaved as they did. Then it was protons, electrons, neutrons . . . All the time the search for knowledge drives them on. All the time trivialists are collecting facts, snippets of info, details. And like scientists, they arrange those details into patterns. Then they arrange the patterns into patterns. They won't be happy until there's one big pattern, joining every dot in the universe, linking every detail to every other detail.

In *Patterns of Discovery*, the book Arthur Miller recommended, Norwood Hanson considers the interconnectedness of facts. 'This way of looking at the world,' he writes, 'leads to bewhiskered questions. Y caused Z, X caused Y, W caused

X, V caused W. Thus back to A. What caused A? Dryden makes
the standard answer pleasing to the ear:

> . . . Some few, whose Lamp shone brighter, have been led
> From Cause to Cause, to Nature's secret head;
> And found that one first principle must be;
> But what or who, that Universal He;
> Whether some Soul encompassing this Ball,
> Unmade, unmov'd; yet making, moving All . . .

Whether or not a scientist or a trivialist ends up with God as
their Big Answer, it seems to me that the Big Question is certainly
being asked. 'Ah,' someone might say, 'but is it? Are you really
after the meaning of life? Couldn't it just be that you like patterns
for their own sake, for the simple reason that patterns are pretty?'

Something tells me not. Otherwise why would my immediate reaction to that have been 'Why are patterns pretty?'

A suspicion lurks that I haven't finished with the issue of
gender. Or that it hasn't finished with me. At some point my
search will return to it.

In the meantime, though, there is one definite conclusion to
be drawn. When women do show an interest in trivia it's trivia
about people, rather than events or dates or places. My perfect
fact must reflect this. A fact can hardly be classed as perfect if
it alienates half the world's population.

And so inspired by that entry on Andrea's mind map, I make
a note:

The perfect fact must help you understand people.

6

A hundred trillion synapses

The amygdala's role makes sense, sort of. The prefrontal cortex seems relatively easy to understand. And I can just about get the point of excitatory neuronal feedback systems. But the fundamental basics of what's actually going on here still elude me.

The next stage of the search is to get inside the head of people who remember trivia. Literally inside their heads: their memories. Andrea and Harry have both pointed me towards this issue. How does the brain store information? What's happening in there? What are the neurological, biological and chemical processes by which a trivialist does his mental filing? The answer, I suspect, won't only be of interest in itself, in tidying up the query raised by Sherlock et al: 'Can the memory fill up?' It might also provide clues to trivia's appeal in the first place. Understand my brain's relationship with this stuff, and I might understand why I love it.

If you want to know about memory, it soon becomes clear, you go to the Institute of Cognitive Neuroscience. Housed over four floors of a Georgian building in London's Bloomsbury, not far from the British Museum, the ICN is peopled by over a hundred academics, from PhD level upwards, engaged in all manner of studies about the human brain. There are groups studying numeracy and literacy, speech, motor control, visual cognition – and one group named Clinical Neurophysiology and Memory. Its head is Professor Emrah Duzel. His current research interests, the ICN's web page reveals beneath a picture of a smiling man in his late thirties with rimless glasses and a trim goatee, include the 'functional organization and neural dynamics of memory'. His work involves 'multimodal imaging using fMRI [the scanners in which patients lie] and electromagnetic techniques in combination with psychopharmacology'. Surely this is a man who can explain how we remember that John Lennon's first girlfriend was Thelma Pickles?[1]

Professor Duzel is happy to be interviewed. But perhaps before we meet, he says in an email, it would make sense for me to read the two attached articles? That way we can avoid wasting time on the really simple stuff. Good idea. We fix an appointment, my printer sets to work, and I settle down with a cup of coffee and two extracts from the *Encyclopedia of the Human Brain*.

The first, 'Memory: Overview', sets up a few initial distinctions. For instance between 'declarative' or 'explicit' memory – facts, experiences, information about events – and 'nondeclarative' or 'implicit' memory. These are the bits not directly accessible to your consciousness, such as skill and habit learning. Trivia, you would assume, belongs very much to the former category. I make a note to this effect. Then we reach 'excitatory neuronal feedback systems'. Neurons, it appears, are at the

1. And indeed that she went on to work in television, and produced *Blind Date*.

core of how our memory works. They are cells, appearing all over our nervous system – brain, spinal cord, nerves – which can be electrically activated, and so process and transmit information. The number in your brain varies throughout your lifetime, but for the sake of ease let's call it a hundred billion. The nematode worm, on the other hand, has three hundred and two. Not much fun for the worm, but pretty handy for scientists, who find it easy to experiment on.

Neurons in themselves, though, aren't a lot of use. It's the connections between neurons which do the real work. These are called synapses. When a neuron gets stimulated it releases chemicals known as neurotransmitters, which form bonds with neighbouring neurons. Each neuron can form synapses with many other neurons. A brain of a hundred billion neurons might contain a hundred *trillion* synapses, and these are what allow us to hold memories. The article doesn't explain how, exactly, but an early layman's suspicion forms that Sherlock needn't have fretted so much.

When a new piece of information is received by the brain, the neurons that get excited, and link to form a memory of it, can set up what are known as excitatory neuronal feedback systems. Otherwise known as 'reverbatory circuits', these entail the neurons continuing to excite each other even after the information has been received. The more this happens, the stronger the long-term memory that is formed.[2] This seems a perfect, if entirely unscientific, metaphor for what happens between trivialists when they swap trivia. The joy at hearing a new fact,

2. As opposed to short-term memory, the capacity to hold information (e.g. a telephone number) in your head immediately after receiving it.

a new bomb of delight, leads you to tell someone else. Constant repetition reinforces it in your brain, each retelling making it that bit harder to forget. But this doesn't explain the excitement caused by getting the trivia in the first place. Presumably we only notice it at all because we find it interesting? And if so, how does the brain define 'interesting'? How do neurons know which bits of information hold interest and which don't? On that the article is silent.

Next up is a section on *where* memories are stored.[3] It quickly becomes apparent that the brain isn't like a computer, with one physical space labelled 'memory'. Neurons all over the brain, both on its surface – the cortex – and inside it – the sub-cortex – are involved. But some areas seem particularly important. The hippocampus, for instance, a small curved region – hence its name, meaning seahorse in Greek – found in both halves of the brain; and the amygdala (Greek for almond – guess what shape it is), of which we also have two. Both areas are in the temporal lobes, the bits at the side of the brain. Damage to the left lobe, the article says, can impair ability to remember verbal material such as stories or word lists, while damage to the right tends to impair non-verbal recollection, like faces or locations of objects. Does this mean that trivia, verbal information that it is, gets stored in the left side of the brain? Another note is scribbled.

The prefrontal cortex gets mentioned. Located, as its name implies, at the front of the brain, this area helps you remember where you first learned information. Those suffering damage to the prefrontal cortex can sometimes remember facts correctly,

3. The 'neuroanatomical correlates' of declarative memory.

without knowing how they know them. Any trivialist will recognise this. It's particularly frustrating when the fact turns out to be incorrect. Sophia Loren wasn't addicted to peanuts after all – but can I remember where I first 'learned' that she was? Can I hell. Which is a pity, because I want to know who to blame.

TOPOT

The Grand Canyon is big enough to store every human being on earth. Not crammed in, either – we would all have a room measuring several feet in every direction.

Not, the article assures me, that my mistake was simply a mistake. No, it was 'confabulation'. This is what the brain does, without our knowledge, when it fails to recall factual information. It supplies false information instead. So when Gareth told me that Chas and Dave had appeared on a Dido track sampled by Eminem, when it was actually a Labi Siffre track sampled by Eminem, he wasn't misremembering; he was confabulating. Must tell him that the next time he's down the pub.

Several pages in and we've still only covered processing and storage[TOPOT] of memories.[4] Remembering them – 'retrieval' – is a whole new topic. It's known that we don't permanently store memories in the same area where we first form them. The permanent storage happens, it's thought, in the outer six layers of the brain.[5] Searching and retrieving these permanent memories is then handled by the inner part of the brain – the 'subcortical nuclei'. Exactly how it achieves this, though,

4. 'Encoding' and 'retention', to give them their proper names.
5. The 'neocortex'.

TOPOT

Steven Spielberg has an accountant called Bruce. Or at least he did during the filming of Jaws. *One of the three fake sharks used was named in the accountant's honour.*

is unclear. Which is a pity, because I would love to know why, when Tim says the policeman who attended Eddie Cochran's car crash was Dave Dee, I remember that one of the soldiers who guarded Rudolf Hess was Bernard Manning. How does the brain do that? What search engine is it using?

The second article[6] outlines different *types* of memory. 'Episodic' is tied to the time or place it occurred – a memory of seeing *E.T.* at the cinema when you were a child, for example.^TOPOT A 'semantic' memory, on the other hand, stands on its own – such as 'Paris is the capital of France.' This seems to imply that trivia is semantic. But that's the problem with these articles: *everything* is implication, rather than statement. Not that I'm expecting the articles to identify 'trivia' as a particular category of memory, as distinct from 'serious' information. The brain obviously won't file heavyweight military analysis of the Battle of Waterloo in one compartment and the fact that Napoleon's piles made him late for it in another. But nonetheless it feels like something is missing: the very basic, simple truth of how neurons and synapses create a memory. It's almost as if instead of sending me chapter one and two from the *Ladybird Book of Memory*, Professor Duzel has sent chapters two and three. It's that opening chapter I need, the one

6. 'Memory: Neuroimaging'.

containing all the really basic, key information. The material I've read has raised as many questions as it's answered.

Good job I've got Professor Duzel to sort them out.

Queen Square has always intrigued me. Among the inhabitants of this quiet little corner of the capital are Great Ormond Street Hospital, the publishers Faber and Faber, the church of St George the Martyr, a statue of one-time resident Sam the cat, and a restaurant called Cagney's, all of whose dishes are named after said actor and his movies.[7] Talk about throwing disparate items together.

Also added into the mix, I now find, is the Institute of Cognitive Neuroscience. It's not often you find yourself waiting in reception next to a young woman announcing that she's 'here for the experiment'. Were it not for Emrah's articles, this could sound alarming. As it is, I know she'll shortly be taken to a room and shown a list of, say, thirty household items and asked to recall as many of them as she can. A bit like *The Generation Game* but with clipboards.

Emrah, who was born in Turkey[TOPOT] and grew up in Germany, appears. He shows me to his office. Beyond the huge flatscreen computer on his desk the window offers a pleasant view of the Queen Square gardens, though not of Sam the cat. The furniture, including the round

> ### TOPOT
>
> *Istanbul is the only city in the world to straddle two continents.*

7. Surely the only restaurant in the world where you would order a Dirty Rat (hamburger topped with blue cheese).

table at which we sit, is light and modern. The whole wall behind me is lined with books.

I begin by thanking him for the articles, then admit that the fundamental basics are still confusing me. Or at least that's the intention. After 'intrigued by the way neurons and synapses work', however, I pause. It doesn't seem easy to admit that I'm being . . . well, a bit thick.

'The connections between neurons get strengthened and weakened according to demand,' says Emrah. 'And according to how groups of neurons are activated together. So if you get input from a certain bundle of neurons to another one and that is always synchronised in a certain way, then these connections get strengthened. And all that can be made permanent. This is what forms the basis of memory. The phrase that's always used is "cells that fire together wire together".'[8]

The articles made it clear that our memory isn't housed in a single part of the brain. Presumably it's not like computer memory, where X amount of data takes up Y bytes? We probably can't say how many neurons it takes to remember a certain amount of information?

'No, we can't. When we represent, let's say, a picture of Jennifer Aniston, there are neurons in certain brain areas that represent perceptual detail – what she looks like. And we know there are neurons in the hippocampus that just represent Jennifer Aniston as a concept – the fact that it's Jennifer Aniston. Information is represented at many different levels in the brain. It's not just a single site where we store Jennifer Aniston.'

8. It was first said by Donald O. Hebb. Hebb, a Canadian academic, is often described as the father of neuropsychology.

Another problem is that with a hundred billion of them inside your head, neurons aren't exactly easy to see. 'When we look at MRI activity we don't see activity at the individual neuronal level. We see activity somewhere in a particular region, but you can't count and say "That was five hundred neurons" or whatever.'

So what exactly happens when you remember a piece of trivia?

'When you first hear a fact,' replies Emrah, 'it's in your working [i.e. short-term] memory. You process it, think about it, make sense of it. Then other processes go on that transfer this information into long-term memory. For example, if you find it really interesting, or if it has what we call an "oddball effect", it's not the usual stuff you hear every day, it deviates from the normal information that you hear, or from your expectation. Certain things drive what gets memorised. This kind of information gets stored into long-term memory. There's a debate as to how that works. One idea is that the hippocampus stores this information for a short period of time, then it gets transferred into other areas. So that's why if you remove someone's hippocampus – because of epilepsy, for example – they can't store new information any more. But they can still tell you about the past.'

The 'interesting' question seems . . . er . . . interesting. How does the brain recognise this quality?

'Studies have shown that emotional words like "murder" get remembered more easily than neutral words like "tree" or "plumber". Even neutral words will be remembered more easily if there's an oddball effect. For instance if you present some words in capital letters and others in lower-case letters, the ones in capitals will be remembered much better.'

Yes, but why? How does the brain know emotional words are emotional in the first place? How does it recognise the oddball effect? This could certainly explain the memorability of trivia, much of which appeals because it's surprising, but how do we *know* it's surprising?

'Usually learning is most efficient when we can relate things to existing knowledge.[9] What we actually learn very much interacts with our knowledge in the sense that constantly, as we learn, we generate predictions. So I know I'm in a certain environment, and I know exactly what type of information I can expect. When I walk out of the door I know where I will go. I have certain expectancies, based on my knowledge, about what type of information I will encounter. The same is true when you read a book, or want to acquire new information – you have certain predictions, and you learn in a context of existing knowledge. Sometimes these things are violated, in the sense that for certain kinds of trivia you don't really make any predictions. These are basically violations.'

He's starting to lose me a bit here, but I try and stick with it.

'Now usually one would think that these are the types of encounters that we should not be able to memorise that well, because they don't fit so well into existing knowledge. But I think that what happens in the case of trivia is that we form new links, because they are not really violations of semantic knowledge, they are basically rewiring of things that were not previously linked together, and maybe we're interested. The

9. Scientists call this knowledge 'pre-existing schemata'.

outcome is you have a new link formed, which partly violates your predictions, and therefore is interesting, but at the same time fits into your pre-existing knowledge and doesn't drop out of memory.'

Now I see it. As with apophenia and Arthur Miller, it's the idea of trivia linking previously unlinked items. Emrah seems to be saying that the surprising nature of such a link is what makes it memorable – but that if there was no link at all, we wouldn't remember the new information, because it wouldn't fit in with our existing store of facts.

'Oddballs and prediction errors,' he says, 'if they are not really meaningful to us, they are not going to be learning signals. They are not going to be really consolidated. So probably trivia is a mixture of these different aspects. [Pieces of trivia] are interesting in the sense that they are kind of unpredictable, in the sense that they're some form of oddball. But in the other sense they basically form new links and extend existing knowledge.'

But trivia isn't equally interesting to everyone. Do different people's brains behave differently?

'People who are good at trivia are probably people who have sufficient interest to generate predictions regarding these things. But when I say "generating predictions", it's often not something very obvious to the person engaged in it.'

It's a subconscious thing?

'That's right.'

I'm reminded of Melissa's point about detail versus the big picture. If trivialists are the sort to be interested in detail in the first place, they'll probably progress beyond the Marcus Aurelius stage – 'Of each particular thing, ask, "What is it in itself?"' –

and generate predictions, albeit unknowingly, asking where each thing – say, Shane Warne always eating pizza – might lead. When these predictions are violated by a link being formed with Ringo Starr, who has never eaten pizza, the memory sets to work.

So it's the prediction error that makes something interesting. But that only begs a further mystery: how did our brain make the prediction from which the error diverged? I feel like Patrick's son on the train, constantly querying, never finding an answer good enough, always coming back with another question. As I'm trying to frame this one, though, Emrah moves on to another point.

'Also there seems to be an element of chance. There is some underlying fluctuation in brain activity. If at the moment you hear something your brain is in a certain state, that thing will be remembered better just by pure chance. It's known that pre-stimulus activity in the hippocampus, a brain wave known as theta, if that's stronger when you present people with a stim-ulus it will be remembered better. So simply normal fluctua-tions in brain activity might help explain why you remember one piece of trivia and not another. Maybe it was just that at the moment you heard one piece you were more receptive.'

By 'stimulus' Emrah means 'something to remember'?

'Yes. When you give people a list of twenty words, and tell them to recall them . . . well, they will never recall the entire list – that basically doesn't happen. They will recall perhaps up to seventy per cent if they are really good. There are some regularities: items from the beginning of the list are remem-bered a bit more, and items from the end of the list.[10] But the rest is chance: it's unpredictable, you cannot predict what the

10. Known as the 'primacy' and 'recency' effects.

subject will remember. And there is now evidence that it's actually the brain state at the moment of stimulus presentation which predicts whether the item will be remembered.'

If that's fluctuating within a list of only twenty words, these waves must be changing *all* the time?

'Yes, very rapidly. We are not quite sure what benefit our brain has of such states. One possibility is we cannot maintain a certain motivational state constantly. I mean that in a physiological sense, of having a certain level of neuro-modulators in the brain that sustain interest or motivation to explore things. In some sense, this is good. It's good that when we are engaging with something our motivational state fluctuates, and is not captured by it constantly. This allows us to disengage and look at other things. There may be such factors involved. But we don't really know. These are phenomena that have just been uncovered, within the last year.'

Another entirely unscientific metaphor occurs: trivialists don't disengage. They don't look at other things. They stay locked on to a subject for longer, hoovering up the details they love so much. That's where their trivia comes from.

I ask Emrah about confabulation, giving the example of Gareth and his Eminem mix-up.

'It's a case of "Use it or lose it,"' replies Emrah. 'If you don't use certain information for a long time you'll get certain aspects of it wrong. There's also a very strong link between the memory and imagination, or future planning. Your plans for the next few years involve some form of imagining – where you want to be, what you want to be doing. This usually activates the memory system. You draw on your past experience to create the future experience. This can also happen when you forget part of a piece of trivia. Your imagination fills in the gaps. It's possible this is what your friend did.'

It is bizarre what the memory can do. In Blackpool, for instance, Patrick, Melissa and I discussed James Bond. Patrick asked if Christopher Eccleston had played him.

'No,' Melissa and I replied, exchanging confused glances. 'He played Doctor Who.'

'Right. And did Daniel Craig ever play Doctor Who?'

'No, he's James Bond.' Perhaps Patrick should be taking more water with it, we thought.

'And was Daniel Craig in *Our Friends In The North*?'

'Yes.' Ah, we began to see . . . 'With Christopher Eccleston.'

Patrick clicked his fingers. 'Got it.'

Even in the short-term memory, though, it seems there are limits to our capabilities. The accepted figure is 'seven plus or minus two' – that is, between five and nine. 'If I tell you a random sequence of numbers,' says Emrah, 'you can probably remember up to the first nine, but that's where it will end.'

Does he mean single-digit numbers or bigger ones?

'That's the thing – you can clump them together to make your memory more effective. So if I say "One, five, six . . ." you can clump them together and remember one hundred and fifty-six, and store that as just one number. You should be able to remember seven lots of three numbers rather than seven individual numbers. The problem is that after a while, if I keep on saying "Three, five, nine, two, eight . . ." it takes you a while to clump them together, so you can't concentrate on the next numbers I'm saying.'

That must be good for remembering phone numbers?

'Yes, that's what some people use it for.'

TOPOT

Not realising how popular Sherlock Holmes would become, Sir Arthur Conan Doyle failed to note every detail, with the result that in later stories Dr Watson's war wound – sustained in Afghanistan – moves around his body. But at least Conan Doyle got the name right, something Charles Dickens didn't always manage between instalments.

What about capacity of the long-term memory? Am I right to suspect that with a hundred billion neurons and a hundred trillion synapses Sherlock Holmes had more room under the deerstalker[11] than he thought?[TOPOT] Could the memory ever fill up?

'That's a very good question,' says Emrah. 'Probably nobody has a clear answer. I guess the basic question is how much do we know at any given time? Is there a linear increase? Or is the amount of knowledge we can reproduce limited to a certain quantity? I think that's going to be very hard to test. It's not just how much our brain can learn, it's also the quality of representation. The amount of information that may be available in the brain may be unlimited, but the amount of information that's accessible could be limited.'

Research in the last decade has influenced our view of this.

11. A piece of headwear never actually mentioned by Arthur Conan Doyle. It derives from Sidney Paget's illustrations for the stories. He only got the job by mistake, the publishers having meant to write to his brother Walter.

Specifically the discovery that the brain experiences neuro-genesis: the production of new neurons. 'We know that there are new neurons until late adulthood. So theoretically one would hope that there's always some new potential for learning additional information. But it's unclear how that's embedded.'

At the word 'unclear' a distant bell sounds. A suspicion starts to form about my inability to grasp the basics of all this. One of the articles used the same word about retrieval of memories. What do we know about that?

Emrah thinks for a moment. 'The more overlap between your current situation and the situation in which you first learnt something, the better you'll remember it. That's why the police sometimes take a witness to the actual scene of the crime. It tends to help them improve their memory.'

Right, I think, but that doesn't tell me what's actually happening in the brain.

'Also if you take people, put them in a different room, change the surroundings, change the background music and so on, their memory is not so good. This is more or less common knowl-edge now – a lot of school and university study tips tell you to find out which room your exam will be in, and try to imagine yourself reciting the facts in that room. Practising with the context in your mind helps when you get to the exam.'

This all makes sense – but still doesn't actually tell me how you remember a piece of trivia. What I want is an account of what the neurons and synapses *do*. How are they extracting a memory from storage and delivering it to your consciousness? How do they store it in the first place? That's what I still can't grasp. My suspicion on that score, however, is getting ever stronger. I decide to confront it. 'Forgive me going back to basics,' I say. 'But could you just run me through exactly how neurons and synapses work?'

Emrah seems momentarily baffled. Then a smile breaks across his face. 'There's a very simple answer to that. We don't know.'

Suspicion confirmed.

'We know a lot about memory,' he says. 'We've understood bits and pieces. But we obviously haven't understood it all, because if we had we'd be Nobel Prize winners and science would be at an end. There's still a lot of ongoing neuroscience. The reason for that is that we haven't understood the brain yet. Basically, there are molecular processes going on in the neurons that have been shown to correlate with memory. But the leap from these molecular processes to "What does it actually mean for an abstract fact to be memorised?" is still a gap.'

So it's not just me. No one understands it. I've been doing precisely what Melissa said: looking for the answer in the details. But the answer isn't there.

'The fact that we don't totally understand memory hadn't occurred to me until now,' I say. 'We're so used to scientists explaining the things they do know, we forget there are plenty of things they don't.'

Emrah smiles. 'There are molecular mechanisms and they're extremely complicated. I'm not sure you'd be satisfied by an answer like that. What would you make of the fact that there's protein synthesis and so on? What would it give you?' His conclusion remains unspoken: the one thing it wouldn't give me is The Answer.

The memory, I'd assumed, was like the internal combustion engine: we knew the one central secret driving the whole thing.

In an engine it's the explosion of petrol vapour. Ever since someone discovered you could use that explosion to provide power, everything else about the engine's development, from Mr Rolls and Mr Royce to the pits at Imola, has been, in essence, tinkering. Building on a core, working outwards from it. But neuroscience isn't like that. We don't know the core. All the research is working towards a secret, not out from one.

It brings back my attempt to verify eight pieces of trivia. Disillusionment set in when things proved harder than expected. My faith in knowledge – in the Natural History Museum's pencils, in the concept of truth itself – was shaken. Now the edifice of this clever thing called neuroscience starts to look equally frail. When they said 'damage to the hippocampus means so-and-so', I looked behind the statement for a deeper truth. But there isn't one. Or at least not one we've yet discovered. Neuroscientists may know what goes wrong when the hippocampus gets damaged, but they don't know what it's going wrong *with*. That's the central secret of how memory works – and it's still a mystery.

Will it ever be solved? Essentially to ask how the memory works is to ask how the brain works, maybe even what consciousness is. Not a small question. Does Emrah think memory can be 'cracked'?

The way he laughs, then exhales like a plumber faced with a tricky boiler, is an answer in itself. 'The problem with the question is that there's not one kind of memory. There are so many different forms. There's memory at the very sensory level, perceptual memory, memory for skills, for knowledge, for events, olfactory memory[12] . . . There are going to be many

12. Memory for smells.

different mechanisms in the brain by which information is, in some form, retained over time, and we call it memory.'

It's not just that we don't know the answer. We don't even know the question. 'The problem at this time is that we don't even know the taxonomy of memory, we don't know how many scientifically separable memories there are. We don't know whether certain forms of memory are really different or not.' He smiles. 'Yes, we have a long way to go.'

I tell Emrah about feeling like Patrick's son on the train. Will his work ever reach an answer? Or does he think there will always be more questions?

'I hope it's the second.'

Because he likes questions?

'Yes. And I like this type of work, of course. But also I hope there will be stages where we can come to some type of conclusion that is meaningful, in the sense that we can help people. It doesn't mean that we will have achieved an end point.'

There's a pause. I get the sense Emrah feels he's let me down, or at least wants to say more about the link between memory and trivia. 'One thing about [what we find interesting] is perhaps the relationship to reward. My work at the moment is focused on the relationship between reward and why we learn things. There is a very close link in the brain between reward centres and memory centres. Certain types of reward, especially when things are novel, can enhance learning. One of the reasons trivia may be interesting for certain people is that it may be rewarding. It's a rewarding experience to tell it to friends and get positive feedback. It's a rewarding experience to tell it to friends and get invited for a beer, to have a laugh or whatever. If all your friends always said, "I'm not interested in that," you'd have negative feedback and you wouldn't do it.'

This certainly rings true. The joy you get from a 'bomb of delight' isn't just the joy it gives you now, it's the joy of looking forward to passing it on. I tell Emrah about Tim's phrase. And Jo saying we're 'hiding from real life'.

'You have a combination of novel information,' he replies, 'plus the anticipation of a rewarding experience when you tell it to your friends later. The two together maybe activate the hippocampus, which is a novelty detector, and dopamine, which is what you might call a "reward hormone". So the dopamine releases at the time when you hear the trivia, because you anticipate reward later, may lead to a consolidation of that information. But your girlfriend is not interested in trivia because she never gets positive feedback from her friends.' He smiles. 'Although she would from you, of course.'

We finish our chat. As I'm leaving Emrah's office, I notice a picture of his wife and baby daughter. He also has a son. He asks if I have children. I say no.

'That explains your interest in trivia,' he replies. 'You've got the time for it.'

As I walk through Queen Square, something puzzling starts to happen. I find myself actually *liking* the fact that Emrah couldn't give me the answer I wanted.

When I checked those eight pieces of trivia and they refused to provide clear answers, it felt frustrating, the frustration of a child unable to get the sweet jar open. But for some strange reason this is different. It feels exciting. Not the excitement of anticipation, either. This isn't the thrill a child gets from eyeing wrapped presents on Christmas Eve. The secret of memory will almost certainly remain undiscovered in my lifetime. Knowing I'll *never* know is what's exciting.

It doesn't make sense. But as I pass the few customers still lingering over lunch at Cagney's, I don't care. I just enjoy the pleasure of all those details refusing to give up the solution, refusing to yield to our clamour.

Assuming, that is, that they hold the solution at all.

It's delightful to learn that scientists whose working life is defined by such phrases as 'functional motor compensation in amyotrophic lateral sclerosis' can also call something 'the oddball effect'.[TOPOT] Indeed, if I've understood it correctly, the fact that I can remember the name 'oddball effect' is itself a result of the oddball effect: the short name is memorable because it stands out from the longer ones. It surprises me. As does the fact that I can remember the astonishing speed at which a greyhound accelerates. Or that an England rugby captain was once a choirboy on a Tina Turner record. Or that a cheap lager was invented for Britain's greatest Prime Minister . . .

There's a lesson here for my search:

The perfect fact must be surprising.

> **TOPOT**
>
> *'Thunderball' was the nickname given by American soldiers to the cloud resulting from a nuclear explosion.*

7

Famously trivial

It was Thursday, 14 July 2005. I was at home, trying to work. This was not easy. The England cricket selectors were due to announce the squad to face Australia in the following week's Test match at Lord's.

Speculation was rife, excitement high among media and fans alike. For the first time in years England were seen to have at least half a chance of regaining the sport's most prized trophy, the Ashes. Riding a tide of success which had left them unbeaten in a home series since 2001 (the Aussies, naturally), they had gelled into a settled side that performed well as a unit. Only one spot remained unallocated, that of number five in the order, a key batting position which would dictate just how many runs England could rack up against the old enemy.

The incumbent was Graham Thorpe, a wily old pro favoured by many for his cool head, his experience, his excellent record against the Australians. Knocking on the selectors' door, however, was Kevin Pietersen, a flashing young blade with the swagger of a young Muhammad Ali, the batting power of a young Ian Botham, and the ego of both combined. Some thought that his character, as opposed to raw talent, was insufficiently proven. Others cited his number of Test matches – zero – as a good thing; he lacked the mental scars Thorpe had accrued from Ashes defeat after Ashes defeat. It was a finely balanced decision. No one could predict which way the selectors would go.

My preference, as I ignored the paragraphs waiting to be written and refreshed the BBC cricket website for the three hundredth time that morning, was still unclear. I could see the merits of both batsmen. Youth and experience, football managers call it, the blend any successful side needs. But there was only one place up for grabs. England could choose youth, or they could choose experience. They couldn't choose both. I genuinely didn't know whether it should be Thorpe or Pietersen.

Except . . . One tiny consideration was pushing me towards Thorpe. Knowing it to be unworthy, I dismissed the thought. I tried telling myself that if Pietersen got what sports journalists insist on calling 'the nod', I would support him, rally to his cause, cheer as he strapped on his pads and strode down the pavilion steps towards a date with Glenn McGrath. But secretly the thought persisted. Every click of the mouse, every breathless wait, every gradually pixillating screen brought the same wish: *Please let it be Thorpe.*

Finally the announcement was made.

It was Pietersen.

And I swear at that moment a tiny part of me died.

Because for the first time ever, I was older than every single member of the England cricket team.

Trivia about heroes – be they sportsmen, film stars, musicians – and about the rich and famous in general, has always held a particular fascination for me. It seems to occupy a special place all of its own in the pantheon of trivia. By which I don't mean that the trivia itself is especially interesting. Very often it isn't; we're talking middle names here, addresses of record companies, dates of movie contracts. Rather it's what the trivia says about the person who knows it.

What has set my thoughts along these lines is Liz Anstee's revelation about knowing when she'd outlived John Lennon and Elvis Presley. Every trivialist I've ever known has displayed this trait. If not an awareness of which celebrity was how old when they died or achieved a certain feat, then at least an accumulation of facts, dates, anecdotes, minutiae of every sort. The celebrity in question doesn't have to be one of your out-and-out heroes (although the most in-depth trivia, the *real* pay dirt, usually is). It might just be a run-of-the-mill star, someone you're aware of without having any real affection for.

Frank Sinatra, for instance. I like his music – who doesn't? – but wouldn't call myself a fan. I own no Sinatra albums, don't even know any of their titles. Yet I know that when he took up acting a newspaper headline read 'Frankie Goes To Hollywood', hence the band's name. I know that he was so annoyed at being the rumoured inspiration for the gets-his-contract-with-a-horse's-head-in-someone's-bed character in Mario Puzo's *The Godfather* that he once verbally assaulted the author in a restaurant. And I know that the kid from Hoboken, New Jersey shouldn't have been called Francis Albert at all. His intended name was Anthony Dean, but the godfather (small g this time) at Sinatra's christening accidentally gave the priest his own name instead. The trivia grips me even though the music doesn't.

TOPOT

In the early days of their courtship, Paul McCartney and the woman who would one day remove his status as the only Beatle never to get divorced were sitting in a Notting Hill pub. No one bothered them, until a quiz in a different part of the pub reached the question 'What was John Lennon's middle name?' One quizzer went across, and asked McCartney if he knew. 'Of course I do,' came the reply, 'but I'm not telling you — it would be unfair on everyone else.'

Dates always figure heavily. I know, for example, that the blues guitarist Stevie Ray Vaughan was born on 3 October 1954, and died, in a helicopter crash, on 27 August 1990.[1] I know that the 2005 Ashes series started on Thursday 21 July and finished on Monday 12 September with Kevin 'Younger Than Me' Pietersen smashing 158 to secure England's victory. But again, it doesn't have to be an area of expertise. Winston Churchill, about whom I know no more than the average, was born on 30 November 1874 and died on 24 January 1965. Gary Lineker, about whom I know marginally less, was born on Churchill's birthday in 1960, and so has the middle name Winston. As did John Lennon, born on 9 October 1940, at the height of the Blitz. (Though he changed his name, upon marrying Yoko, to John Ono Lennon.)[TOPOT]

When it comes to Lennon trivia, though, that's not even the tip of the tip of the iceberg. He was, after all, in the biggest

1. Particularly galling as I had tickets to see him two weeks later.

band ever. And there are lots of people who know lots of trivia about the biggest band ever.

Midweek, early evening, a quiet riverside pub in the verdant corner of England that is Richmond. Tim (who's been working in a studio nearby) and I are here to meet up with Tim's friend, and fellow voiceover artist, Dave. There are several things I remember from my two or three previous encounters with Dave. The sly, even cocky grin that frequently crosses his rounded face, giving the air of a mischievous late-thirties cherub. The deft flick of the ash from his cigarette as he engages, never half-heartedly, with whichever topic is under discussion. The sense – much as I got from Melissa – that he's judging you, waiting to be impressed, not in an antagonistic way but simply because his judgements take time. But above all, I remember that Dave knows the name of the New York police officer whose interview led to the rumour that Mark Chapman said 'Mr Lennon' immediately before pulling the trigger even though he didn't.

Dave arrives, fresh – or, to be more accurate, exhausted – from a session recording the voiceover for a high street bank's corporate film. Judging from the script's length it was written by Tolstoy, so after two hours of negative amortisation and accelerated depreciation, he's even more happy than normal to talk Beatles trivia.

He starts with the observation that trivia is about 'belonging'. Meaning?

'People who are into trivia generally don't fit in. Socially, I mean. They want to belong.'

Including himself?

'Yeah. That's how it all started for me, when I was a kid. I wanted to be liked, to fit in. And to engage with my dad. He was a very quiet father, I felt there was little connection with him. He was a Geordie, he'd come from the north-east to work in racing [Dave grew up in Newmarket, where his father was a groom in the stable yards]. He was always silent. He'd just sit there, in silence. To try and get a response from him I found out about the things he was interested in: racing and rugby. So I'd know which horse had won which race, the rugby results from years gone by. But you had to get it right. He would always say, "Empty vessels make more noise." Every detail had to be right.'

What about the wider social picture?

'Oh, I was chronically shy. I couldn't even take a Rubik's cube back to the shop to be mended.[TOPOT] I wanted people to like me, to feel comfortable with me. So I found out about things. I'm the same now. If someone tells me they're into golf, I'll be able to say that Faldo's won more majors than any other European. It's insecurity. You just want to make a bond with someone. Feel that you fit in.'

Shades of Melissa again. The thought strikes me that perhaps Dave's distance, and indeed Melissa's, isn't distance at all, but rather a mask for insecurity.

> TOPOT
>
> *A Rubik's cube has more combinations than light travels inches in a century.*

I ask about the Beatles. Just why does Dave know so much about them?

He thinks for a moment.

'It's closeness again. Like I was trying to get close to my dad, I'm trying to get close to the Beatles. Knowing all the dates and facts and stories, it's wanting to know *them*, the four of them. The more arcane the better. Like,

> ### TOPOT
>
> *Paul McCartney's dad wanted him to change the refrain in 'She Loves You' to 'Yes, yes, yes'.*

the "Hey Jude" mistake – you know that one?'

I don't. I know the 'Good Day Sunshine' mistake, McCartney fluffing a piano phrase, which, as the Beatles recorded in primitive stereo, you can isolate by listening just to the right channel. But I don't know the 'Hey Jude' mistake.

'Paul started on his own,' says Dave. 'Ringo was running to the drums, and as he sat down he knocked the high hat, and it happened to be in time. They left it in. Little things like that are exciting because it shows that even though they were great, they were ordinary too. They weren't from outer space. We like the trivia because we want to understand them, to know they were human. You know them through the trivia. If you want to get to the soul of a great artist you need to know this stuff.'TOPOT

Is it, perhaps, even more than understanding them? Is it wanting to *be* them? Bob Willis, a cricketer from the good old days when scorecards included initials,[2] was known to every schoolboy (even those in their sixties) as R.G.D. Willis. The D wasn't there from birth, though; it stands for Dylan, in tribute

2. J.W.H.T. Douglas being the only England captain ever to have four.

to Willis's idol, coincidentally also called Bob.[3] And there's a Status Quo fan who changed his name, also by deed poll, to Status Quo. This has always scared me. Not content with admiring an artist or a band, you actually want to take their *name*. Is Dave's Beatles trivia a similar attempt?

'No,' he says. 'I know what you mean, but for me that's not what it's about. I don't want to be them, I want to know how they *felt*. If I learn a Beatles lick on the guitar, it's like knowing how Paul felt when he wrote it. It's "Walk A Mile In My Shoes".'

Tim gets the reference: an Elvis song about trying to understand someone else's point of view, experience things as they do. 'If we could find a way to get inside each other's minds . . .'

'I went to Bridego Bridge once,' he says. Neither Dave nor I need telling what that was the venue for: the Great Train Robbery. 'I just stood there, putting myself in their position, thinking, God, imagine what it must have been like that night, waiting for the train, wondering if it was all going to work.'

I think of the trivia I know about that event: the name of the farm where the gang hid out (Leatherslade), how they played Monopoly with the stolen money, the fact that the robbery took place on 8 August 1963, Ronnie Biggs's thirty-fourth birthday. Are all these details a way of doing what Tim did literally – putting myself in their position? Knowing how they felt?

'The trivia adds to the songs,' says Dave. 'You might listen

3. Another fan was Mark Feld, who changed his 'k' to a 'c', then made a surname from the the first two letters of Bob and the last three of Dylan. Not to be confused with Mark Felt, who was Bob Woodward's 'Deep Throat' source in the Watergate investigation.

to "Let It Be" and "The Long and Winding Road" and think, yeah, they're both great. Then you find out that McCartney wrote them on the same *day* . . . It makes you see them in a new light. You think about that when you listen to them, it helps you feel closer to them.'

Dates again. Do they play a big part in Dave's trivia?

'Oh yeah. That "Hey Jude" mistake, for instance – 29 July 1968. Exactly one year before I was born.[4] And my mum's eighteenth birthday – 11 February 1963 – was the day the Beatles recorded their first album in twelve hours.'

George Harrison's twenty-first birthday, I respond: it was 25 February 1964, the day Muhammad Ali won his first world title.[5] Dave didn't know about Ali, but he did, of course, know Harrison's birthday. Does he know who shares his own birthday?

He laughs. 'Daley Thompson. And Andi Peters.'

'Not as bad as me,' I reply. 'I've got ex-BBC political editor Robin Oakley, and assassinated Indian politician Rajiv Gandhi. Oh, and David Walliams – same year in his case – and Robert Plant. I suppose they're moderately cool.'

'You think that's bad,' says Tim. 'I've got no one.'

'You must have,' Dave and I chorus. 'Everyone knows at least someone who shares their birthday.'

Tim shakes his head.

4. And exactly 13 years before Charles and Di got married. I had the commemorative mug for ages.
5. The famous pictures of the Beatles in the ring with Ali in the run-up to the fight might never have happened. Cassius Clay, as he was then still called, was the underdog. John Lennon was angry with Brian Epstein for not getting them a photoshoot with the champion Sonny Liston.

'When is it?' we ask.

'June the twenty-seventh.'

I smile. 'Forget birthdays. You've got something better than a birthday.'

Tim gives a quizzical look.

'On your sixth birthday,' I tell him, 'the UK's first cashpoint was opened . . . by *Reg Varney*.'

There's a respectful silence. Then: 'You're right. That is way better.'[6]

Dave's mention of his mother has intrigued me. As well as knowing that I'm exactly the same age as David Walliams, I know that my mother is exactly the same age as Cher, my father exactly one week younger than Eric Clapton, and my brother exactly one day older than Robbie Williams. This sort of trivia has always intrigued me. It invites comparisons. Comparisons of wealth, of happiness – as much as he scores on the former, Robbie Williams seems far less contented than my brother – but above all comparisons of achievement. The Walliams discovery was a relatively recent one, but for many years now I've known that Roy Keane is ten days older than me. Each Premiership trophy, each FA Cup winner's medal, each towering midfield display left a niggling sense of 'That's not fair.' The fact he played for Manchester United provided a cloak for my envy. Everyone hates United.

And deep down the childish sums would always be computed. If I worked really, *really* hard, could I change career, become

6. Later research shows Tim sharing his birthday with Tommy Cannon, Meera Syal, Michael Ball and Tobey Maguire, as well as the dastardly Kevin Pietersen (born 1980).

astonishingly good and play in the Premiership within ten days? As absurd as you know them to be, thoughts like that never really go away. They're what the Pietersen thing was all about. When you're eight, dreaming of playing cricket for England, you tell yourself the only thing stopping you playing cricket for England is the fact that you're eight. Then you get older, and it becomes clear you're not even good enough to play for your school, but still, you tell yourself, there's time. You read interviews with Test players who were 'late developers', 'took time to find their feet', 'didn't start playing the game until their teens' . . .

Then comes the day – sometime in your early twenties – when someone younger than you is picked for England. You can't now fall back on age as an argument. And you realise you're trapped on the grim conveyor belt known as maturity. Growing up isn't a process of bravely accepting responsibility, swapping youthful rebellion for middle-aged restraint, achieving a sense of worth. It's not about achieving anything – in fact the very opposite. It's about accepting, however reluctantly, that you will never walk down the steps at Lord's to bat for England. The message is hammered home that bit more conclusively every time one of the older players is dropped. The younger and younger models that replace them bring the team's average age further and further below your own. Until the final indignity strikes: Kevin Pietersen replaces Graham Thorpe, and you're older than the lot of them. *And so we beat on, boats against the current, borne back ceaselessly by England cricketers who weren't even born when we started secondary school* . . .

It's not just sportsmen. We realise that Tim, being slightly senior to Dave and me, is already older, in the Craig Dynasty, than James Bond. If David Cameron wins the next election, Tim will be older than the Prime Minister.^{TOPOT} Faced with this stark truth, he retreats to the bar.

I ask Dave if he does the 'comparisons' thing.

'All the time. A while back I noticed it was the anniversary of Andrew and Fergie's wedding. I remembered that day, watching it with my parents, twenty-one years ago, and I thought, How far have I come since then, what have I achieved . . . I do it with other people, too. If I see an Elvis thing from '74, I'll think, Right, he's got about nine hundred days to live . . .'

He reaches for a cigarette, a smile playing across his lips.

'What's so funny?'

'When Tim was forty-two, I worked out exactly, to the day, when he'd got to the age Elvis was at his death. I rang him up, said, "You're about to fall off the toilet," and put the phone down.' Tim, needless to say, got the reference instantly.

What about sports stars and their achievements?

Dave winces. 'Remember Michael Owen at the '98 World Cup? He blew it for all of us.' That goal against Argentina. Aged 18. It just isn't fair.

'Have you ever heard Harry Carpenter's radio commentary on the Rumble in the Jungle?'

Dave hasn't.

'When it's obvious that

> **TOPOT**
>
> *After the 1997 general election, the average age of the British Cabinet was for the first time ever lower than the average age of the Rolling Stones.*

Foreman isn't going to get up,^{TOPOT} and Ali's won, Carpenter goes into shock. "Oh my God," he says, "he's won the title back at thirty-*two*!"[7] I remember turning thirty-two and thinking about that. And about Captain Oates. The day he walked out of the tent

> ## TOPOT
>
> *George Foreman's sons, of whom there are at least four, possibly five, are all called George.*

and said he "may be some time" was his thirty-second birthday.' Thirty-two, I remember later, is also the upper age limit for SAS applicants. Somewhat academic in my case. But in a way that's the point.

Dave does some mental arithmetic. 'I'm now slightly older than McCartney was when Lennon was shot.' He sighs. 'Do you know what he was working on in the studio that day? The Frog Chorus. He shelved it for a couple of years.' Understandable. At least Macca can comfort himself with the thought that since Heather the song is no longer his biggest mistake.

Tim returns with our drinks. 'My Abbey National hedgehogs have just been on,' he says. You get this sort of thing when you're drinking with voiceover artists.

We fill him in on our conversation, the theme of achievement. Is trivia an achievement-substitute? I wonder? Even if

7. The age question was also raised by legendary darts commentator Sid Waddell: 'When Alexander of Macedonia was thirty-three he cried salt tears because there were no more worlds to conquer. Eric Bristow is only twenty-seven.'

knowing everything about a hero isn't a quest to *be* them, maybe it's a quest to match, or at least share in, their greatness?

'I don't think so,' says Tim. 'I really don't go in for the arcane Elvis stuff. I'm not interested in which take of "It's Now Or Never" they used, but I get a real buzz from knowing that Elvis's pilot was called Milo High. The trivia's got to have humour.'[8]

Dave agrees. 'It has to be something that captures the imagination. Like George being the only Beatle to go to America without being famous. His sister Louise lived in Chicago. He went to visit her in '63. He kept going into shops asking for Beatles records. No one had any. Six months later he went back and got mobbed.'

The 'human story' element is certainly important. While I don't know as much about Elvis as Tim does, or about the Beatles as Dave does, I still appreciate the drama of the stories. The first singer to achieve that level of fame, then the first band. Who wouldn't be fascinated by the lives as well as the music? Elvis's reputation yo-yoing along with his weight, the four friends from Liverpool descending into hate-fuelled rivalry . . .[9]

And yet sometimes, like the W in George W. Bush, it's amazing what *isn't* known. 'I only found out the other week about Elvis being a twin.'

8. Like the 'impersonator' statistic. In 1977, when Presley died, there were 170 Elvis impersonators in the world. By the turn of the millennium that had grown to 85,000. At that rate of growth, by 2019 one third of the world's population will be Elvis impersonators.
9. Which is why their late-sixties autographs, all on the same sheet, are worth so much more than those from the early days. By that stage it was rare for them to be in a room together.

Tim nods. 'Jesse. He was a few minutes older than Elvis. Stillborn. They buried him in an unmarked grave.'

'That's such an important detail in someone's life,' I say. 'You'd think it'd be one of the most well-known facts about him. People know his middle name was Aaron, he never visited England, his house was called Graceland . . . and yet how many people know he had a twin?'

There's a pause. Dave takes a sip of his lager. Then he says, 'You know, it's funny, talking about children . . . When you mentioned that Big Ben thing earlier [the radio experiment] my response was "I want to tell my children that."'

'I feel the same,' I reply.

'Me too,' says Tim.

It's a pity, therefore, that none of us have children yet. One of the things that attracts me most to the idea of parenthood is the ability to pass on knowledge, share its capacity to delight. I think of Marcus's daughter, her eye for the 'silly fact'.

Tim points towards the river. 'There are some buildings down there designed by an architect called Quinlan Terry. One of them has four scallop-shaped things at the top, a little tribute to Prince Charles's ears, because he's a fan of Terry. I told my seven-year-old niece about that.' He shakes his head. 'She couldn't have been less interested.'

Later, as the District Line takes me clatteringly back to the city, I ponder the achievement question. With respect to Tim, it still feels like there's something there. Vim Fuego, Adrian Edmondson's character in the Comic Strip rockumentary *Bad News*, said, 'I could play "Stairway to Heaven" when I was twelve. Jimmy Page didn't write it until he was twenty-two. I think that says quite a lot.'

If it's correct that humour is exaggerated truth, many trivialists – certainly those who had guitars when they were young – might recognise themselves in this even as they laugh at it. And while Tim and Dave are perfectly well-adjusted, easy-going, successful men, I still can't rid myself of the feeling that hero trivia has some link to achievement. Not in any literal sense, of competing to see who knows most. When Tim gleans new information from a fellow Elvishead he doesn't resent them for knowing more. He relishes the trivia, probably swaps it for some of his own. No, the relationship is more complicated than that.

Several years ago, researching a newspaper piece about obsessive fans, I interviewed Mark Knopfler, whose song 'Rudiger' was based on a real-life autograph hunter. 'This guy would get anyone's autograph,' he said. 'He didn't care, as long as they were famous. I said, "You'd want Saddam Hussein's autograph, wouldn't you?" and he said, "Yeah, of course."[TOPOT] I think maybe it's wanting to collect people's talent. If you get their autograph, you could say you're getting a small bit of their talent. So if you collect thousands of autographs, it's almost

---

TOPOT

During a meeting in which Clare Short was holding forth, Alastair Campbell passed Tony Blair a note: 'Saddam had one of his ministers taken out and shot once – shall I get a gun.' Blair replied, 'Yes.'

like having a talent of your own.' Could the same be true of trivia? More than wanting to be close to a hero and know how they felt, could there also be a subconsious longing to share in their achievements? If you know every date and fact and quote and story about the Beatles, do you become part of them? Is it 'I'm with the band'?

If so, then for someone as talented in his own field as Dave it remains subconscious. Yet for those whose outsider status persists, who never (in Dave's word) 'belong', things can go awry. Just as trivia can be a way of indulging your love of a star, it could also be seen as fulfilling precisely the opposite function. Knowing that Paul McCartney used 'Scrambled Eggs' as the working title for 'Yesterday'[10] is doubtless a delight for most Macca fans, a secret insight that helps them feel closer to the most recorded song ever. But you might also say it's a way of belittling the song, of mocking it. Saying 'Look how much trivia there is about this man McCartney, look at all these useless, stupid facts' allows you to demean him. 'If there's all this trivia,' goes the charge, 'he must be trivial.'

Maybe this thought occurs because we've been talking about the Beatles. Mark Chapman was once a fan of the band, and especially of Lennon. Very few people ever take the route he did, thank God, but nonetheless the theme of unrequited love – as a fan's love must always be – turning to hate is a common one. In fact love and hate are often said to be the same thing, the opposite of love being not hate but indifference. Both the four-letter emotions depend on intensity of feeling. And intensity is what fuels trivialists. For almost all of us it stays healthy,

10. The second line being 'Oh my baby how I love your legs'.

but that intensity is there. And for it to stay there, for the engine to keep turning, the intensity itself needs fuel.

Is achievement – or ambition to achieve – what provides that fuel?[11]

The date thing won't leave me be. An early episode of *QI* comes to mind, in which John Sessions displayed his staggering knowledge of the birth and death dates of various historical figures. Sessions, said the presenter Stephen Fry, knew virtually everyone's dates, and invited the other panellists to test him. They did, and Fry was proved right. Sessions, while unable to resist showing off his knowledge, at the same time seemed ashamed of it. With every mumbled '1682 to 1751' came an apology.

The memory of his memory intrigues me. An email gets dispatched to Sessions's agent: might he be willing to talk to me?

That Sunday evening, I venture to the pub for one of my occasional dalliances with its weekly quiz. Gareth is in, and we form a team with Richard (speciality: the flags of almost every country in the world), Gary (speciality: those flags missed by Richard), and Tony (speciality . . . well, we'll get to that).

11. Later that evening, Tim sends a text: Anna, in a break from her usual antipathy to trivia, has revealed that a policeman is not allowed to arrest you unless he's wearing his helmet. Researching it, I find reports that a pregnant woman is legally entitled to relieve herself into a policeman's helmet. Sadly both rumours prove untrue, though Tim and I long for the first to be correct and the second incorrect. That way a policeman could arrest you for relieving yourself into his helmet, but only by putting it back on.

The quiz is being run this week by Michael, who normally works behind the bar. Barely 20, he's a star of the village cricket team, and annoyingly modest with it. Why can't talented people have the decency to be big-headed, so providing an excuse to dislike them? Michael's in the corner, making last-minute checks on his questions. The last time Gareth ran the quiz he asked, 'Who was the last British Prime Minister not to have had a wife?', thereby ignoring the convention that a trick question is the last refuge of a scoundrel.[12]

He asks how the book's going, which soon leads to us telling the others about the Eminem–Chas and Dave saga. Gareth provides the mistaken Dido version, I cap it with the Labi Siffre correction. (Later on this will provide ammunition to anyone disputing Gareth's suggested answers.) Mentioning the word 'trivia' to four grown men primed for a pub quiz is like putting a flame-thrower under an ammunition dump. Soon facts are pinging around like crazy. Richard reveals that Heather Graham's father used to be the head of the CIA, while according to Gary the first country to adopt the euro was East Timor, in tribute to their old colonial masters Portugal. Unfortunately both assertions turn out to be false. Mr Graham was a humble FBI agent (if such creatures exist), while East Timor, having toyed with the euro, opted for the US dollar. This level of accuracy may explain our eventual showing in the quiz.

Someone whose accuracy can't be faulted, however, is Tony. As we discuss sports trivia, he mentions that he knows the entire line-up of both teams from the 1954 World Cup Final. The rest

12. The answer being not, as several teams thought, Ted Heath, but Margaret Thatcher.

of us, who weren't even born then, knew Tony was a bit older than us, but when he recalls watching the match as a 15-year-old we realise he must be at least ten years older than we thought. His memory's wearing well, too. As the West Germans rattle by[13] we wait patiently, certain that sooner or later Tony will trip up. But as the Hungarians start to fall – Grosics, Buzanszky, Lantos, Bozsik – a tension falls over the table. Tony has to pause before summoning forth Lorant, and Toth gives him a bit of trouble too ('Was it him or Budai? No, that's it. Budai was dropped after the semi'), but then he's skiing divinely through Zakarias, Czibor and Kocsis, and when Hidegkuti disappears only one player remains. With a quietly triumphant 'Puskas' Tony raises his glass. Four others clink against it, and we cheer. Everyone else wonders why we're so pleased with ourselves before the quiz has even started.

Tony has the grace to look slightly embarrassed in his triumph, but he needn't fear any 'anorak' taunts from us. We recognise ourselves in what he's just done. Maybe not that match or even that sport – but all four of us have things we know, arcane and useless details lodged in the recesses of our brains. Remembering them has no purpose other than the comfort and reassurance of knowing that we *can* remember them.

We discuss how this stuff ends up in our minds in the first place. Gareth thinks it results from the capacity to concentrate at the exact moment the information is received. 'I always give my total concentration to something. If Sue [his wife, like him a teacher] asks me to read something to do with her work, within five seconds she'll say, "What do you think of that paragraph

13. Turek, Posipal, Kohlmeyer, Eckel, Mai, Liebrich, Walter (O.), Walter (F.), Schäfer, Rahn and Morlock.

there? Maybe if . . ." And I'll say, "Please, can I read it first, *then* we'll discuss it?"'

'Women can multi-task, you see,' says Richard.

'Of course,' replies Gareth, 'but is that necessarily a good thing?' Isn't "multi-tasking" just another word for "easily distracted"? You may be able to do eight things at once, but how much concentration are you giving to each one?'

The discussion is cut short by Michael starting the quiz, but Gareth has set me thinking. We're back to intensity again, the ability to lose yourself so completely in a subject that its details get burned into your memory without you even trying. Is this a male thing? It would certainly explain *Spinal Tap*. Put two or more men over the age of 30 in a room together, get one of them to say 'How much more black could this be?' and two hours later they'll have done not just the rest of that scene but the rest of the film. I can see why women shake their heads in bemusement at this. It's pretty childish, after all. They probably think we go out of our way to learn the lines, sitting there hitting rewind on the DVD as we practise ('these go up to eleven' . . . 'these go *up* to eleven' . . .), but we don't. It's simply that we love the film so much, and have watched it so many times, that the lines have just gone in there.

Andrea's mind map contained, on the 'male' side, the entry 'quick info (short attention span)'. Yet men's attention spans are actually very long. And, as Gareth points out, deep. For all its connotations of shallowness, trivia often comes from a real love of something, be it a film, a band, a hobby. It's a way of deepening that experience, of prolonging it. The Beatles haven't released any new albums since 1970, so Dave needs something

> **TOPOT**
>
> The Silence of the Lambs' *author Thomas Harris has never seen the film, lest Anthony Hopkins influence his image of Hannibal Lecter.*

to keep him going. When I watch *The French Connection* (or rather segments of it – a whole sitting is too much, even with a film you love), it adds to my enjoyment that I know the actor playing the villain, Fernando Rey, was chosen by mistake.[14] Or watching *The Silence of the Lambs*, that Anthony Hopkins modelled Hannibal Lecter's voice on that of HAL the computer in *2001: A Space Odyssey.*[TOPOT] The trivia section of the Internet Movie Database website is now a regular port of call. 'Making of' documentaries, added as DVD extras, open up a whole new world. Films about films – trivia's going meta.

The quiz continues, but I can't help thinking about this, and being worried by it. As J.D. Salinger has Holden Caulfield say in *The Catcher in the Rye*, 'You take somebody that cries their goddam eyes out over phoney stuff in the cinema and nine times out of ten they're mean bastards at heart.'[15] Is it healthy to have

14. An assistant misunderstood director William Friedkin's description of the man he wanted. It was only when Rey arrived in New York that the mistake was realised, by which time it was too late to back out.

15. A writer friend once mistakenly attributed this sentiment, in a national newspaper, to Graham Greene. Even worse, when quoting it several years later on *Woman's Hour*, I somehow convinced myself Matthew had written 'Joseph Goebbels'. The double confabulation only came to light while checking this book. Between us, we misled millions of people.

a relationship with a film? Shouldn't this sort of intensity be reserved for relationships with people? Do men engage in the first because they're scared of the second?

The high point of the quiz is Michael's question 'How many of Snow White's seven dwarves had beards?' Improvising a supplementary, he offers an extra point if we can name the one who didn't. As it dawns on him what he's done, the poor lad's face turns the colour of a brand new cricket ball.

Shamefully, I find myself making a note to remember this the next time he hits a perfect drive through extra cover.[16]

A few days later an email from John Sessions's agent arrives. John would be happy to talk, though because of filming commitments it will have to be by phone.

The first thing Sessions does is apologise for how long it took to respond. This was all of ten days, which in celebtime equates to about a nanosecond. I mention the episode of *QI* on which he displayed his dates knowledge. There's a groan of embarrassment. 'The guy in the *Independent on Sunday* said he wanted to murder me. I can understand that. I thought I came across as Violet Elizabeth Bott.[17] It's an illness.'

At the risk of mocking the afflicted, I ask if I can test him on a few dates. His reply of 'Sure' contains the same mix of shame and eagerness he displayed on the programme.

16. The beardless dwarf was Dopey.
17. For years I felt foolish about my long-held assumption that Richmal Crompton, the annoying schoolgirl's creator, was a man. Discovering that my editor, Nigel – he of the Tichbornes – made the same mistake has been a great relief.

'Churchill.'

'November thirtieth 1874, January twenty-fourth 1965.'

'Hitler.'

'April twentieth 1889, April thirtieth 1945.'

This would feel like being a spectator at a Victorian freak show, were it not for the fact that I knew those dates as well. Half-exhibit, half-spectator.

'JFK.'

'Don't know the birthday, died November twenty-second 1963.'

'Mozart.' I know he died at 35, but not the years. If Sessions knows this, I lose my 'exhibit' status.

'1791 to . . . no, hang on, he *died* 1791. December the fifth. Born . . . yeah, born 1756.'

'Martin Luther.'

'1483, 1546.'

'Descartes.'

'Er . . . was it 1599? This is where my claim falls to the ground. Died 1650, I think. Yeah, I'm pretty certain about that. *Think* he was born 1599.'

'1596, I'm afraid.'

'Argh . . . Well, there you go.' He sounds disappointed, but also relieved.

'Florence Nightingale.'

He's straight back: '1820, 1910.'

Deciding to end the test on a high note, I ask Sessions how he knows all these dates

'When I was a small boy we had this magazine called *Look and Learn*. It appealed to the nerdy person, but it exposed me to pretty much everything I've been interested in ever since. Great paintings, great musicians . . . You remembered things because you wanted to remember them. It's too grand and highfalutin and in bad taste to say it verges on Asperger's – I know people who have children with Asperger's – but there's definitely that element to it.'

I guess he must read a lot of biographies?

'I do. But I think most of what I know I knew at twelve. A vast number of these dates went in then. Although I have picked up others since. I look at someone's dates and for some mad reason I want to remember them. What I'd *love* to remember are very complex theories by great philosophers. I've tried to. I've read Spinoza and tried to hang on to what he believes and it just slithers right out of my head. I'm a bit of a numbskull when it comes to a grasp or understanding of abstract intellectual thoughts. I'm a [he puts on a nasal "accountant" voice] facts and figures man. I should have been shot at the end of *The Thirty Nine Steps*. I would have found the submarine tricky, but if it had been the dates of all the German spies . . .'

I can't resist mentioning the thirty-nine-steps-at-the-old-Wembley fact.

'I'm so pig ignorant on football,' says Sessions. 'I know Manchester have red jerseys, but that's about it.TOPOT It's not an affected "I don't *do* football" – I have great and glorious friends

> TOPOT
>
> *In the 1997 Charity Shield, David Beckham's shirt read, 'BECKAM'.*

who are big football fans, and I envy them the passion. I want that feeling of it really mattering.'

But some football fans can be – to use his word – 'nerdy' about the game. A quality which never seems far away when trivia's being discussed.

'There was always that kid at school, wasn't there?' he says. 'At ours it was this lad who knew every kid's timetable, where they'd come in class . . . He was your absolute movie school swot. He had the glasses. He looked like John Lennon in *How I Won The War*, those round glasses . . . but without the grooviness of John Lennon.'

I mention my chat with Dave, how he would know exactly when Lennon made that film. And all the Beatle birthdays, of course . . .

'Shall I try them?' interrupts Sessions. 'You see, I have to do it . . .' He lists all four birthdays, and both death days.[18] 'Ringo's birthday is the same as Mahler's . . . Fuck, when it comes out of my *mouth* like this.'

In an attempt at reassurance, I say every trivialist I know is the same.

'Yes, but there are many other things I'd like to be able to do. Like when you're trying to get a computer to work, or a fuse goes, all that stuff, I'm just . . . oh, I'm like a child. Pathetic. I can't even drive. I'd give every date I know for a driving licence.' He pauses. 'A driving licence and being able to drive. I think that's important.'

18. John 9 October 1940–8 December 1980 (unless you use British time, in which case it was 9 December), George 18 February 1943–29 November 2001, Paul 18 June 1942, Ringo 7 July 1940.

How many times has he taken the test?

'Three. I don't *want* to be able to drive, though, that's the trouble.'

As in deep down, subconsciously want? The logic of that is that he *does* want to know dates.

'I guess so.'

What does that say about him?

He thinks for a moment. 'Some sort of order? It's not as though I have any great facility with numbers. My mental maths is OK, but no more.' Does he remember phone numbers? 'I would say reasonably but not especially. It's that history thing, that thing of the past. I'm really into the past. Too much so, in my own life and in time. I daydream of being in previous times.' He laughs nervously. 'Particularly the end of the nineteenth century. Even with all the drains and everything. I wish I had a big moustache and a bicycle.' There's a pause. 'Anyway, we're supposed to be talking about trivia; you don't want to hear about me.'

But an obsession with dates and a love of the past seem closely linked, I say. In my experience trivialists are often nostalgists as well. I mention Dave reminiscing about a royal wedding. Alan Clark comes to mind, too. A self-confessed 'passage of time' addict – a trait inherited from his father – his diaries are littered with entries starting 'Today it is X years since I . . .' Does Sessions do this?

'Oh yes. Constantly.'

Too much?

'Yeah. It's a compulsive way of looking at things. "It's twenty-four years since I did whatever" or "I've been in this job for however many years it is" . . .'

It's self-reference, self-reflection. An obsession not just with *the* past but *my* past. If hands are going up to this charge, mine's there too.[19] Not for the first time on my search the question of narcissism has arisen. Does Sessions see a link?

'Because the purpose of doing it is to show off? It's not as though you're doing it to show off like being a great tennis player, or a great footballer. When you look at it like that it's no wonder the guy in the paper wanted to smack me.'

Not narcissism in the sense of showing off, I say – rather of having a relationship with yourself. Relishing trivia about your own past, or how your life compares with the lives of others. I tell Sessions that I once worked out, to the day, when I would become as old as my dad was at my birth.

'That's pretty impressive. I don't tend to do that, although I occasionally think, God when my dad was this age I thought he was so ancient. Like now. I've got my mid-fifties coming up, which I can't *bear*. [We're talking a couple of months before Sessions's fifty-fifth birthday.] I get panic attacks. I don't just feel young inside, I feel *childish*. But the mirror's throwing back this guy with grey hair. All these people I know who are teenagers or young adults, they're driving around, doing all this stuff. You think, bloody hell . . . Sorry, we're getting way off again.'

But again, I don't think we are. Though Sessions hasn't directly addressed my narcissism question, his concerns about

19. A favourite game is that of seeing where your lifespan reaches if you go backwards. Born in 1971, for instance, at the age of 26 I was back in the Second World War. Now, only twice my lifespan takes me into the nineteenth century. Five times my father's puts him back before the English Civil War. As a reminder of how closely we're linked to the past (how little real change there ever is?), it takes some beating.

ageing show how easily the topic of date obsession resolves into that of self. Doesn't everyone feel childish? I want to ask. A friend of my mother, also in her mid-fifties at the time, once confessed to feeling *more* childish as she grew older, on the grounds that she simply didn't care any more. This strikes me as the norm, and Sessions's worries as groundless. I resist prying, though, and stick instead to the wider question of achivement. Does he compare his own position to that of famous people at the same age?

'I did – and this is the name you should never mention, this is the one that makes psychiatrists reach for the pen – I did a show about Napoleon. BEEP! Red light, red light, red light! He died at fifty-two,[20] that's nearly three years younger than me. Not that I'm saying [adopts maniacal voice] "I wish I'd done what Napoleon had done, invaded all these countries." But yes . . . And the year after next I'll be the age Hitler was when he died.'

What about people whose accomplishments *didn't* centre on invading countries?

'Oh yes, absolutely. Dickens – the energy of that guy. And Mozart . . . And you think, they weren't doing it in a big comfy room; they were in garrets, they were cold, there was death, they were sick. Newton was half-blind – he took one of his eyes out in an experiment . . . I just don't have that kind of energy. I can throw myself into something, but also I have this terrible lassitude, just staring at four walls. It's terrible.'

He mentions Jools Holland, whose autobiography featured on the radio this morning. 'I was listening to him and I was saying

20. Another rare lapse in the Sessions database – Napoleon actually died at 51.

"Fucking *hell*, look at what he's *done*." The energy of the guy, and the achievement, and he's still so sweet and charming, and he works like a brigand. Oh, and Stephen, and Ken Branagh and everyone – and there's old Johnny, plodding along.'

There is real feeling in Sessions's voice. No self-pity – and, he emphasises, no envy, either ('They're all my buddies and they're doing great and I think it's brilliant') – but obviously a heartfelt dissatisfaction, far beyond what seems reasonable for a man who's achieved so much. I ask how often he's happy with his own work. He laughs ominously. His TV series *Stella Street*, for instance. It was widely seen as brilliant – does he think it's brilliant?

'It's a weird thing to say, but not enough.'

B.B. King's lyrics float into my head. Sessions strikes me as a man looking down too much.

We return to talking about dates. Are they a male way of relating to people?

'That seems to be borne out by the evidence,' says Sessions. 'It goes back to the guy at school who knew all the cricket averages. It's kind of a part of "bloke equipment".'

What about dates as a subsitute for *being* someone else?

'That's what impersonation's like. Impersonation is a lot to do with wanting to be somebody. Like wanting to be Al Pacino, or wanting to be Keith Richards...'TOPOT Sessions is noted for his impersonations of both. Knowing

> TOPOT
>
> *Bruce Willis prides himself on his impersonation of Al Pacino's performance in* Scarface.

that he made a film with Pacino, I can't resist asking if he did Al for Al. 'There was no way I was going to do that. He was always saying "John, do Laurence Olivier" or whoever, but I told the assistant director, do *not* get me to do Al for Al.'

'What about Keith for Keith? Yes, I did do that. That was probably the biggest meeting of all for me. Keith, in the dressing room at Wembley, just before they went on.' He groans with embarrassment. 'Oh, do you know the first thing I said to him? "What was it like working with Jean-Luc Goddard?" Keith looked at me for a moment, then he said, "French."' We mention Keith singing at the Queen's coronation. 'I think it's so brilliant he did that,' says Sessions. 'It's such a Keith thing to do. Rather than get a knighthood, sing at the coronation as a child, then become the Prince of Darkness.'

On the personal identification front, does Sessions know who shares his own birthday?

He sighs. 'Arthur Scargill. Not the same year. The hair's getting the same way, though. My best mate shares a birthday with Jack Nicholson.'

Undeniably cooler than Scargill. My computer happens to be logged on to Wikipedia. A quick search reveals that 11 January is indeed a cool-free zone. Mary J. Blige is as about as good as it gets. Sessions is exactly one year younger than the American golfer Ben Crenshaw, four years older than the English footballer Bryan Robson. Has he stumbled across www.deadoraliveinfo.com? I ask.

'You know, I think I have. I certainly do a lot of that stuff on the internet. "I wonder what were so-and-so's dates?" and looking them up.'

The site reveals that in 47 days' time Sessions will outlive Peter Sellers. Twenty-three will take him past Rudolf Nureyev. Seventeen days ago he overtook Roy Kinnear. At this point we get sidetracked into anecdotes. The one about Kinnear and a theatre director[21] leads to the one about the actress Coral Browne telling a screenwriter he 'couldn't write "fuck" on a dusty Venetian blind'.

'Oh, listen to us,' says Sessions. 'Never mind trivia, anecdotitis is a terrible disease.'

Perhaps. The symptoms are similar, though. Sufferers of one invariably seem to contract the other. As trivialists swap facts, so they swap stories. Talk of just how much money Alec Guinness made from his supposedly nominal percentage in *Star Wars*[22] will lead to the story of a young fan, who'd seen the movie literally hundreds of times, asking for an autograph. 'I will sign,' said Guinness, 'if you agree never to watch that film again.' Mention *Marathon Man* to any trivialist and they'll reply with Laurence Olivier's riposte to Dustin Hoffman who, in true method-actor style, stayed up all night to simulate his character's exhaustion: 'Dear boy, why don't you just act?'

And what is an anecdote but an excuse, for just a few seconds,

21. In a heavyweight play (Ibsen? Chekhov?), the director started rehearsals with 'Roy, I've spotted a new way into your character. No one's ever concentrated on his relationship with so-and-so before. I think what you could do is—' Kinnear interrupted: 'I'm going to do it short, fat and sweaty, all right?'
22. The most authoritative estimate being £12,000 a week for the rest of his life. Director George Lucas once asked how he was investing it. Guinness replied that he paid it into his Post Office savings account.

to be the person it concerns? As you deliver the punchline, you become its original author. Very often you'll do it in their voice – and, as Sessions says, impersonations are themselves born of wanting to be someone else. I can't help feeling that all this stuff goes a little bit deeper than just wanting to know how our heroes feel. At least part of us wants to *be* them. School-boys don't just know what they want to do when they grow up, they know who they want to *be*. When I was at school I wanted to be, among others, Ian Botham. To this day, it doesn't matter how many documentaries they make about the 1981 Headingley Test, I will watch them all. Every bit of trivia about the match gets relished every time: Botham scoring 149 not out, Richie Benaud saying that the ball went 'into the confectionery stall and out again', Botham greeting his new partner Graham Dilley with 'Right then, let's have a bit of fun.'

When you ask a schoolboy who he wants to be when he grows up, you're assuming that males *do* grow up. Even now, when I'm eleven years older than Botham was at the time he played that innings – and after I've realised he's not quite the flawless hero he seemed back then, in fact in some ways he's a bit of a bore – part of me wants to be him. The trouble is, you can't be Ian Botham.

Someone got there first.

Another thought about young achievers.

The afternoon of my thirtieth birthday was spent glued to the television, watching Mark Butcher score 173 not out to beat the Australians. Post-match interviews revealed that in three days' time he would turn 29. A twinge of envy ran through me.

Later, I listened to Jonathan Agnew discussing the innings on the radio.

'It must be such a great feeling,' he said. 'Mind you, he also has to know that however long he plays the game he's never going to achieve anything this good again.'

Thinking of that Olivier/Hoffman anecdote has reminded me about *Rain Man*. I was supposed to check if Liz was right about it ending with Hoffman on a bus, as *The Graduate* and *Midnight Cowboy* both do.

One trip to the video library later, Jo and I have a date with Charlie and Raymond Babbitt. The first sight of Tom Cruise brings the obligatory complaints, although we quickly agree this is about the only film he doesn't ruin: he's *meant* to be an arse. Equally the first sight of Dustin Hoffman warms the heart, and soon the famous scenes are showing up like long-lost friends: repeating the Abbott and Costello 'Who's on first?' routine, counting the toothpicks, knowing the waitress's phone number. Inevitably, with a laptop to hand, I start reciting from imdb.com's trivia section. The names Raymond has memorised the phone book up to, Marsha and William Gottsegen, were Hoffman's real-life in-laws . . . After three weeks' filming, Hoffman was so unsure of the performance that would win him an Oscar, he wanted to pull out . . . Several airlines edited Raymond's roll call of plane crash statistics from their in-flight versions, though not Qantas, who he (incorrectly) credits with never having crashed . . .

'Can we just watch it?' says Jo eventually.

'Sorry.'

This happens to be at the moment Raymond is constantly reciting a radio jingle, much to Charlie's annoyance.

'I know how he feels,' Jo says.

'Thanks.'

The film reaches its end. Charlie wants to look after Raymond, but agrees it's best his brother returns to the institution. As they gently touch foreheads, and Raymond spells out Charlie's name (his sign of intimacy), I start sniffling. It feels good, like crying at movies always does, but also, now, troubling. What was that Holden Caulfield said?

Jo squeezes my arm and calls me silly.

'You don't cry at films very much, do you?' I say.

'Suppose I don't. I cry when things go wrong.'

'Mmm.'

'I cry at real things, you cry at make-believe.'

After all that, Liz was wrong: Hoffman ends the film on a train, not a bus. Not that I'm really bothered. I'm too busy mulling over what Jo said about my interruptions annoying her. The thought has occurred of a similarity – a remote one, but there nonetheless – between a love of trivia and Raymond's autism. Of course this isn't to say that anyone who loves trivia is autistic; that would be absurd. But the film has reminded me about John Sessions's mention of Asperger's syndrome. A love of facts, an incredible memory for dates . . . Is there something here?

I do some digging on the internet. Things get intriguing

when I find the web page of the Autism Research Centre, whose director, Professor Simon Baron-Cohen,[23] is the country's leading authority on the condition. He views it in terms of what he calls the 'extreme male brain'. If the female brain is characterised by empathising, he says, and the male brain by systemising, the autistic brain is simply an exaggerated version of the male. A cautionary note is that 'female' brains can be possessed by men just as 'male' brains can be possessed by women, but each gender *tends* towards the appropriate type. This helps explain, says Baron-Cohen, why 80 per cent of people with autism are male.

Apparently a 'systemising' brain is typified by, among other things, a love of facts. Such a brain will stick with a particular topic until it has exhausted everything there is to know. Systemisers also like arranging the knowledge they gain into patterns . . . Curiosity takes over, and before I know it an email is on its way to Professor Baron-Cohen.

The next morning, regret sets in like a hangover. How could I have been so flippant? This guy spends his life engaged in serious, heavyweight research. The condition he's investigating has profound consequences for those who display it. In extreme cases it can destroy their ability to interact socially or form any kind of relationship. He's a very busy and very senior academic. And I've asked him if he'll talk to me for a book called *The Importance of Being Trivial*.

For a while I consider sending an email of apology, but decide against it. Least said and all that. Maybe the first one didn't even get through. Let's hope so.

23. If the surname seems familiar, yes, he is indeed Borat's cousin.

A couple of days later I get a reply:

dear mark,
your new book sounds very important. i think the ability
to retain 'trivia' is actually not trivial! i'd be happy to do
an interview.

As I look back on my last few conversations, it strikes me how
often the theme of childhood has occurred. John Sessions gaining
most of his knowledge by 12, and still feeling 'childish' at 54 . . .
Tony remembering every footballer from a match he watched at
15 . . . Vim Fuego playing *Stairway to Heaven* at 12 . . . School-
boys deciding who they want to be when they grow up.

And I realise that this theme was there at the very start of
my search, when Marcus told me about his daughter's eye for
the 'silly fact'. Only now, after all I've learned about how fundamental trivia is to us – that it results from our quest to understand the world, our tendency to perceive patterns, our love of
'Why?' – do I see how key the question of the next generation
is. If curiosity and wonderment and delight in knowledge sum
us up, then so do our children, because – in the most literal
sense possible – we are our children and our children are us.
The date trivia tendency is so redolent of achievement, a sense
of our own mortality; and trivia in general, I now see, can be
viewed as a desire to leave something behind, a statement of
who we once were and what we once knew. Dave's comment
about telling the Big Ben fact to his children makes even more
sense to me now than when he said it. Standing outside Parliament that day with my radio made me feel like a child again,

so great was the excitement of hearing the chimes reach the speaker before they reached me from the tower. How much more exciting, then, would it be to have a child of my own, one I could take to London, hand a radio to, say 'You're not going to believe this . . .'

Another conclusion has been reached:

The perfect fact must be one you can pass on to your children.

8

All the world's a system

S ometimes it's nice when a cliché comes true. Movies and television dramas always portray Cambridge as one big bicycle track, handlebars weaving and bells ringing as eager undergraduates pedal their way hither and thither.[TOPOT] Surely that can't still be the case? There's time to spare before my appointment with Professor Baron-Cohen, so I spend a pleasant half-hour wandering the city centre. It's like the Tour de France dressed by Gap.

As I pass the ancient colleges, the bookshops catering to their students, the university library (which, like its counterpart in Oxford, is entitled to a copy of every book published in Britain), I'm reminded of the small Midlands library from my childhood:

TOPOT

The Olde Mitre pub just off London's Hatton Garden is technically in Cambridgeshire. The Bishops of Ely used to have a residence near there, and Cambridgeshire council took responsibility for the land.

the place where all human knowledge is stored. Cambridge has a much better claim to that title than my old library. Still not a perfect claim, of course. Nowhere, not even the internet, has that. But the thought still excites: a mythical Home of All Knowledge.

The Autism Research Centre, part of the university's School of Clinical Medicine, is housed in a large Edwardian building. I find Professor Baron-Cohen's office on the first floor, and he welcomes me in. Despite being the boss he has a room as small and basic as everyone else's. There is a desk, some bookshelves, and two easy chairs either side of a low table. Simon himself is a tall, fresh-faced man with fair hair and glasses, and a voice so soft and relaxing that if he ever wanted a change of career he'd be a natural at hostage negotiation.

I explain the role that gender has played in my search so far, and why I'm interested in his notions of the 'male' and 'female' brains. The first thing to ascertain, it seems, is that I've understood the science correctly. The idea that men's brains are hard-wired for trivia, and women's aren't, might be a convenient one for my book, but life probably isn't that simple, is it?

Simon smiles. 'Not exactly.' To explain the systemising/ empathising theory he fetches a chart and places it on the table between us. It comprises two axes forming a big plus sign. 'The vertical axis denotes empathising. By that we mean the ability to identify another person's thoughts and feelings, and to have an appropriate emotional response to those thoughts and feelings. The horizontal axis is systemising: how interested you are in analysing, exploring or constructing systems. Like football league tables, or car engines.'

He has developed measures for both qualities. 'Some of them

were questionnaires, where people had to agree or disagree with statements like "I can easily tell if someone else wants to enter a conversation" or "If I were buying a stereo I would want to know about its precise technical features." We also gave them tests, for instance pictures of pairs of eyes with four adjectives around them, where people had to pick which adjective best described the person's expression.'

This gave each respondent an empathising score and a systemising score. High on the former (vertical axis) and low on the latter (horizontal) would put you in the top left corner of the chart. Vice versa, you're in the bottom right. 'What we found was that the largest group in each sex had a bias towards one rather than the other. Fifty-four per cent of men had a bias towards systemising [he indicates the lower right section of the chart], forty-four per cent of women had a bias towards empathising [the upper left]. The rest of each gender was split between those who had biases the other way – for instance women who systemised – and those who were equally strong on both.'

So while of course it isn't true to say that all men are systemisers and all women empathisers, the general trend is clear. Which might explain why most of the trivialists I've encountered have been men. Would Simon say it's fair to see a connection between trivia and the male brain?

'If you're interested in systems, one assumption is that unless you're good at retaining a lot of detail, you're never really going to understand the system.' He picks up his mobile phone. 'This is a system. Say you want to change a setting – the alarm clock, or the predictive texting facility – there's a whole sequence of buttons you need to press. To do that you need to remember a lot of what you could call trivia but I'd call detail. If you can remember it, it gives you an advantage in systemising. So it's not just retaining trivia for the sake of it. It's actually got a purpose, which is that it'll help you understand how things work.'

To which the obvious question is: 'That phone is useful. The fact there are no letters in "Hull City" that you can colour in is use*less*. Totally. Why would you remember that?'

'It's true,' says Simon, 'that that particular fact has no use. But equally there are lots of things you can do with this phone that may have no use. You can punch in whole sequences of numbers that won't do anything. But when you're trying to understand a system it helps if you don't start off with any prior assumptions about how the system works. That means you collect all the detail without any prejudice as to which will be important and which will be truly trivial – or let's just say "unimportant". So if you're walking along through life you don't know which of the things you spot will be important. A systemising brain starts off by trying to absorb and retain as much as it can about everything, and then starts looking for patterns.'

Our old chum the pattern. I tell Simon about interviewing Arthur Miller, how he said some brains look for patterns all the time.

Simon nods. 'Sometimes the patterns will be important. For instance, "This is the only company that hasn't made a loss in the last five years." You can use that information to decide which shares to buy.^{TOPOT} Or it might be which players to buy for your football team . . .'

But most of the time the patterns won't be important. The

TOPOT

In the 1880s Charles Bergpresser formed a company with two other New York journalists. No matter how they tried to incorporate his name into the firm's title, however, it just wouldn't fit. So only his partners' surnames became famous – Dow and Jones.

male brain doesn't know that, though – is that it? Such a brain takes in detail whether its owner tries to or not?

'Yes, that's the annoying thing: it all sticks. And when you get to the extreme – autism – a lot more detail sticks. That's down here . . .' He points to the very bottom right-hand corner of the chart. 'People who are very strong systemisers but have great difficulties in empathising. Most of them have autism. Another way of saying that is they've got an extreme of the male brain.'[1] He looks up. 'I don't know whether you saw the film *Rain Man*?'

We talk about all the things Raymond remembers, from phone numbers to plane crashes. 'They're extreme cases,' says Simon, 'of a systemising brain trying to understand the world.'

As we're on the film, I ask Simon what he thought of Hoffman's performance.

1. The extreme male brain theory was first hinted at by Hans Asperger, the Austrian doctor after whom the condition is named. Unfortunately the hint came in 1944, in German. Only with a 1991 translation did the English-speaking world take notice: 'The autistic personality is an extreme variant of male intelligence.' It was 1997 before anyone set out to test this theory. The anyone being Simon.

'It was good. Inevitably they took characteristics from lots of different types of autistic people, and combined them into one character. But it was good.' He mentions the fact that Hoffman returns to his institution because he feels safe there. 'But there are people with Asperger's syndrome who are "high-functioning" – they live independent lives, have jobs and maybe relationships, manage their own money and so on. As a group they are more likely to suffer from being aware that they're different. They're trying to make friends and hold on to relationships, but may get it wrong because of the empathy difficulties. They often say the wrong thing, putting their foot in it with a faux pas, so people may not want to stay in touch with them. They can get lonely and depressed. That's a part of autism where there are problems.'

Other people with autism are 'low-functioning'. Simon recalls one child he encountered. 'He's got limited language, and I don't know how much social awareness he's got. He may be less troubled by the fact that he's different. He likes bouncing on a trampoline for hours and hours, or watching the same video again and again. The repetition of certain activities is very predictable, very systematic. It may not bother him that he doesn't fit into social groups.'

It reminds me of Jeffrey Bernard's comment that thinking is the greatest cause of unhappiness. But now I feel guilty for so readily agreeing. It's all very well wishing your mental faculties away, spouting a smug theory about why you'd be better off without them – until you hear about a boy on a trampoline. *There but for the grace . . .* you think. *Ah*, says your logical side, *that's only because you have the mental faculties to see the alternative in the first place.* Being logical doesn't stop something feeling callous, though.

We return to the non-extreme section of the chart. I ask Simon about the comfort a systemising brain finds in facts and details. This seems to explain the pleasure my friends and I get from trivia. Would Simon agree?

'Yes. When you're looking for patterns, you're seeing if the facts you came across before come up again in exactly the same way. Someone told you about Hull City. If someone else tells you as well, then you've got it from two sources, so it's probably true. It's a way of checking. It may be that that's why it's reassuring. If you're into fact-checking, however trivial, it's a way of sampling reality. You know that it's really reality out there, not fiction.'

As Tim said, we only love this stuff because it's true.

I tell Simon about Toby and his Charlton Heston films. He didn't *try* to find the world-about-to-end pattern.

'That's because he has that sort of brain,' says Simon. 'There are other people who would watch those films and not notice the pattern. Part of what I think is so impressive is that a brain like that has evolved to be a pattern detector.'

Although Simon's initial research was psychological, he's now working at the neurological level: looking for actual, physical differences between systemising and empathising brains. 'For instance we've found that your ability to do the "eyes" test of reading emotions correlates with activity in the amygdala.[2] We've done the test while people are lying in the MRI scanner. In a normal person the amygdala lights up when they do that

2. The almond-shaped region mentioned in the article Emrah Duzel sent me.

test. People with autism don't show as much activity in the amygdala. And there are sex differences on average in both the function and the size of the amygdala.'

At this point Simon issues a timely reminder about these being generalisations, that neither are all men the same, nor all women. But overall, these are how the differences play out.

'Another thing is sheer size of brain. On average, the male brain is bigger than the female brain, and in autism the brain is even bigger than the male brain. Not that size relates directly to intelligence, but it might well have something to do with what you're interested in, what trivia you store.'

At that moment there's a knock on the door. One of Simon's PhD students, Bonnie, needs a form signing. As Simon does the necessary, this bright young American woman listens eagerly to a brief explanation about my book, then happily explains her current research, which concerns testosterone levels in amneotic fluid. Male babies produce twice as much testosterone in the womb as female babies, and Bonnie is testing whether higher levels can be linked to autistic traits in childhood.

'It's very exciting,' says Simon when Bonnie has left. 'No one else in the world is doing this work at the moment.'

It raises the nature/nurture question. How much of a brain's systemising tendency (be it extreme or otherwise) was there from the start, and how much is learned, or reinforced, through social interaction? Was I always going to have a brain that retained trivia, or did, for instance, playing Top Trumps at primary school *make* it so?

Simon's sure that cultural and social factors play their part, but equally they're not the whole story. Two of his former students tested newborn babies at a Cambridge maternity hospital. One student, Jennifer, smiled at the babies. Another student held a mechanical mobile over their cots. Made from a ball the same size as Jennifer's head, it showed her features rearranged so that they no longer formed a recognisable face. The babies' reactions to each object, one at a time, were videoed, then analysed. Girls looked for longer at the face (a social object), while boys looked more at the mobile (a mechanical object). 'This was on the first day of life,' says Simon. 'It strongly suggests that biology plays a role.'

And so helps influence whether you're a systemiser or an empathiser?

'Yes.' Simon returns to the chart. 'Incidentally, I call these dimensions "systemising" and "empathising", but other psychologists might call it "detail" versus "gist". People on the systemising axis would be good at detail, people on the empathising axis good at gist.[3] Or, in the technical jargon, "local versus global processing". These two accounts are not incompatible. When you empathise, the most important thing to do is look at the big picture. When Bonnie walked in she immediately realised that we were having a meeting, rather than what kind of watch you were wearing. But if she was very detail-oriented, she might have focused on irrelevant detail. In fact, Bonnie is very good at both axes. [Simon points to the top right-hand corner of the chart.] She's right up here, very good at both systems and empathy.'

'Irrelevant detail' is how a lot of people would define trivia. It's encouraging to know that a detail-loving brain is just that: a brain working independently of its owner. Arthur Miller raised that idea. Now Simon is adding a new element: that of gender.

3. If the devil is in the detail, could God be in the gist?

'The brain has evolved over millions of years,' he says. 'It doesn't have a preset idea of what's going to be important. The best design principle for a brain that's going to understand systems is "Collect as much information as you can and then sort it out afterwards into usable and useless." Arguably what's happening in people who are better at empathy is that they're starting out with assumptions, such as "When you walk into a situation, don't pick up all information, go for what's relevant, like this is a work meeting, so I should behave in this way."'

Simon's still holding his phone. It reminds me of his email confirming our meeting. It contained his mobile number, which ended '007'. I instantly thought of Jeffrey Archer. A previous owner of the novelist's famous London flat was John Barry, composer of the Bond theme, whose personalised phone number included '007'. Archer, ever the fan of the fantastic, has kept it to this day.^{TOPOT}

It seemed a bit nerdy to mention that before. But now, as we chat about systemising brains, it feels appropriate. Another example of pattern-spotting.

Simon nods. 'It's a case of where retaining trivia might be

TOPOT

The building housing Jeffery Archer's flat is next door to Tintagel House, where the Metropolitan Police team investigating the Kray twins were based. Scotland Yard's headquarters contained informants who may have tipped the Krays off.

---

useful in aiding your memory. Now you've got another way of remembering my number – it's got some of the same digits as Jeffrey Archer's.'

A quick Bond conversation soon takes us back to *Rain Man*. 'By the way,' says Simon, 'I meant to say: the film was based on a real person – whose name I annoyingly can't remember right now – who had total recall. He would read books, mainly on history, which was his big interest. He read both pages simultaneously, not the left then the right. And if you asked him in which of those thousands of books a particular sequence of words occurred, he could tell you not just the book but also the page number.'[4]

I mention Liz's memory of Hoffman ending the film on a bus, when it was actually a train.

'That's a case,' replies Simon, 'of someone distorting a memory because they've gone for gist over detail. If they were a good systemiser they wouldn't have made that mistake. An empathiser will go for the fuzzy some-kind-of-transport category, and lose the important detail.'

To be fair to Liz, it was a memory I shared. And it's nice to know we've both got *some* empathising qualities.

I like the irony of Simon being unable to remember the name of a man with total recall. What's his memory like generally? Is he much of a trivialist?

4. The trivia section of imdb.com takes over where Simon's memory leaves off. The man in question is Kim Peek. Hoffman met him while researching the role, and was so moved that he made Peek's father promise to 'share Kim with the world'. Peek now makes regular public appearances, displaying the Oscar given to him by the film's screenwriter. This is said to have aided his self-confidence.

'I'm jealous of people who can do it better than me. The fact that right now I'm stumped on that name ... I wish I could remember things like that. I don't see it as trivial in the sense of "useless"; I see it as a gift.' He points at the bottom right sector of the chart. 'The market for things like *Schott's Miscellany* and Trivial Pursuit show there must be a fair number of people down here.'

Is he a systemiser or an empathiser? Has he done his own questionnaires?

'I try not to take the tests myself. Because I designed them myself, my own particular test scores probably wouldn't mean much.'

What about other signs? Does he remember phone numbers?

'You know when you live with someone, and they're better at remembering phone numbers than you are, that you've got limitations.' That's the case with him? 'Yes. I look numbers up in my phone rather than from my memory.' He plays bass guitar in a blues band. 'There are nine of us. Some, the systemisers, remember every note we've played, that we played a C sharp there before, for example. That's a real skill, it helps you musically. You can approach music as an empathiser, though. "Does what I'm doing fit, does it contribute to the whole?" I am attracted to both: I like the detail but I also focus on the whole.'

I wonder if Simon wishes he was even more of a systemiser. He points out that anyone working in science 'must be quite detail-oriented', but also talks about the shortcomings of an empathising brain. 'You could say that people who don't have systemising brains are being blind to the world. They don't notice many details. You could see that as a limitation.'

In the same way, he sees those with extreme systemising

brains – those with autism – as an untapped resource. 'There are people who know lots of trivia but do nothing with it. At some point [most people] stop collecting information and reflect on it. They think, How could this be used? – be it science, or programming computers, or some other field. For instance a scientist might look at his or her data and see a pattern, which might lead to a breakthrough. But people with autism may not reach that point. I think there's a great waste of talent there. Many have a great capacity for absorbing data but may never stop collecting; they may never pause and do something with the information.'

He gives the example of collecting data on thousands of horse races, then using it to make a prediction. Like Charlie getting Raymond to count cards in a Las Vegas casino, I say.

'Yes, but recall that in the movie it's someone else who gets him to do it. Raymond might not have done it on his own. An extreme systemiser might say, "I'll wait for one more race." There's always more information out there. It can paralyse them, whereas if they put that talent to use they could achieve more.'

Simon's favourite example of a non-autistic systemiser harnessing their talent is Jim Simons, an American mathematics graduate who used his skill with numbers to establish an investment company. Now a multi-billionaire, he employs the best mathematicians and runs computer-based models to predict financial changes, basing his trading on the results.

'The remarkable thing,' says Simon, 'is that because he has a child with autism, he has set up the Simons Foundation to fund research into autism.'

'So someone here,' I say, tapping the chart's inner bottom

right sector, 'is using his talent to help people here [the extreme bottom right]?'

'Yes,' replies Simon. 'That's one of the nice twists about it.'

As I'm leaving, I notice a poster in the corridor outside Simon's office. Produced by the National Autistic Society, it achieves every poster's goal of being eye-catching in a superbly literal way: it shows an eye. A close-up of an iris and pupil is super-imposed with text:

When a person with autism walks into a room the first
thing they see is:

A pillow with a coffee stain shaped like Africa,
a train ticket sticking out of a magazine,
25 floorboards, a remote control,
a paperclip on a mantelpiece,
a marble under the chair,
a crack in the ceiling,
12 grapes in a bowl,
a piece of gum,
a book of stamps
sticking out from
behind a silver
picture
frame.

So it's not surprising they ignore you completely.

'People with autism,' continues the text underneath, 'see too much detail in everything, so they can't always tell what is important.'

It echoes Simon's comments about the *non*-autistic systemising brain: detail being another word for trivia, systemisers liking detail, empathisers preferring gist. And this in turn echoes what I've heard before, from Sandi about female intuition, from Melissa about men seeing the devil in the detail.

The thrust of Simon's theory is clear: if your brain works that way, your brain works that way. I can't help feeling his work gives a clue as to why trivialists – with their love not just of facts, but facts that are organised, patterned, arranged into systems – are usually male.

Jo said we were hiding from real life. But what if this *is* our real life?

That evening, Jo and I sit with sheets of A4 paper on our laps, quietly making crosses as I read out a list of statements.

Simon's book, *The Essential Difference: Men, Women, and the Extreme Male Brain*, has an appendix containing the systemising and empathising questionnaires given to his respondents, together with instructions on how to mark them. Jo and I have each drawn up columns headed 'strongly agree', 'slightly agree', 'slightly disagree' and 'strongly disagree'. We make the appropriate cross for each statement.

'"I like to be organised in day-to-day life,"' I read, '"and often make lists of the chores I have to do."' Jo makes a snorting sound, which I ignore.

Later: '"I find it difficult to read and understand maps."' I make a snorting sound which Jo ignores.

Later still: "'I am at my best first thing in the morning.'" We both make snorting sounds.

Marks are awarded for the various crosses, giving a quotient, or score, for each quality. Jo's Systemising Quotient is 14 (most women score about 24), mine 32 (most men are around 30). Her Empathy Quotient is 51, slightly above average for women, mine is 25, below average for men.

Neither Jo nor I are surprised at the results. My 'systemiser' status, she thinks, sheds light on some of my tendencies. The fact that I 'get twitchy' (her phrase) if she buys a new brand of coffee. That I get 'especially twitchy' if cutlery is placed handle-up rather than handle-down in the drying rack.[5] That I insist on following instruction leaflets to the letter.

For my part, though I keep this to myself, the results provide disturbing evidence for my trivia-as-narcissism worry. Disinclined to empathise, does a trivialist turn inwards? Dave spoke of us as people who struggle to fit in, to belong. Is this what it means to have a male brain? Should I be making more effort to let people in? To spend a bit more time relating to them, a bit less time crying at films?

But isn't the other side of this coin that our brains are the way they are? That we *can't* see things from another perspective, can't (sorry, Elvis) walk a mile in someone else's shoes? Can a male brain ever really understand a female brain?

Jo and I have this little argument which gets reprised from time to time. It's never very serious, but the fact it keeps

---

5. All right, this does sound a bit anal. Though I maintain it's only to aid identification. The times I've got a fork when I've been going for a spoon . . .

cropping up has always struck me as somehow significant. The 'somehow' was a mystery, until now. If Jo happens to start speaking while I'm concentrating on a TV or radio programme, I'll quickly say 'Shush.' She'll get annoyed at my rudeness. It's reminiscent of the Frank Skinner line: 'During the football results, when they say "West Bromwich Albion" a girlfriend will say "oh, West Brom, that's the team you support isn't it, Frank?" And then she stops, and the guy's saying "Charlton Athletic, one."' 'Shush' may appear rude, but 'Excuse me, darling, would you mind waiting one second while I listen to this important detail?' would itself obscure the detail you're trying to catch. Jo and I have tried discussing this, seeing it from the other's point of view. But every time the same thing happens.

It's not that I don't see where she's coming from. Even though my argument is logical, I know there's more to life than logic. Witnessing my father 'shushing' my mother in the same way, the rudeness of it hit me like a wet haddock. Yet knowing isn't the same as feeling — as empathising. Whenever the argument happens, true colours break out. I get irritated, Jo gets offended.

But she's right. I know she's right. While I'm wrestling with detail — analysing the length of phrases, searching for an alternative to 'Shush' that's less brusque but equally brief — Jo just knows the gist: it's rude. She sees the bigger picture, knows instinctively what the reality is. While women have intuition, men have intensity. It drives them onwards into a jungle of detail, a maze of trivia. They're searching for the answer, at the top of Everest, on the moon, inside an atom.

But as someone once said, the more you find out, the less you know.

There's this feeling I sometimes get: life is a book women have already read.

With Simon's help, I have reached another conclusion about the perfect fact. Trivia appeals to systemising brains. And so:

The perfect fact must relate to a system.

9

The perfect fact

Time for the search to enter its final straight. Somewhere along that straight I will have to find the search's goal: the perfect fact. As I round the final corner, it seems a good idea to run through the criteria:

- *The perfect fact must be true.*
- *The perfect fact must be charming.*
- *The perfect fact must link together two or more disparate items.*
- *The perfect fact must help you understand people.*
- *The perfect fact must be surprising.*
- *The perfect fact must be one you can pass on to your children.*
- *The perfect fact must relate to a system.*

Keeping these elements in mind, each and every fact I encounter has to be judged, assessed, prodded from all angles, tested to the limit. Failure on a single one of the criteria will render the fact worthless; only perfection is good enough here. But perfection, I sense, can't be judged *solely* by these criteria. They are necessary qualities, but they're not sufficient. Somehow the perfect fact will stand out from all others by dint of . . . well, by dint of standing out. I'm after the 'elephant' quality: hard to describe, but you know it when you see it.

How, though, to put myself in the way of these facts in the first place? We already know that trivia finds you, rather than the other way round. Look for it and, like the policeman when you need him, it will elude you. No, this calls for lateral thinking, an indirect approach, some way of looking without looking. I need to sidle up to the facts, pretend to be doing something else, then catch them unawares.

It's a tough one. But inspiration comes from the old martial arts dictum: use your opponent's strength against him. If trivia itself is tangential, why not be tangential with trivia? Instead of putting myself in the way of facts, I need to put myself in the way of people who put themselves in the way of facts. People who encounter them on a daily basis.

People, in other words, who have turned trivia into a business.

Eleven o'clock on a Thursday morning, and I'm heading for a one-bedroom flat in a brand new development 400 yards from St Albans' train station. The flat is home to a woman who can answer any question.

This modern-day equivalent of Mr Memory, the *Thirty-Nine Steps* character John Sessions mentioned, is Chantel Sankey. She is 27 days younger than me (the reason for knowing this will become clear), supports Spurs, and knows, among much, much else, that Whitney Houston's godmother is Aretha Franklin.

1. Checking the spelling, I find that St Ives has also dropped its apostrophe. But King's Lynn hasn't.

Chantel, you see, is one of the longest-serving employees of AQA.

Any Question Answered is a service that does exactly what its name implies: text a question – any question – to 63336, and, for the princely sum of one pound, they will text you back the answer. (Or at least *an* answer – the distinction is important.) Established in 2004, the business has enjoyed word-of-mouth (word-of-text?[2]) growth to the point where they now answer seventeen thousand questions a day. Not all of them are trivia. In fact the service wasn't designed with trivia in mind at all, the original idea being to act as a concierge for the man in the street, offering train times, restaurant recommendations and the like. Soon, however, trivialists got to hear of it. And things were never the same again.

'In the early days,' co-founder Paul Cockerton told me, 'we would spot spurts of questions, like "Which three footballers have scored for opposing teams in the FA Cup Final?"[3] The conclusion was obvious: pub quiz. 'I've seen messages saying "We won the pub quiz thanks to you." Mind you, I've also seen "We lost the pub quiz thanks to you."'

It's not just quizzers, though. 'We know there are people,' Paul said, 'who will go away from a conversation, text us, then go back and say, "You know, I've thought about it. I'm sure it was Hermann Hesse who wrote *Steppenwolf*, and that's why the band's called Steppenwolf." I was talking to someone the other day who'd used the service for a year and a half. All his friends thought he was the font of all knowledge. His nephews always

2. Wdvtxt?
3. Bert Turner (1946), Tommy Hutchison (1981), Gary Mabbutt (1987).

ask him things. They think he's the most amazing uncle. He knows things about popular culture they'd never expect him to.'

Don't they spot that his blinding insights always coincide with trips to the loo? 'Apparently not.'

The success of the venture has taught Paul how 'important trivia is in people's lives. It is predominantly a male thing. Women won't chance a pound so easily. They'll wait to hear from several people before asking a question they think is really worth it. Whereas men think, A pound is a third of a pint in London. A lot of it is power. Knowledge is power. People like to be seen as the person everyone has to come to to get the answer.'

What really excited me about AQA was that perhaps it could achieve what neither my childhood library nor Cambridge University managed: it could be the place where all knowledge was gathered together. I had images of a vast HQ, a repository of wisdom where eager young boffins consulted huge databases – OK, and probably Google too – answering queries from all over the world.[4] Even if it wasn't located where your fantasy might want – atop a Manhattan skyscraper, perhaps, or hidden inside a Swiss mountain – at least it would inhabit a really big open-plan office. Sort of like a call centre, but dispensing joy instead of misery. The truth, though, is that AQA isn't located in one single place at all. Its researchers, over 800 of them, work from home.

Researchers like Chantel. A cheery and engaging dark-haired woman, she meets me at the station. It takes only slightly longer

4. The service works from anywhere on earth that has mobile coverage, as long as you have a UK phone.

to reach her flat than it did to cross from the opposite platform. As she makes coffee, I can't help noticing the piles of books on the sitting-room floor.

'They're my library books,' she says.

'All of them?'

'Yeah. You're allowed twelve at once.'

'How long will that keep you going?'

'About a fortnight.'

'A *fortnight*?'

'I'm a quick reader. It's a habit I've always had.^{TOPOT} I was brought up in a little village near here, and we used to have a mobile library that came and parked opposite our house. When we got older we were allowed to borrow more books. It was a rite of passage.'

Chantel grew up to become a librarian herself. 'I wanted to do something that helped people, but where you didn't get too involved. If you do something like social work it's very emotion-ally draining, it drags you in. I couldn't deal with that. Librarianship seemed ideal. People come in and want information or books and you help them, but they go away at the end of the day.'

Engagement, but not on too deep a level: some would say that's what trivia's all about.

'I prefer old libraries,'

> ### TOPOT
>
> *Ex-US President Jimmy Carter, as well as being the most famous peanut farmer ever, was a speed-reader. The skill allowed him to devour incredible numbers of official documents.*

Chantel continues. 'I know we have to have new ones, but if you go into a library that's been there for years and years it's almost like a church where you can feel the history of all the people who've worshipped there. You get a sense of all the people who've used that library. You don't get that in modern libraries.'

The same is true of individual books, I reflect. Looking at the date stamps in a library book, I would always think of the other children who'd borrowed it, wonder whether they enjoyed it, what they'd taken from the story.

One particular pile of books, however, belongs not to the library but to Chantel herself. Perching obediently next to her computer, it includes *Guinness British Hit Singles and Albums*, *Schott's Miscellany*, *England Football Facts and Trivia*, *How To Walk In High Heels – The Girl's Guide To Everything* (advice including how to cure a hangover, how to use chopsticks, how to remove contact lenses, how to send an attachment . . .), *AA Members' Handbook*, a London Tube map, a map of Paris, *True Colours: Football Strips from 1980 to the Present Day*, *Whitaker's Almanac 2007* . . . Yes, these are Chantel's work books.

Her favourite websites number in the hundreds. They're divided into categories from 'business' to 'crosswords' to 'films and TV' to 'maps' to 'politics' to 'translations' . . . Each category is itself subdivided into squadrons of web pages waiting patiently for active service. Someone on a bus in Bradford wants to know the only footballers to have scored in every season of the Premiership? A plucky private from 'sport:football' steps forward to reveal that Gary Speed and Ryan Giggs are the only two still in the running, though Giggs has yet to score in the current season.[5] Curious of Cardiff yearns for Madonna's IQ? 'People:pop stars' does the necessary: 140.[6]

Before Chantel can hear from the eager questioners, she has to log on to the system. AQA's researchers work whenever they want to. 'We've got lots of students,' Paul told me, 'lots of parents who work for a couple of hours a day in between changing nappies. Also a lot of retired people, disabled people . . . anyone who can't do full-time work, or has commitments at home. But we also have a few guys who do have jobs, but answer about twenty questions a month – the really difficult ones, just because they love doing it.'

Chantel logs on, and is presented with a screen divided into several sections. The main one offers her the next question available for answering. She doesn't have to take it, and any question skipped by five researchers gets transferred to a 'hard' list, which everyone can see. At this time of the morning the system is relatively quiet – 86 hard questions and 91 normal ones waiting to be answered. Chantel's next is 'How do I get to the postcode area YO30 1XW by car from the A1(M)?' The excellent streetmap.co.uk gives her the postcode's location – Skelton, just outside York – and with a flurry of junction and road numbers, an answer is winging its way within seconds. Chantel is 30 pence richer. Top researchers answer about six thousand questions a month; others are more modest, just doing a few hours for pin money.

5. He rectifies this several weeks later.
6. This might not surprise – Madonna seems a canny lass. Less expected is Liam Gallagher's IQ of over 160.

Other common non-trivia uses of the service include: 'What were last week's Lottery numbers?' (which Chantel finds 'bizarre – they've already spent a pound on the ticket'); 'What are next week's Lottery numbers?' (AQA issues a random prediction);TOPOT and 'What is the meaning of life?' As for any question, researchers can consult a database of previously offered answers. On this last one they include 'Life is the result of a complex sequence of chemical reactions and has no underlying meaning. Assign yourself a meaning – find out what you love and do it.'

Periodically AQA checks its most-used answers. As Paul said, 'It's one of the things we're very conscious of: the truth changes. What you actually think you've got down as a completely uncontestable truth can change. There's an ongoing debate about Omega 3, for instance – is it good for you?' There's also so much misinformation out there. 'Out there', of course, meaning the internet. 'Things like oysters climbing up trees. And there are huge debates about whether banana trees can walk. The banana isn't in fact a tree, it's something like a herbaceous bush. They generate roots, and after time the roots get put into the soil. They do inch closer and closer towards the sun, but they don't actually walk.'

The company was only a few weeks old when Chantel started. 'You had to do the research yourself,' she says. 'That was how the database was built. I feel a sense of

> ### TOPOT
>
> *You are more likely to correctly guess a stranger's UK telephone number than next week's winning Lottery numbers.*

ownership about it.' It strikes me that if the 'Knowledge is power' theory is correct, Chantel must be something approaching a superhero.

Lottery numbers and the meaning of life are all very interesting, but it's trivia I'm here for. Looking back through Chantel's previous answers, we learn that Rudolph wasn't one of Santa's eight original reindeer, as named in the 1823 poem 'A Visit from St Nicholas', better known by its opening line 'Twas the night before Christmas'.[7] We learn that the first football club in England to have an all-seater stadium was Coventry City. We learn that lips are red because they comprise skin containing no melanocyte (pigment cells), so allowing blood vessels to be seen through them.

But none of these seem as pleasing as the fact that a zebra's stripes are white on a black background, as opposed to black on white. The question was actually 'How many stripes does a zebra have?' to which Chantel answered, 'Around two hundred and fifty – they increase in number from birth to adulthood.' But researchers are encouraged to use up the text's 153 characters with extra information. And 'extra information' is often where the real gold is found. As Harry said about Wikipedia, the original object of your research can pale next to one of its own footnotes. Within seconds you're down a long but fascinating side alley.

Could this be a definition of trivia itself? Paraphrasing John

7. He first appeared in 1939, in a book given out to children by the American chain store Montgomery Ward. Rudolph is, however, the son of original deer Donner, whose colleagues were Dasher, Dancer, Prancer, Vixen, Comet, Cupid, and Blitzen.

Lennon, could trivia be what happens when you're busy making other plans? Initially I wondered whether working for AQA, dealing with trivia day in day out, might not dull the appetite for it. Now, though, I see Chantel isn't dealing with trivia, at least not actively. She stumbles across it just as inadvertently as any trivialist. The question was how many stripes a zebra had; only in the hinterland of 'supplementary info' did the white-on-black gem appear.

Perhaps the stripes fact appeals because it's the answer to a question you can't believe you never asked. Another such query appears further down the list: 'Why do the numbers go down on a phone, but up on a calculator?' 'Eighteen layouts were tested,' reads Chantel's answer, 'before keypad phones were introduced. It was thought least confusing to have 1 top left as few people had used calculators then.' Yet more appear in *The End of the Question Mark*, a 'greatest hits' book published by AQA. 'On my coins,' runs one, 'I've just noticed that directly underneath the Queen's neck are the tiny initials IRB. What does this stand for?' The answer: 'Ian Rank-Broadley. He is the artist responsible for the Queen's updated portrait.' After reading that, I check the coins in my pocket: all bear the initials.[8] Every one of us handles these coins dozens of times each day, yet how many of us notice the initials? At least one person did. And unearthed a fact that, as the best trivia often does, threw new light on the commonplace.

Other highlights from the book include the fact that in 1989 the pre-Oscar-announcement 'And the winner is . . .'

8. Because all date from 1998 onwards, the year in which Rank-Broadley's portrait was first used.

was replaced with 'And the Oscar goes to . . .' to protect the losers' feelings;[9] that Attila the Hun died of a nosebleed; that the only female in *Lawrence of Arabia* is Gladys the camel; that the 5 button on every mobile phone has two tiny raised dots to aid blind people; that Maine is the only US state to be adjacent to only one other state (New Hampshire);[10] that red-headed people are more sensitive to pain, and need more anaesthetic before operations; that Ho Chi Minh once worked as a pastry assistant in London's Carlton Hotel; that the G-spot was named (initialled?) after gynaecologist Ernst Gräfenberg . . . It's no wonder pub quizzes ban mobiles.

A common question, according to Chantel, is 'What was number one on the day I was born?' Further evidence though this may be of trivia's narcissistic side, I nonetheless ask Chantel to check mine. The answer is 'Get It On' by T.Rex. Satisfyingly cool, I childishly think. It was a close thing, mind you: the next day Diana Ross took over with 'I'm Still Waiting'. What's worse for Chantel, the record was still there three weeks later, when she made her entry into the world.

While we're on pop, Chantel asks what the following five songs have in common: 'Stranger on the Shore' by Acker Bilk, 'Last Christmas' by Wham, the expensively packaged 'Blue Monday' by New Order, 'White Christmas' by Bing Crosby and 'Angels' by Robbie Williams. The answer is they're the only five records ever to sell a million copies in

9. The statue was named by a librarian at the Academy of Motion Picture Arts and Sciences; it looked like her uncle Oscar.
10. Maine is also the only state with a one-syllable name.

> ## TOPOT
>
> *Ultravox's 'Vienna' was kept off the number one spot by Joe Dolce's 'Shuddupayaface'. Or however it's spelled.*

the UK without getting to number one. Wham at least had the comfort of kowtowing to Band Aid. Robbie Williams came second to the Teletubbies.[TOPOT]

Inevitably some answers have to be estimates. Occasionally AQA will conduct their own research, as when someone asked how many Cornish pasties would fit inside Buckingham Palace,[11] though often it's a case of reporting others' work. The number of cars in the world, 350 million, seems surprisingly low, while the number of grains of sand in the world, seven sextillion – a seven followed by 21 zeroes – is so large as to be meaningless. Or *is* that its meaning?[12] Even when an estimate is used, AQA still fill up the reply with bonus info. An informed guess that there are 82,000 cat's eyes on the M25, for instance,[TOPOT] was accompanied by the fact that Percy Shaw invented the device in 1933, after seeing a cat walk towards him at night.[13]

Like Chantel, Paul has turned into something of a walking encyclopedia. 'I'm intrigued by trivia when I see it on the system. Your ears always prick up when someone makes a grand

11. Calls to pasty manufacturers and examination of Palace plans elicited the answer forty-nine million.

12. And if so, what meaning can we take from the fact that there are fewer grains of sand in the world than there are atoms in a glass of water?

13. Ken Dodd offers the thought that if the cat had been walking the other way Shaw would have invented the pencil sharpener.

sweeping statement, some fact that's bound not to be true. Except some of them are.' Like the one about coconuts killing more people each year than sharks. Or the one about a human baby being able to crawl down the artery

of a blue whale. Though not the one about cutting a child's hair to make it grow back thicker. 'I've got a two-year-old daughter, and last year her aunt said that. I said it's rubbish: hair is dead once it leaves your head.'

The total number of answers sent out by AQA now stands at over ten million. But do any of them, I ask myself as I scan Chantel's screen, contain the object of my search: the perfect fact?

The criteria soon set to work, as vicious and unforgiving as *X Factor* judges. 'Zebra stripes are white on black' is charming, but doesn't help you understand people. The million-sellers-who-didn't-get-to-number-one list unites some disparate elements (New Order and Acker Bilk), but lacks any real element of surprise. 'Buckingham Palace would hold forty-nine million pasties' might have a certain charm, but doesn't relate to a system . . .

So I have to move on, and find somebody else who has turned trivia into a business.

The Q in *QI*, unlike the Q in AQA, doesn't stand for 'question'. It stands for 'quite'. The *I* stands for 'interesting'.

QI is more than just a television programme presented by

Stephen Fry which allows John Sessions to impersonate Violet Elizabeth Bott. It also produces books like *The Book of General Ignorance*, which reveals that although Nelson did indeed say 'kiss me' rather than 'Kismet' to Hardy,[14] his very last words were actually 'Drink drink, fan fan, rub rub' (he was thirsty and hot, and his chest was being massaged to ease the pain). *QI* is a website too, with a forum allowing members to discuss topics like 'Scrabble two-letter words', 'Why does a week have seven days?' and 'Names for things you didn't realise had names'. The metal or plastic tag on the end of your shoelace, apparently, is an aglet.

More information obtainable from the *QI* website concerns Justin Gayner, the firm's media coordinator. 'Despite getting 6 A levels aged 17, Justin is quite comfortably the most ignorant member of the *QI* team. So ignorant, in fact, that he is frequently pelted with fruit and vegetables in research meetings . . . Professionally, Justin has masqueraded as a FTSE 100 headhunter, a dot-com entrepreneur and a journalist on the *Daily Telegraph* and *Daily Mail*. Justin was recruited by *QI* in 2005 after John Lloyd [*QI*'s founder] saw him streak during the finals of the Babbacombe Lawn Bowls championships in Torquay.'

Despite the obvious untruths (six A levels at seventeen? Come off it), I email Justin to enquire if he might care to talk trivia with someone in search of the perfect fact. Evading the tomatoes for a minute, he replies that he'd love to. We arrange to meet in a pub near his west London home.

* * *

14. Hardy's christian name was Thomas. No relation to the writer, although Oliver Hardy did claim to be descended from Nelson's aide. Then again he was in showbusiness.

There can't be many friendships which have bonded over a badger's penis bone. But that's exactly what happened between Justin Gayner and John Lloyd.

Justin, with his fair hair and Peter Sellers glasses, has a charm bordering on the raffish. A confident manner belies his age: last weekend was spent celebrating his thirtieth birthday. Several years ago, when he was working as a gossip columnist and the first series of *QI* ran on television, he interviewed Lloyd.

'I hadn't heard of him, much to my embarrassment. I asked him what he'd done. He said *Not the Nine O'Clock News*, *Blackadder*, *Spitting Image* . . .' Despite this unpromising start, Lloyd liked the resulting article. 'He said it was one of the first times a journalist had understood the concept of *QI*. The fact we bonded over was that Victorian gentlemen used badgers' penis bones as tiepins. I think it's called a baculum.'[15] Straighaway we have a contender for perfect fact. It certainly unites disparate elements, though not in a way the badger can have been very happy about.

Gayner and Lloyd seemed to click. 'Ridiculous phone bills were run up talking about everything. The universe, family life . . . The *QI* philosophy was very different from my world at the time, the Fleet Street mentality of trying to break stories about celebrities, the rich and famous. I was trying to unearth facts, that's what you do as a journalist. But John got me into facts in a different way.'

15. It is indeed, the word being Latin for 'stick'. Bacula are found in mammals that require extra rigidity during copulation, though not in humans, which must be a source of disappointment to some. A walrus's can be as long as two feet.

Hang on. 'A different way'? The '*QI* philosophy'? Isn't it just about . . . well, things that are 'quite interesting'?

'The primal drives for humans,' replies Justin, 'are seen by biologists as food, sex and shelter. But we argue there's a fourth – curiosity. If you look at human history we've only evolved because someone has been curious about something, or experimented with something, or gone on an adventure to places no one's ever been. And trivia [though Justin dislikes the word for its 'geeky' connotations, he uses it as shorthand] allows us to do that – to explore the world around us in a way that text-books can't, novels rarely do, our average school lesson hasn't been able to achieve.'

But don't different people find different things interesting?

'I think there are things that everyone finds interesting. Anything that overcomes a previously held belief, for instance, something you thought was true and turns out not to be. It makes you think, Wow, what I thought was true is hogwash. That's universal, I think. It's like a scandal, primal and gossipy. It's exciting, your neurons get shaken up and you start looking at something differently.' Justin cites examples from *The Book of General Ignorance*, from Nelson's last words (and, as noted by Andrea Barham, his lack of an eyepatch) to the fact that the tallest mountain in the world isn't Everest, it's Mauna Kea, an inactive volcano on Hawaii. Current mountain convention is that although 'highest' means from sea level to summit – on which Everest, at 29,029 feet, wins – 'tallest' means from bottom to top.[TOPOT] At 33,465 feet from seabed to summit, Mauna Kea stands tallest of all.

This example smacks a little of pedantry, but I take Justin's general point.

'Something else that's universal is sex stuff,' he continues. 'At *QI* we say our favourite fact is that the kangaroo has three vaginas. People love that. It immediately sets you thinking, Why three? What are the implications for the male kangaroo? What would it be like if I had three vaginas, what would I do with them?' That's another thing about trivia – it gets you thinking. It's not spoon-feeding, like reading a newspaper or watching the news. It gets you feeling creative, thinking about the possibilities of things.'

> ## TOPOT
>
> *After becoming the first man to conquer Everest, Sir Edmund Hillary is said to have announced: 'Well, we knocked the bastard off.'*

Justin's right: I certainly want to know why the kangaroo has three vaginas. Before asking, though, I pick up on something from earlier: schools not being able to interest their pupils. Why does Justin think this is?

'There is always the odd teacher who can do it. There are usually two reasons for that: the way they delivered the information – entertaining or fun or warm – and they gave you pieces of information which made you forget you were studying a subject. Made you interested in a story, or made you look at it a different way.'

How was Justin at school?

'Disruptive. My parents had got divorced when I was at a difficult age. I had an authority problem. I disrespected adults, teachers, the older boys [Justin was at Eton]. Lots of people have the same problems there, because it's such a hierarchy.' But he was always a reader. 'One of my first childhood memories was being in English when I was six. We'd been given a book to read, and I read it all in a night. The next day I referred to the last page and a middle page, and the teacher didn't believe me – she thought I was cheating. I got told off for it.'

Reading remains a habit. 'If you came to my house you'd be disgusted by the lack of personal space; there are books everywhere. I love reading lots of different things. If I'm in someone else's house and I see *Agriculture Weekly* magazine or *Tractor Monthly*, something I think I would actively dislike, I'm more interested to read it. When I read stuff like that – no matter what it is, a piece of marketing junk, or an airline mag – I'll read it quickly, and find the gem that gets me thinking.'

This, for Justin, is what characterises great trivia: the one interesting fact among a lot of dull ones. It can prove the key that unlocks a whole subject, and is why he disagrees with those who call trivia shallow. 'It's completely the opposite. People who are interested in trivia are more profound, more interesting than any common-or-garden academic, who are interested too often in posturing and giving their own opinion. Trivia isn't about your view or my view, it's about what is *true*; it has to rely on being *true*. If you look at learning as a mining operation, trivia is the gold nugget right at the bottom of the mine, and all the other stuff – the bland facts – are the stuff you have to sift through.'

I like this metaphor. It's the exact opposite of trivia's usual image: lightweight stuff floating on top of 'serious' knowledge.

And for Justin the mining, the sifting, is itself part of the fun. 'There is a difference to me between someone who just reads trivia books and repeats them, and someone who looks into a subject for themselves and uncovers something. It's always tempting when you're researching a *QI* series to buy *The Most Amazing Facts About Engineering* or whatever. The problem is, a) very often they're untrue, b) they've been heard a lot before, and c) they miss out all the story along the way. People think that trivia's just about the one fact you tell a mate at the bar, but a good insight should lead to another, then another, in an unexpected way, so it tells a story. Rather than just a one-off "Look at me, don't I know a lot."'

The one-fact-leading-to-another element is what stops Justin being able to get excited about the Hull City fact, which cropped up earlier in our conversation. 'It's a bit of a "Yeah, so?" It doesn't tell me anything new about football. It tells me nothing new about language. A good fact has to be surprising. The reason Hull City is unsurprising is no one's ever thought, I wonder how many football teams have no letters you can colour in?'

It's good for winding up football bores, I say.

'Yes, that's a good game. But it's not, in itself, good trivia.'

The spirit in which *QI* presents information is important, says Justin. 'It has to be entertaining, warm . . . People do say they like *QI* because it's not abrasive, in the way panel games can be. They can be quite cruel.' And it's not just the audience who benefits. 'I've been a lot happier since working on *QI*. It's made me a nicer person than when I was working for the *Daily Mail*. It was a good gig, but there was always that gnawing feeling that I wasn't doing anything useful. That I wasn't improving myself, or doing anything for the people reading or consuming what I did. Whereas with *QI*, no one's been hurt by what we do. It's totally life-affirming, it doesn't diss anyone.'

There's something very British about this image. It resonates with the nice-cup-of-tea side of our national character. Would Justin call trivia a peculiarly British trait? 'No. Our book was bought by twenty-two countries around the world. So we know there's an international appetite for trivia. Everyone is interested in something – be it film, plants, football – that's a universal thing. It's a universal desire to be interested.' The only two countries who requested changes in the book were France and, as with Andrea's book, America. 'Doesn't that tell you something in itself?'

What about the website forum? What sort of trivia interests people there?

'Animals are always hugely popular. Language is very popular, etymology. Everyone uses language, when you understand where it comes from you can't help but be interested in that. Humble pie, for instance. It was a pie made in, I think, the eighteen hundreds, from the entrails of deer which were called umbles. The finer cuts of the venison would be eaten by the lords of the manor, the entrails would be eaten by the workers. It developed into humble pie.'[16]

Also popular are countries, in particular 'anything that gives you a different impression of a country. For example the Swiss are one of Europe's largest consumers of dog meat – not the food you give to dogs, but humans eating dogs. You wouldn't expect that of the Swiss.'[TOPOT]

16. Justin also reveals the original name for table tennis: wiff waff.

QI's research has shown the website is popular with young people. 'There are a lot between sixteen and twenty. They're the bright kids at school, I suspect, the ones who don't find socialising particularly easy, are too embarrassed to say anything.'

> TOPOT
>
> *The European Union exports more to Switzerland than it does to China.*

A more surprising fact, certainly in view of my experiences so far, is that *QI* is marginally more popular with women than with men. Not that this translates to the people responsible for it, however. 'We only have one female researcher, out of six or seven. We'd love more.' The same applies to guests. 'I was talking with John recently about women in comedy – there just aren't that many funny women. It's not a sexist thing. Jo Brand is one our most regular and most loved guests, and one of the funniest people in the world. We'd like more female guests on the show, but there just aren't any out there.' I'm reminded of what Steve Punt said: comedy is in the detail. And who does detail?

Conversation moves on to the relationship between thinking and happiness. Justin's certainly aware of the Jeffrey Bernard problem, but also that thinking can rescue you *from* unhappiness. That's how *QI* was born in the first place. He tells me about John Lloyd's history, how a lifetime achievement award from BAFTA and staggering amounts of money made in advertising left him chronically unfulfilled. The awareness struck him that he didn't actually know anything, that real happiness was to be found in the stuff that interested you . . . But after a minute or two he stops. 'Why don't you get all this from John himself?' he says. 'I'm sure he'd love to talk to you.'

And so we arrange that Justin will put me in touch.

I'm not to know it at this stage, but it's a meeting that's going to lead me to the perfect fact.

Despite the onward march of technology, where adverts can target an inbox or a mobile phone quicker than you can say 'pop-up', some marketing is still best done by good old-fashioned flyers. Across London, wherever those with spare time and money are to be found waiting – by the till in a café, in a theatre's foyer, at a hotel reception desk – racks of brightly coloured leaflets expound the merits of various museums, musicals and day trips. In most of these racks, standing out from the garish reds and day-glo yellows by simple virtue of being plain white, are elegantly fonted sheets promoting the virtues of another company which makes money out of trivia: London Walks.

As its name implies, London Walks has no truck (literally) with those who would exhibit the city to visitors by cramming them on an open-top bus and driving around for a couple of hours, while someone with questionable microphone technique delivers scripted extracts from an A level history syllabus. For this firm, revealing London's secrets is a pedestrian affair. But only in the strictest sense of the phrase: each walking tour is led by a guide who, although they probably know the A level syllabus backwards, can bring their information to life with judicious use of gossip, scandal, offbeat detail and general oddity. In a word, trivia.

It's this aspect of London that has always, for me, made it the city it is. From the horizontal Monument reaching the spot where the Great Fire started, to Angel Tube station's escalator being the longest in Western Europe, to one of the bricks at the top of Canary Wharf being ten millimetres higher than all the others, London is soaked in trivia. There's Burlington Arcade, the posh shopping gallery off Piccadilly, where tradition forbids visitors to 'whistle, sing or hurry'. There's Of Alley, near Charing Cross, on land once owned by George Villiers, Duke of Buckingham, who insisted on every word of his name and title being commemorated in local streets. There are the official measurements of an inch, a foot and a yard on a brass plaque on the north side of Trafalgar Square which defines the lengths at '62 degrees Fahrenheit'.[17] There's Eros, who points the wrong way: the statue is meant to be firing its arrow up Shaftesbury Avenue, so 'burying' its 'shaft' there . . .

The sheer variety of a city like London is reflected in London Walks' excursions. Among the 130 or so on offer are Old Mayfair, Darkest Victorian London, the Beatles In My Life Walk, the Along The Thames Pub Walk, the Inns of Court, the Old Jewish Quarter, Ghosts, Gaslight and Guinness, London and the Da Vinci Code, Spies' and Spycatchers' London . . . The company also offers a walk that once caused me some confusion. Walking through Whitechapel, I was stopped by two Japanese tourists who asked if I knew 'wiper'. 'I'm sorry?' 'You know wiper?' 'Sorry, I don't understand.' One of the

17. The south side of the square gets in on the act too – a small pedestrian island houses the plaque from which all road distances to London are measured.

tourists drew a finger across her throat. 'You know – wiper, Jack the wiper.' I directed them to Tower Hill Tube, where at any given time dozens, often hundreds of people are stacked in groups, waiting to walk around and hear about five murders which will never be solved.^{TOPOT}

A call to London Walks soon finds its owner, David. Inevitably, he is American. (He didn't start the company, however. That was done nearly 50 years ago by someone called Keith. He wasn't American. He was Australian.) I explain that I'm writing a book about trivia, at which word David lights up, and soon we're swapping London facts like kids with cigarette cards. David has most of the cards already, of course, but he's happy to swap anyway. The only 'fact' he can't help with is one I've heard somewhere – *somewhere* – but can't verify: when added together, the Square Mile's streets and alleys (no roads, remember) total 48 miles in length.

David's happy for me to join a guide on one of the walks, and suggests Tom, a 'recovering barrister'. The walk in question covers the City itself, from St Paul's to the Tower of London. On the appointed Sunday afternoon I make my way to the pavement outside the Tube station that shares the great cathedral's name and find two dozen people milling around, waiting to be called to order by a middle-aged man who clearly can't be Tom. Medium height, wearing a baseball cap over a bald head and sporting a pink

TOPOT

One of the few things we know for certain about Jack the Ripper is that he was left-handed.

T-shirt, black leather jacket, black jeans and trainers, there's no way this character could ever have practised at the Bar.

'Tom?' I ask, to elicit an explanation of why Tom couldn't make it.

'Mark? Pleased to meet you.'

Tom, his tones fruity and full, even a little camp from time to time, takes some latecomers' money, then marshals the group around him. He asks where people are from. There are Americans – 'Welcome home' – some Germans – 'Thank you for the Royal Family' – as well as French, Polish, Russian and a smattering of natives. He gets the housekeeping out of the way, including a reminder about looking the correct way when crossing the road. It's not only Australia, New Zealand and South Africa who drive on the left, reveals Tom: 68 countries share our preference, over half the world by land mass.

Then we're off. First stop is St Paul's itself, where Tom points out the gilt copper pineapple atop the west entrance. New and exotic in Christopher Wren's day, the fruit was a symbol of hospitality. Thousands of times I've been past here, and not once have I noticed it. We view Cheapside, and learn that its first syllable is an old word for 'market', hence the adjoining Bread Street, Milk Street, Honey Lane . . . Moving down to the Thames we hear about Elizabeth the virgin queen (Tom laughs derisively after the penultimate word) burning incense on her boat to mask the river's smell, and hear that although the plumber Thomas Crapper didn't invent the flushing toilet – some word derivations are just too good to be true – he did popularise it.

Passing the Globe Theatre on the opposite bank – its straw roof the first permitted in London since the Great Fire – we

reach Stew Lane, 'stew' being an old word for brothel. Land-
lord to these establishments was the Bishop of Winchester, who
permitted the women to ply their trade as long as they wore
uniforms of white dresses. Hence their nickname of 'the Bishop's
geese', and hence our modern term 'bird'. Reaching the headquarters of the Worshipful Company of Skinners, Tom tells us
about livery companies, the guilds of tradesmen dating back
centuries[18] and still being created today. Recent additions include
the Information Technologists (1992), Management Consult-
ants (2004) and Tax Advisers (2005).

On we go, wending our way through the financial district,
its Mammon-inspired streets now empty on the Lord's day. Tom
points out Wren's churches, such as the one in Walbrook
dedicated to Saint Stephen, with its neighbour dedicated to
'Saint Arbuck' (think about it). Many of the buildings we pass
were damaged in the Blitz, whose blackouts were the reason
white lines were introduced down the middle of roads. Early
motorists thought you had to drive along the line. A stop outside
the Lloyd's building reveals that both Rudolf Nureyev and
Betty Grable insured their legs there, while the site of Samuel
Pepys's house inspires Tom to the tale of the diarist proposi-
tioning three women during the same church service – all of
them successfully.

Our twenty-second and final stop overlooks the Tower of

18. The first 12 organised themselves into order of precedence in 1515.
Only the Skinners and Merchant Taylors failed to agree who was more
important, and ever since have alternated yearly between positions six
and seven. Sadly the phrase 'at sixes and sevens' doesn't, as some believe,
derive from this disagreement: Chaucer used it over a century earlier.

London itself. Tom relates the site's bloody history – some executioners were less than competent, one taking eight chops of the axe to dispatch Simon of Sudbury – then performs a modest bow as his delighted audience break into applause. Several hang around with supplementary questions about various aspects of the walk, to which Tom knows all the answers. Then he and I retire to a pub over the road, the Liberty Bounds.[19] Tom apologises that his voice wasn't all it could have been: today is his first day back after a fortnight's holiday in Spain.

'Surely that means your voice would be at its strongest?' I say.

A shake of the head. 'Not warmed up yet.'

Tom now earns his living exclusively from guiding, preferring not to practise law 'for reasons of sanity'. But did the two livings share an attraction? I ask. Namely the chance to . . . er . . . 'I'm trying to find a nice way of saying "show off".'

Tom smiles. 'I don't have a problem with that. Whatever anybody does, if they enjoy what they're doing an element of that will be showing off. It's part of you.'

He holds the Institute of Tourist Guiding's Blue Badge, the industry's gold standard. Taking two years to complete, it covers 'a core of everything – history, art, architecture, law, the monarchy, religion, politics, music . . .' – and allows Tom to guide just about anywhere, even Westminster Abbey and the Tower of London itself. Not that London Walks insist

19. So called because it lies just outside the boundary of the area, or liberty, controlled by the City of London.

on the qualification. It wasn't even how Tom himself got started. 'During my Bar training I saw an advertisement for an organisation called British Tours. I went along and enjoyed it. Suddenly I realised I was reading as much on London as I was on law.'

Tom was born and brought up in Cornwall. I put to him a long-held theory: those who love London most aren't from the city originally. He agrees. 'It's a case of not taking it for granted, isn't it?' Maybe it's because we're not Londoners that we love London town. 'I think it's a never-ending thing about London trivia that you're never in your lifetime going to know everything you might like to know. You'll discover, with things you've never thought about before, that as you start finding out about them, one thing just leads to another. You do get this feeling that there's a depth to the whole thing. Also it's a way of touching the past. I don't think you can touch the past by saying "Samuel Pepys wrote a diary from 1660 to 1669" but you do when you start talking about how people behaved, how relationships worked, even talking about the stews and all that. It has a sense of reality about it. Giving the past to the future, perhaps.'

It's nice to hear trivia cited as the best way into 'proper' history, rather than an optional adjunct to it.

'I particularly like silly details,' replies Tom, echoing Marcus's daughter. 'I think one of the most tedious things to do is simply relay a whole list of facts. Which you could do – you could go date, date, date – but if you don't have any hooks to put anything on, it won't capture people's imagination. I think the wrong attitude is that knowledge is about talking facts at people. That's not going to get you anywhere. Presentation is important. Interaction is important too.'

Tom gives an example from today's walk: he deliberately mentioned the statue of a swan outside St James's Garlickhythe[20] because it was at the right height for a young girl on the walk. Does he do much of this individual tailoring?

'All the time. On this one you could go from St Paul's to the Tower on fifteen or twenty different routes. And walks can branch off as a result of questions that are asked. This morning I did a Westminster walk where people asked questions about Parliament, and so we branched off into the differences between Lords and Commoners, the role of the Queen and so on. It's a tangent, so out comes information I wouldn't otherwise have given.'

Does the information ever travel the other way – does Tom learn things from the people on his walks?

'Oh yes. Not so much in the City and Westminster, but certainly in the village places like Notting Hill and Highgate. Locals will give me bits of information. For instance, I found out recently that there's some property in Notting Hill that's owned by Enron. And in Highgate somebody who was obviously older than she looked said she could remember people in her family looking after animals that were driven down to Smithfield. The animals were fattened up in Highgate before the drovers took them to the market. She remembered relations who had looked after sheep in

20. The church has links with the Vintners' Company, who together with another livery company, the Dyers', own those swans at Windsor not reserved for the Queen.

TOPOT

Holloway Road is so named because the cattle being driven down to Smithfield market hollowed it out.

---

the fields around Kenwood House. That sort of thing is priceless.'^{TOPOT}

What feeling does Tom get for the reasons people come on the walks? What's the attraction of this stuff?

'I think they want to feel part of something. They want to know what makes the place tick, historically and contemporarily.'

The last three words sum up what has always struck me as one of London's most magical qualities: the way it mixes new and old. Prince Charles couldn't get it more wrong when he talks about 'monstrous carbuncles'. To insist that good architecture, good design of any sort, belongs to a particular century is to view biscuit tin lids through rose-tinted spectacles. Take Lord's, for example. The beautiful old pavilion, now a listed building, faces the spaceship-like 1990s media centre. Both represent their age. Both are stunning.

Tom agrees. 'At Bank junction you have that amazing juxtaposition of the nineteenth-century neo-classical Royal Exchange^{TOPOT} next to the new glass Stock Exchange.'

This interplay between the ages, he says, is particularly appreciated by Peter Ackroyd. 'He has an exceptional understanding of the organic nature of civilisation and cities, London especially. He's got a most extraordinary ability to knit the history together. The idea that it keeps coming back and biting people is true. One of his programmes featured a

TOPOT

*The Royal Exchange's grasshopper symbol, now adorning
the matchboxes in the ultra-modern bar inside, comes
from the institution's founder, Thomas Gresham. Born out
of wedlock, he was left to die in a field, and only survived
because a young boy stumbled across him. The boy had been
chasing a grasshopper.*

building near London Wall which bridges over the road. That's
very near where one of the exits from the City used to be,
where there was a gate over the road. It's London coming
back and biting you.'

It occurs that London's capacity for 'amazing juxtapositions'
helps explain its affinity with trivia: both of them unite disparate
elements. Queen Square gave a hint of that the day I went to
see Emrah Duzel.

I ask Tom if he can help with the Square-Mile-streets-total-
forty-eight-miles thing.

'I've never heard that, no. But I have to say, even if I had,
I wouldn't have found it particularly memorable. It's one of
those pieces of trivia which in a sense is leading nowhere. You
might say "So what?".'

This brings back Justin's disenchantment with the Hull City
fact. Neither statement moves you on, gains you an insight, deepens
your appreciation of anything. As much as the sheer stupidity of
Hull City will always delight me, I see where the critics are coming
from. Great trivia thrives on tangents, but these facts cut off those

tangents. They leave you stranded. They clearly, then, can't be contenders for the title of 'perfect fact'. But can their imperfection point me towards a fact that is? It feels as though there's a lesson here. For a second I think I've got it . . . something stirs in my subconscious . . . but no, the lesson eludes me.

Something Tom said earlier caught my attention: that you could never 'know everything you might like to know'. It prompts the question: *does* he want to know everything?

'In a sense, yes. There's this completely unattainable state of being sure you know absolutely everything about a particular place. But it *is* totally unattainable. Which in some ways drives you on more, to find layer on layer, knowing that even if you were to reach this impossible state, in one day's time it's gone. Something will have happened.'

His words stay with me after we part. It's dark now, and the lights around the Tower of London blaze off the thousand-year-old walls. Surely there's nothing in the capital to beat this sight? But then my gaze slips past to Tower Bridge: just as beautiful, and an incredible feat of engineering to boot. Then again, there's Docklands in the distance . . .

All the time I lived in London, I searched for its centre. Its heart, its core, the one place where the whole city came together and was defined. The candidates queued up: Piccadilly Circus, clichéd comparison for busy places everywhere, but nothing actually *happens* there . . . so then you try Trafalgar Square, with Nelson watching over it, but then you're nearly at Parliament, so you head down Whitehall to Big Ben . . . but then you're just down the road from Buckingham Palace . . . the

royals aren't real, though, you want what London is *now* . . .
so you try Oxford Circus, but everyone's just passing through
. . . over to the City – finance is where the real power is –
the Bank of England's good, but you can't see in, can't really
experience it . . .

Even now, every time I come back to London, I play the game.
But nowhere's good enough. No one place is perfect; wherever
you are it's never a destination, merely one great place leading
on to other great places, an endless chain of inspiration. Like
Tom's state of total knowledge, London's heart is unattainable.

A few days later I make what will prove the final journey on
my search for the perfect fact.

QI's headquarters are an eighteenth-century townhouse in
the middle of Oxford, between Exeter and Jesus Colleges.
Having visited Cambridge, it's nice to get the matching
pair.[TOPOT] In the early nineteenth century, part of the building

TOPOT

*The BBC's John Snagge used to do his radio commentary on
the Boat Race from a small craft following the competitors.
Obviously this angle wasn't ideal, so Snagge relied on an
official running along the riverbank, lifting a dark- or light-
blue flag depending on whether Oxford or Cambridge was in
the lead. Years later Snagge met the man, and marvelled at
his skill in keeping up with the race. 'Oh I never bothered,'
came the reply. 'I just used to listen to that bloke on the radio.'*

was used as a coffee house.[21] An old guidebook mentions 'libraries [being] founded in our coffee houses . . . There are books suited to every taste . . . instruction and pleasure go hand in hand . . . learning no longer remains a dry pursuit.' *QI* aims to follow in that tradition: its ground floor contains a bookshop, while the upper floors form a private club in which members can drink and dine, as well as enjoy quizzes, lectures, comedy performances and all manner of interesting pursuits.

I've arranged to meet John Lloyd in the first-floor lounge. It's post-lunch, so the place is empty. John is running late, and I kill time by perusing the books arranged around the room. There is Boris Akunin's literary thriller *The Winter Queen*, *The Pig That Wants To Be Eaten: 100 Experiments for the Armchair Philosopher* by Charles Panati, *How To Win at Poker and Bridge*, a book about extinct animals entitled *A Gap In Nature*, a copy of the Beatles' *Anthology* . . . There is everything, in other words, except books of trivia. It echoes Justin's *Most Amazing Facts About Engineering* point.

Alex, the club's smartly suited meeter-and-greeter, brings me a coffee. We get chatting. He asks what I'm interviewing John about, and within seconds we're swapping trivia. Alex says he was born in the year that the first ever 3-D pop video was made.

'You mean "Money For Nothing" by Dire Straits?' I ask.

---

21. On the London walk we passed the original site of the coffee house where Edward Lloyd (no relation) started his insurance business. Back then, Tom told us, coffee was seen as a man's drink, hence the less dainty shape of its cup compared to that of a tea cup.

'Yeah.'

That was 1985. For *God's* sake. I was at university before Alex reached primary school. This unfeasibly urbane six-foot-two personification of charm was younger than me, I knew that, but not by *fourteen years*. He looks like he should be running an investment bank, albeit a particularly hip and fashionable one. By the time he's my age he probably will be. I have what can only be termed a John Sessions moment.

Rising above it, I notice the sheet music on the upright piano standing in the corner. It's entitled 'Grieg's Concerto in A Minor'.

'That was the piece in the Morecambe and Wise sketch with André Previn, wasn't it?' The sketch being over a decade older than Alex, I toy with an explanation about 'all the right notes but not necessarily in the right order'. Alex, however, says he knows the episode. He doesn't know whether this is the music from it.

Muttering something to myself about every good boy deserving fun, I slowly piece together the notes in the first chord, then play it. I'm halfway through working out the second chord, keeping my fingers on the first so I don't forget it, when Alex, standing an octave to my right, takes a cursory glance at the music and faultlessly plays the first four chords. They establish that this is indeed the music from the André Previn sketch. They also come dangerously close to provoking some very petty behaviour from a man fourteen years Alex's senior. Fortunately for all concerned, John chooses this moment to arrive.

He looks remarkably youthful for a man of 55. Tall and

trim, he's wearing a shirt, jeans and trainers, none of which bear trendy logos, but nevertheless the impression is 'cool' rather than 'uncle-at-the-disco'. Vivid blue eyes peer out from a face whose absence of lines is clearly due to something far cheaper than surgery: intensity. It's no surprise that Lloyd has produced some of the most successful comedy programmes of the last 30 years. He exudes energy, but not in the way of Billy Connolly or Robin Williams; his drive is quiet, contained, tightly focused.

Once he's procured a double espresso, we settle ourselves at a table. I mention the books, the fact that none of them are collections of trivia.

'You should see the library upstairs,' replies John. 'We've got three editions of the *Encyclopædia Britannica*. In fact one of them is the way . . . well, there are many ways *QI* started . . . but one of them is, when my children were born I thought, I'm going to apply the way I work to being a parent, which is obsessively perfectionist. So I went out and bought a copy of the *Encyclopædia Britannica*, intending to read the whole thing, in order to be the best possible dad. I'd know everything they asked me.'

What was that Andrea said? 'Knowledge is safety.' The female approach to parenting is to nurture, cherish, feed your child, let it know it is loved. The male approach is to tell it the capital of Albania.

Not that Lloyd even got as far as the 'Al's. 'The 1911 edition is almost like science fiction, the sense of joy at discovering how exciting and wonderful the world is. It's marvellous, like poetry. But the one I'd bought, from the early nineties, is *so* dull, it's just lists of mid-American towns. Anyway, we had this thing in our house, and I'd look up something I wanted to know. The article would be dull, but the one next to it would have fantastic facts. I remember reading that William Pitt was so thin he was known as the Bottomless Pitt, and that he was advised for health reasons, to relax and so forth, to drink a bottle of port a day. Which he did, then died of cirrhosis of the liver.'

And so a seed was sown. 'It started this idea that interesting information is never collected in one place. I'd read about koalas and find they never drink, and think, *What*? Then a year later I'd be reading some other reference book, and it would say koalas eat so much eucalyptus that close up they smell like giant cough sweets. And you say, "But that wasn't in the other encyclopedia!"'

I've dreamed of a place where all knowledge is gathered together. John wanted a place where all interesting knowledge is gathered together.

'The one thing we don't do, though,' he continues, 'is judge what is an important piece of information and what isn't. You don't have all the information to know whether it's important or not. Is a potato more important than the planet Jupiter? Obviously one is much bigger than the other, but the potato has all sorts of personal values . . . Why is it that people are so obsessed with how the universe began, and get angry to the point of violence about whether you believe in the Big Bang or not, when it has clearly no effect whatever on us? Whereas people won't talk about how to get on better with their wife, or whether you should hit children or not, which is actually very important and can make a big, big difference to your life.'[22]

John dislikes the way the word 'trivia' has become degraded. 'People say, "Oh, it's just useless information." You learn at school that the steam engine was invented by James Watt. Actually it wasn't. The first recorded steam engine was in Alexandria in about 100 AD, built by a man called Heron. It was a metal sphere with two arms on it. They would heat it and the air inside would expand. They got it up to fifteen hundred revolutions per minute. People say, "That's just trivia," and you say, "Hang on, if it's not trivia to teach them at school that it's James Watt who invented the steam engine, which is wrong, why is it trivia to say it was Heron, which is right?".'

To illustrate how supposedly trivial information can be a route into 'serious' learning, John mentions the kangaroo with its three vaginas, providing the explanation I forgot to get from Justin. 'All marsupials have forked peni, with one stalk and two outlets. The female kangaroo has three vaginas, two of which connect to wombs, so both are fertilised simultaneously. But only one is triggered into producing a baby kangaroo. The little joey crawls out – they're still almost embryos when they crawl out into the pouch, half-grown – and they live in the pouch for a bit, sucking on milk pads. If that kangaroo survives to be a

---

22. John quotes Buddha: 'In the search for truth, there are certain questions that are not important. Of what material is the universe constructed? Is the universe eternal? Are there limits or not to the universe? What is the ideal form of organisation for human society? If a man were to postpone his search for Enlightenment until such questions were solved, he would die before he found the path.'

year old, the dormant embryo inside the second womb just atrophies. But if the first one dies, even by an accident, ping, the second one is triggered. Isn't that great?'

He's right: instantly you want to know even more, learn *how* the second one gets triggered, what the third vagina does . . . To pursue this, though, would sidetrack us. I let John continue.

'We live in a culture where people who want to know feel they have to apologise for it. Aristotle said, "All men by nature desire to know." Maybe he meant women as well. Probably not actually, they were all terribly sexist, the Greeks. Aristotle averred that women had more teeth than men did. He was married at least twice; he obviously never bothered to look in his wives' mouths and count. Complete genius, Aristotle, but full of weird mistakes.'

Sounds like Newton, I say, recalling my chat with Arthur Miller.

'Did you know that Newton spent some time as MP for Cambridge?' John replies. 'His only speech was to ask the Speaker if somebody could open the window. Also he lost his first tooth at the age of eighty.'

'Ralph Richardson started smoking at eighty. He said at that stage he had nothing to lose.'TOPOT

TOPOT

Appearing in the West End, Ralph Richardson paused mid-speech, went to the front of the stage and asked, 'Is there a doctor in the house?' A man in the third row put up his hand: 'Bloody terrible play, isn't it, doctor?' said Richardson.

'You see,' says John. 'That's the thing about this – the connective nature. You saying something interesting, it sparks something in me, I reach a memory level that I'm not generally able to access. All information is in the hard drive somewhere, but we'd go mad if we had open access to it all the time, so there's a thing called the defensive grid which locks it down. We live in this ridiculous little biography. If I asked you to tell me who you are you'd say "I went to this sort of school, then I went to university . . ." and there'd be this sort of Wikipedia article. Whereas there are millions of things in there under the grid. *QI*'s a very quick way to get to them. I might say "I've just found out the most amazing thing about giraffes" and somebody might reply "There are only three kinds of giraffe" and I'll ask how they know that, and they'll say they used to live in Kenya, their dad was a game warden – and suddenly you're in, under their defensive grid.'

'I thought you were going to say they were the gayest animal.'

'What?'

'Giraffes are the gayest animal on the planet. I read it in a book review. There was something about lesbian hedgehogs, too.'

'This is fantastic,' says John, reaching for a pen.

Annoyingly, I now can't remember the details. 'Hang on, it might be that giraffes engage in more lesbian activity than any other animal. Or it could be more homosexual activity generally . . .'

'A lesbian giraffe is funnier than a homosexual giraffe,' says John. 'I don't know why.'[23]

At this point his phone rings. 'Would you mind if I took this?'

'Of course not.'

As John leaves the room, I notice that a club member, a learned-looking woman in her fifties, has popped in for a coffee. Her newspaper, though, remains unopened. 'That kangaroo thing was incredible,' she says.

When John returns, we discuss the notion of, as he calls it, 'interestingness'. 'If I give you a piece of interesting information you go "Yes," you've had a little bit of joy, and it begs the question what are we here for, what's the point of anything? The problem with modern scientific neo-Darwinism is they say "There is no point, shut up about meaning, there isn't any." The trouble is, nobody on earth, apart from when you're very depressed, thinks that. Otherwise why does every language in the world have a word for why? Why do people ask questions, why do they want to know? Why did Aristotle say "All men by nature want to know"? There's a lot of why. The world consists of whys.'

It's exactly the question that came to me in Blackpool: 'Why is it always why?' For the first time I sense that John has looked at all this from the same angle, that he views trivia – learning,

23. Sadly from a comedy point of view, later checking reveals that giraffes are merely the gayest animal generally: 90 per cent of all sexual encounters are males mounting males. I was right about the lesbian hedgehogs, though: 10 per cent of long-eared females engage in sex with each other, including oral sex.

knowledge – in a similar way. A feeling starts to grow that I'm nearing the end of my journey. That the perfect fact could be very close.

John's mention of depression raises a theme that was there from the start: the link between thinking and unhappiness. Sitting with Marcus at the pub quiz, I happily viewed trivia as a way of forgetting that life is meaningless. Yet my journey has made me question that: perhaps trivia *is* a search for meaning? I raise the point with John.

'It's just your opinion that life has no meaning,' he replies. 'It's not a fact. You've thought about it. Probably not very much, is my belief.'

The abruptness of his statement certainly gets my attention.

'I bet you haven't read the *Bhagavad Gita* from cover to cover, for example.'

'No.'

'Have you read any Chinese philosophy?'

'No'

'Do you know what Sufism is?'

'No.' I feel as though I should be taking offence, but somehow it fails to appear. John isn't highlighting my ignorance to belittle me, merely to question my assumption. My lack of religious belief holds firm; faith in any god – Christian, Hindu, Muslim (Sufism being an aspect of Islam) or any other – is fundamentally a matter of instinct, and my instinct says there is no god. But John's greater point is persuasive: to search for knowledge is to search for meaning. Thinking isn't a threat to happiness; it's a threat to unhappiness. Certainly that's been his story.

'I was hit, aged forty-two, by a major midlife crisis where I couldn't see what the point of anything was. I had a crisis of meaning, which is what Jung calls it. The thing is, you would not be able to live if you really thought the universe was meaningless. You would not go on. That's what happens to depressed people. I didn't know who I was; there was no point. It may not be a religious thing, but your life has to be meaningful otherwise you wouldn't go on. When it goes you certainly know about it.'

How had he got to this point?

'I had everything. I had a wife and children, two cars, two houses, lots of money in the bank and a wall full of awards. [The last two were unconnected: producing comedy might get you BAFTAs, but it doesn't make you rich. By then Lloyd had turned to commercials.] I was working too hard, so I took three months off just to think about things. After a couple of weeks the terror came in: I realised I didn't know anything. I'd never thought about anything seriously. So I started. I came across fifth- and sixth-century BC Athens, which was an area about the size of Hertfordshire where they discovered almost everything, from coinage to philosophy to mathematics. I went to Foyles' classical department and said, thinking, How clever am I?, "Have you got a book on fifth-century Athens?" The guy said, "That wall there." I staggered back, thinking, Shit, I'm forty-two years old, I haven't got time to read all that.'

But perseverance won the day. Soon John was teaching himself physics – even the much-feared Theory of Relativity – then philosophy, theology, molecular chemistry, biology . . . Much of his learning came from books, but as the nineties progressed and the internet developed, he came to value websites more and more. 'It's inconceivable that *QI* could have existed before the internet.' Not that the web is used indiscriminately. 'All the researchers are urged never ever to cut and paste a Wikipedia article; you have to cross-check it. It's that thing about information being dispersed for some reason, like someone has cut up the interesting bits and spread them around, so you have to use multiple sources. The best research is this wonderful pudding made up of raisins from here and currants from there and orange peel from there. Some of the stuff on the database is fantastic: you know that nowhere else in the world is there *that* article on cats or Bolivia or guitars.'

His experiences have informed John's view of education. 'It's always said we must know the basics, Tory MPs banging on "They don't know the basics, give them the dates, the facts." Well actually these are the things that are the trivial things. It's not interesting to know the date of the Battle of Copenhagen, it's just a fact. But if you know what happened at the Battle of Copenhagen – that Nelson did this, and then that happened, and so on – then you're cooking. The basics should be learned last. Education shouldn't be about delivering answers, it's about asking more questions.^{TOPOT} The geniuses of our society, and all the burglars, are people who go "Why's that then?" and people go "Shut up, SHUT UP. I'm not interested in what you think, I'm trying to tell you that the past participle of whatever . . ." I've got a friend who's a brilliant musician. He got so fed up with his kids not liking music lessons that he wrote them simple versions of their favourite pop songs. They learned the basics last. Once they could play a tune enjoyably and well they said, "Dad, how does a scale work?" "Oh, you want to know how scales work now, eh? You want to know what a minor key is? You've just played one.'"

This is all fine, but it's taking us away from John himself. It's clear he's developed a view of knowledge, a relationship with it even, which intrigues me. I want to know how he got there. I ask about his schooldays.

TOPOT

The documentary maker Michael Cockerell, who has interviewed every Prime Minister from Harold Macmillan to Tony Blair, saw only one of them use their fingers to count: Blair.

'The real education in my life happened before I was ten. My dad was in the navy. We were shipped all round the world, meeting people from completely different classes and backgrounds. I spoke Spanish before I spoke English, because my father was in Gibraltar for a year. I was on a plane ten years before anybody I knew had flown. I saw Manhattan, which to most people was a picture. I saw a *fridge*. Nobody else I knew had seen a fridge in the early fifties. And then I went away to prep school, and you're sitting there learning irregular French verbs. "Why are we doing this, sir?" "Right, see me in my study. Six of the best for you." Everyone's born curious, they're all curious up to the age of seven, then it's beaten out of you at school by this thing that's supposed to be so valuable – discipline, subject categories, staying to the point, having a curriculum.'

Retaining your curiosity, he adds, isn't just of benefit to yourself. 'The thing is that being interest*ed*, that's what makes a person interest*ing*. My wife, for example. People often come up to me at parties and say, "Your wife is the most fascinating person I have ever met, she's absolutely amazing. How did a git like you marry her?" So I go to Sarah and say, "What the hell did you say to that guy?" She says, "I didn't say anything, I just listened."'

This human bonding aspect is important to John. 'There's a famous episode of *Star Trek* where Spock's mind gets put into a human body. His first words are "My God, it's so lonely in here." Vulcans meld, they're a group entity, but human beings are very isolated from each other. A lot of life – fear, embarrassment – is about loneliness. The things that make it better are friendship. What's better than having three good friends? You join up. Information is the same. It's a passport to being a little bit less isolated from another person.'

John's mention of subject categories, of sticking to the point, brings back Steve's remark about academic expertise in the modern age: achieving it means concentrating on an area so small as to leave time for nothing else. But John seems to be heading towards the opposite view: to understand anything you need to understand, or at least be interested in, *every*thing. It reminds me of the writer C.L.R. James: 'What do they know of cricket who only cricket know?'

Links between supposedly disparate subjects featured in another of Steve's comments too: that of comedy and trivia both depending on such links. Given John's pedigree, it seems foolish not to ask him about this.

'The person who discovers what comedy is,' he says, 'will discover everything else. It's about as mysterious as consciousness, I think. But you can pick away at the edges of it. Unquestionably one clever thing in comedy is when you join two universes. The further they are away and the neater the join . . . that's what a pun is. It's like a wormhole in space: you're suddenly in a completely different part of the universe. Something about that triggers the joy response. It's very close, I think, to interestingness, which is another thing where we don't know what it is. Did you know the Romans had no word for "interesting"? How did they manage?'

Now John's brought back memories of Emrah Duzel, of me wanting to know how a neuron in your brain knows what's interesting and what isn't. This conversation, it seems, is conjuring up highlights of all my others, a Search for the Perfect Fact Greatest Hits package. And by doing that – the sense of this gets stronger all the time – it's leading towards the central truth of everything I've discovered. Towards the perfect fact itself.

As we discuss physics, John mentions Heinrich Hertz, the man who discovered radio waves but failed to see they could be used for radio.[24] I mention my Big Ben experiment, which John loves. His surprise is not just at the radio waves beating the sound waves; he didn't even know Radio Four broadcast the chimes live.

'Really?' I reply. 'I thought you'd have known that.' He was once a Radio Four producer, after all.

'No, no idea. You see, you've given me pleasure, you've made my life better, just by telling me that. And I will tell other people. It's a bit like spreading the word, isn't it? A lapping thing, the waves going out.'

In wave-making mood, I mention the Chas and Dave/Eminem fact. John likes this too. 'What's interesting about that is you've

24. Asked about the possible consequences of his discovery he replied: 'Nothing, I guess.'

made a surprising connection. Heraclitus, the great Greek pre-Socratic philosopher, said, "A hidden connection is stronger than an obvious one." In other words the things you don't know about are much more interesting than the things you do know about. That's what great about trivia – it advances you. We have a terrible problem at *QI*, because once you've done all the research, it's stopped being interesting and you crave new stuff.'

At this point a middle-aged man enters the room, dressed mostly in tweed – the waistcoat is a particularly nice touch – his rounded face and slightly unkempt hair creating the impression of an Edwardian gentleman of leisure. John introduces him as John Mitchinson, research director of Quite Interesting Limited, the man with whom he started the whole thing. The two are scheduled to do a phone interview with an America radio station, plugging *The Book of General Ignorance*. It's going to mean a break from our interview.

I'm glad of this chance to collect my thoughts, and as it's a sunny day I go for a wander round the streets of Oxford. John's words run on a loop through my mind: interesting information is never collected in one place . . . an interesting fact always making you ask another question . . . everyone's born curious . . . the things you don't know about are more interesting than the things you do know about . . . It feels fitting to consider these thoughts in Oxford, yet another place where all learning is supposed to be gathered together but isn't. The impossibility of total knowledge seems a theme of John's message, yet *exactly* where that message leads, its ultimate conclusion, remains stubbornly out of reach. I have a strange sense of calm about that, though. Right from the start I've known the perfect fact would find me, not the other way round. That's how it feels now. It's just a question of waiting.

Back at *QI* HQ, the two Johns show me the library, a room on the top floor lined with books every bit as eclectic as those in the lounge, including the three sets of the *Encyclopædia Britannica*. We sit at one end of the table running the length of the room.

> TOPOT
>
> *In their song 'Lola', the Kinks had to change 'Coca-Cola' to 'Cherry Cola' to comply with TV advertising laws.*

I ask John Lloyd how he turned *QI* the idea into *QI* the business.

'Basically I spent a long time after my midlife crisis creating a long computer file of things that were interesting, everything from bizarre interpretations of Dante's *Inferno* to amazing things about physics. It was what I used to do to stop myself going mad. I'd go and do a commercial, and if they'd mucked around with it and made it worse I'd come back absolutely furious but a lot richer.[TOPOT] And so in the evenings or on Saturdays I'd just start tinkering around with this stuff.'

Then, one day, inspiration struck. 'I can remember it now, just standing there, I suddenly thought, Jesus, I know what this is. I remember writing frantically in notebooks – it could be a radio station, and then there could be a documentary arm, and there'd be shops . . . I got so excited. I felt I'd discovered a new chemical element: interestingness.[25] What makes a good play?

25. Despite sounding a recent invention, the word was first used in 1759 by Adam Smith: 'The axe, the emblem of having been beheaded, which is engraved under those heads, sheds a real dignity and interestingness over their characters.'

What makes a good corporate brochure? What makes a good ad? Interestingness is there before anything. Before it's funny, before it's important, before it's informative . . . You've got my attention if you tell me something interesting.'

The firm has just produced its first corporate video, introducing the new chief executive of an insurance company. 'The idea was that the world is rapidly becoming an uninsurable place for all the reasons we know about: the weather's gone nuts, diseases, earthquakes and all that. So we went to interview six different people – mainly professors of IT, biodiversity and so on – and made a film that this chap showed in his speech in Florida. It was fantastic. If you can make an insurance corporate video interesting you can do anything.'

John Mitchinson brought to *QI* the expertise gained in a publishing career which, despite including a mail order catalogue so comprehensive as to be too large to fit through a letterbox, had proved very distinguished. More importantly, though, he brought a belief in the project exemplified by the fact that his wife calls his brain 'the skip'. 'I like to think of it as hardware and software. What trivia is about is finding a way of communicating the knowledge. That's what *QI* is. We don't invent anything, we're not original, we're not doing original research. Sometimes we find stuff that's been forgotten so it appears to be original, but what we really do – whether it's the TV show or the book – is find a way of presenting the stuff and make it interesting.'

And like John Lloyd, he hates the implication that 'make it interesting' means 'dumb it down'. 'Everything now is so demeaning. I used to be a member of the Young Ornithologists' Club. I found a whole stash of my birdlife magazines – they treated you like you were interested in birds, not like you had to have everything done in crappy little comic characters, with nothing on the page other than puzzles and games. I'm very happy to say to people that *General Ignorance* is a loo book. On the other hand I say you should see what's in my loo. It sits next to the *Upanishads*[26] and *North Atlantic Seafood*. What's wrong with a loo book? It just means it's something you can read in small chunks. Some of the great works of literature are read in small chunks.'

I like his point about facts being exciting in themselves, and recite Tim's point about trivia's appeal stemming from its truth. 'That's why I don't like science fiction,' I say.

'As a former big fan of science fiction,' says John Lloyd, 'I'd say that great science fiction is as true as anything else. The science fiction writer Theodore Sturgeon was once asked, "Isn't ninety per cent of science fiction crap?" He said, "Ninety per cent of everything is crap." The great exponents of the genre are as good as absolutely anything.'

Just as when he tackled me on Chinese philosophy, John's manner is forthright and feels as though it should provoke me . . . but somehow it doesn't. In fact, just as before, he makes me question myself. I feel ashamed of my closed mind, the haste with which I've dismissed an entire body of work. Too ready to spout answers, I'm not taking enough time over questions. And the value of a question is something I'm learning a lot about today.[27]

John mentions Douglas Adams's *The Hitchhiker's Guide to the*

26. A Hindu text.
27. A message which Sturgeon himself would have underlined: his philosophy was to challenge every assumption, to 'ask the next question'. Around his neck he wore a symbol of a Q with an arrow through it.

Galaxy. 'One of the interesting things is how much of it has been taken up by scientists. Richard Dawkins is a huge fan, and was a big friend of Douglas [as was Lloyd himself]. Lots of scientists quote *Hitchhiker* in their books. It was very close to a lot of the things we have now. The *Guide* itself is basically a combination of a laptop, Google and Wikipedia.' He laughs at a memory. 'Did you know the Hubble constant[28] was forty-two? There was a brief time when they'd got it to this value [42 also being the answer to 'life, the universe and everything' in *The Hitchhiker's Guide to the Galaxy*]. Douglas said, "I told you! I knew the secret!" Six months later they revised their figures. But it was a wonderful moment.'

John feels that in *Hitchhiker* 'Douglas asked all the interesting questions, but had none of the answers. He was very young.' Adams was 25 when he wrote the radio series from which the book developed.

Which prompts the ages-at-which-people-succeed question. John Mitchinson laughs and points over my left shoulder. 'We've got the book on that.' He retrieves a paperback called *Tolstoy's Bicycle: Who Did What When?* Its title stemming from the fact that Tolstoy took his first bicycle lesson at the age of 67, the book chronologically details the achievements of just about every person you've ever heard of, and several you haven't. Glancing at the early pages, I find Mendelssohn writing the overture to *A Midsummer Night's Dream* at 17, Joan Baez making the cover of *Time* magazine at 21, Aristotle Onassis becoming a millionaire at 23 . . . The author Jeremy Baker got the idea when life was going badly for him at 35 – my age when I started writing this book.

28. A statistic associated with the Big Bang theory of how the universe started.

John, however, looks at the full half of the glass. 'This book is great – it gives you a real feel for how late some people start.' True enough, the later pages reveal Gladstone becoming Prime Minister at 58, Francis Chichester breaking the round-the-world sailing record at 65, the American artist Grandma Moses having her first solo exhibition at 80 . . .

And so my time at *QI* continues to reprise themes from earlier research. No perfect fact yet – but then we start on a discussion about evolution.

It's triggered by our earlier mention of the man once called 'Darwin's Rottweiler', Richard Dawkins. Although both Johns agree with most modern evolutionary theory, they criticise those who countenance no dissent from it at all.

'I say "So?"' says John Lloyd. 'There's evolution and we evolve – so? How does that help me? We've evolved from lemurs, and before that starfish. Right, very interesting idea, but how does that help me not lose my temper when I'm driving my car? "Well," they'll say, "as an ape on the savannah, probably you would . . ." There's no mechanism, because all the things that are really difficult, like self-discipline and self-control, don't apply to apes. They're instinctive creatures that act like automatons. But we clearly *do* have the ability to make moral, ethical and decisional choices of all kinds, and *that's* the bit that interests me. That's what makes you a person.'

Playing devil's advocate, I respond that understanding, say, testosterone, and how it kicks in when you're angry, may not stop the testosterone making you angry, but it does help you deal with the anger.

'But you're back to the same question,' replies John

Mitchinson, 'because what testosterone doesn't tell you is what's causing that surge in testosterone. Then you get back to the mystery of consciousness, which is how can chemicals be affected by things that aren't chemicals? The interesting thing is, what's making you angry? The mystery is still the interaction between what is physical and what is apparently not physical. There are interesting theories, but no one's solved it. My view is that we're never really going to close the book on the important questions.'

'It doesn't matter how you slice this stuff,' says the other John. 'It's like atoms, there's always a smaller bit. Interestingness doesn't run out. In fact it's fractal: the closer you look at something the more interesting it becomes.'

Mitchinson agrees. 'We know that because bright scientists spend their whole lives looking at one tiny little detail, and the deeper they get into it, the more doors open up.'

Part of the appeal of '*QI*' as a name, adds Lloyd, was that, being 'IQ' backwards, it partly repudiated this answers-in-the-details approach. 'We're more interested in intuitive thinking, rather than measurable intelligence. It's more an "idea" way of thinking.'

I say that intuition versus detail has proved a theme of my search, especially in relation to gender.

John nods. 'Men like visible information, the stuff that can be logged as specific – football scores, names, data. They tend to read the surface signals. One guy asks another how he is, gets the reply "Great, I've just been promoted, it's going really well." Men are much more straightforward than women, you accept that. Then your wife says, "God, he looks terrible." You say, "No, he's fine; he told me he's just been promoted." She says, "I'm telling you, that guy's marriage is in serious trouble, he's obviously having an affair with somebody . . ." all that kind of stuff. How do they know?'

A thought crystallises in my mind, a new way of seeing the male-love-of-detail/female-intuition point. 'What you need for a perfect understanding of the world,' I say, 'is to be both male and female at the same time. The male you would solve every last detail, the female you would have the intuitive feel for things that can never be found even when you have every last detail. A creature like that would finally see the ultimate answer; it would finally understand the meaning of life. But a creature like that could never exist. It would be sexless, so it wouldn't be able to breed. There have to be two different sexes to keep life going – but the very fact we're different means we're doomed never to understand the *meaning* of that life.'

There's a moment's silence during which I feel slightly foolish. But then John Lloyd smiles. 'That's rather good,' he says.

John Mitchinson nods. 'I like that.'

We talk on for a while, swapping thoughts about this and that.

But I'm there now. I know I'm there.

And after the three of us have parted, as I walk slowly back to the park-and-ride stop, I mentally rehearse the meaning-of-life theory over and over again. The need for both male and female understanding gives a whole new meaning to the phrase 'my other half'. The High Street bustles past, shoppers heading home, students planning nights out. I wait at the stop, the criteria for the perfect fact sitting in my memory like cereal packet tokens: *the perfect fact must be true . . . charming . . . must link disparate items . . . help you understand people . . . be surprising*

. . . be one you can pass on to your children . . . relate to a system. Can they be redeemed for the perfect fact?

Various contenders step up. Elizabeth I burning incense to mask the Thames's smell might help you understand her, and is charming and true – but it isn't that surprising and doesn't relate to a system. White lines on the road originating in the Blitz relates to a system, but doesn't help you understand anyone. Rudolf Nureyev and Betty Grable both insuring their legs at Lloyd's links disparate items, but wouldn't make much sense to your children. As for telling them about a kangaroo's three vaginas . . .

But none of this worries me. Because as I think back over the afternoon one quote more than any other keeps reappearing: 'The things you don't know about are more interesting than the things you do know about.' And now I see the fact that meets all my criteria:

The perfect fact is that there is no perfect fact.

For a while I fight against it. This conclusion occurred to me almost as soon as I started the book, the possibility that I could zoom around and chat to my interviewees, pick up lots of trivia, scatter the book with it, say whatever there was to be said, then finish with 'Hey ho, can't find a perfect fact after all, never mind though, it's all bit of a laugh, isn't it?' And I *really* didn't want that. I *really* wanted to find the perfect fact.

But now, on Oxford High Street, I know that I have found it. Saying the perfect fact is that there is no perfect fact isn't some clever bit of wordplay, a neat way out at the end of the book – it's what I really believe. It's where the search has led me. It's true, and it has surprised me, and charmed me. It links together every disparate item – every fact – in the world, makes you realise they're all part of a system. And it helps you under-stand people. Because the whole *point* about us, about our love of trivia, is that every fact we ever learn is linked to other facts. Trivia isn't a game, a hobby, something to tell your friends when the conversation dries up; trivia is what we *are*. John was right: we're born curious. Tom was right: complete knowledge is un-attainable. Sandi was right: as soon as we learn something we wonder where to go next. Like sharks in the water, the moment we stop moving is the moment we die.

Now I understand why I got excited when Emrah couldn't give me the secret of memory. It was there in the Einstein quote: 'The most beautiful experience we can have is the mysterious'. That is the most valuable fact you can ever pass on to your children: the journey is everything, they should enjoy every second of it, discover as much as they can – but know that they'll never discover The Answer. No one fact is ever going to be perfect. I see it now. Just like my search for the heart of London, my love of trivia is destined to keep on going. I'm never going to be satisfied.

That is the perfect fact.

A few days later I'm in a second-hand bookshop. They sell audiobooks too, and there's a cassette copy of the original *Hitchhiker's Guide to the Galaxy* radio series. I remember the shame I felt when John challenged my cynicism about science fiction. The cassette gets bought.

Over the next week or so I take it out on my walks. It's fun ambling through the Suffolk countryside listening to the transgalactic adventures of Arthur Dent and Ford Prefect. Seventeenth-century cottages look very different when you've got Zaphod Beeblebrox in your ear. The trivialist in me delights at the discovery that this is where the internet translation service Babel Fish got its name. In the story it really is a fish, one which lets you understand anything said in any language.

Then the famed 42 episode arrives. A computer called Deep Thought has been constructed to find the answer to the ultimate question of life, the universe and everything. After seven million years it does indeed find the answer – 42. Only then does it become clear that no one understands what the question is. The computer can't find out either. And I think about no fact being perfect. Because facts are answers. It's questions that are interesting.

The final episode's credits include the members of the BBC Radiophonic Workshop responsible for the sound effects. One of them is called Harry Parker. Harry-who-I-interviewed-with-Sandi-Toksvig is a Harry Parker. I know it can't be him, because this is the late seventies and he can't have started at the Beeb that young, and anyway the coincidence of an interviewee in Chapter 9 leading me to something that was worked on by an interviewee in Chapter 5 would be just too much. But I send Harry an email just in case.

'Sadly the dates do tally,' he replies. 'Happy days. Douglas Adams getting all excited about synthesisers . . . Geoffrey Perkins [the producer] playing "Lady Madonna" on the piano ad infinitum . . .'

What was that about everything being connected?

The only road in Britain . . .

After several months of living with me as I researched this book and wrote it up, and having read various drafts of it, Jo finds herself in a black cab in London. The driver, a friendly enough bloke, is enlivening the journey with trivia-related questions.

'Which building used its windows to beat a council's rules?'

'I don't know,' says Jo.

'The Oxo tower. The council wouldn't let them have illuminated Oxo cube adverts, so they built two circular windows and one in the shape of a cross. Next question: what's the smallest city in the world?'

Jo doesn't know this either.

'The City of London.' I'd have questioned the cabbie on this. Yes, the Square Mile's got its own police force, but that's hardly the definition of a city, is it? Besides, the usual answer to this one is Vatican City. Anyway . . .

'Which road,' says the cabbie, 'is the only one in Britain where you have to drive on the right instead of the left?'

Jo sits up straighter in her seat. She fixes the cabbie's gaze in the rear-view mirror. And she says, 'The road between the Strand and the Savoy.'

Apparently his face was a picture.

Index

Index